Sea Trial

Sea Trial

SAILING AFTER MY FATHER

Brian Harvey

Published by ECW Press
665 Gerrard Street East
Toronto, Ontario, Canada M4M 1Y2
416-694-3348 / info@ecwpress.com

Cover design: David A. Gee
Cover photo: © Jonathan Stead/Millennium Images, U.K.
Map: Jessica Albert
Author photo: Theo Harvey

LIBRARY AND ARCHIVES CANADA CATALOGUING
IN PUBLICATION

Harvey, Brian J., 1948-, author
   Sea trial : sailing after my father / Brian Harvey.

Issued in print and electronic formats.
ISBN 978-1-77041-477-8 (softcover)
ISBN 978-1-77305-339-4 (PDF)
ISBN 978-1-77305-338-7 (EPUB)

   1. Harvey, Brian J., 1948- —Travel—British Columbia—Vancouver Island. 2. Harvey, Brian J., 1948- —Family. 3. Sailing—British Columbia—Vancouver Island. 4. Vancouver Island (B.C.)—Description and travel. 5. Harvey, John Edgar, 1912-2008—Trials, litigation, etc. 6. Trials (Malpractice). 7. Parent and adult child. 8. Autobiographies—I. Title.

PS8615.A77383Z46 2019   C813'.6
C2018-905307-0   C2018-905308-9

The publication of *Sea Trial* has been generously supported by the Canada Council for the Arts which last year invested $153 million to bring the arts to Canadians throughout the country and is funded in part by the Government of Canada. *Nous remercions le Conseil des arts du Canada de son soutien. L'an dernier, le Conseil a investi 153 millions de dollars pour mettre de l'art dans la vie des Canadiennes et des Canadiens de tout le pays.* Ce livre est financé en partie par le gouvernement du Canada. We acknowledge the support of the Ontario Arts Council (OAC), an agency of the Government of Ontario, which last year funded 1,737 individual artists and 1,095 organizations in 223 communities across Ontario for a total of $52.1 million. We also acknowledge the contribution of the Government of Ontario through the Ontario Book Publishing Tax Credit, and through Ontario Creates for the marketing of this book.

ONTARIO CREATES

ONTARIO ARTS COUNCIL
CONSEIL DES ARTS DE L'ONTARIO
an Ontario government agency
un organisme du gouvernement de l'Ontario

Canada Council for the Arts

Conseil des Arts du Canada

Canada

PRINTED AND BOUND IN CANADA   PRINTING: NORECOB   5 4 3 2 1

MIX
Paper from
responsible sources
FSC
www.fsc.org   FSC® C103560

For Chris,
who could fix
almost anything.

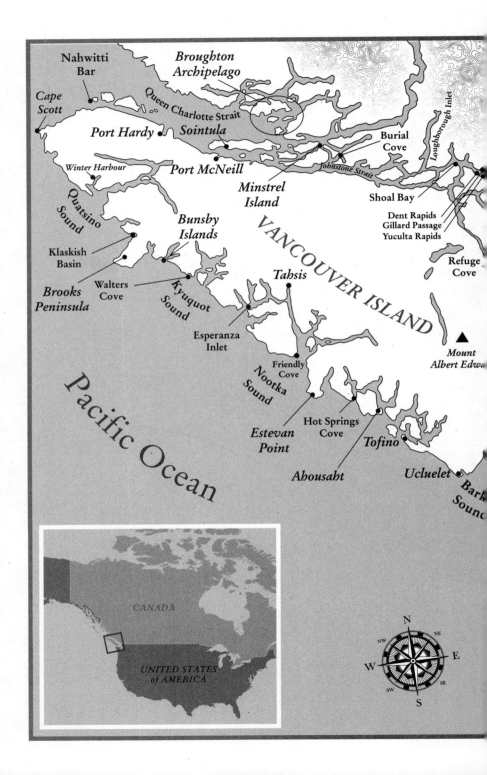

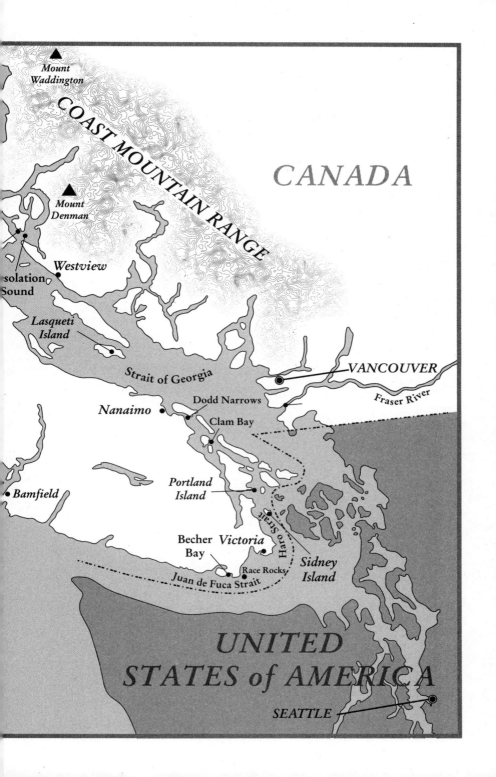

The Nahwitti Bar

Vera was a glowing little island surrounded by drizzle and fog. I could just make out the sickly yellow arc lights on the loading dock where the fishing boats had delivered their catch the night before. It was 4:45 in the morning, and I hadn't slept much. Hatsumi made coffee and poured it into a thermos; neither of us ate. We put on our rain gear. Then I started the engine; turned on the radar, the GPS, and the depth sounder; and crept over the slippery deck to get the anchor up.

"Can we do this?" said Hatsumi when I rejoined her in the cockpit. Her voice sounded small. She put the engine in gear and *Vera* began to slide forward.

"I'm not waiting here another day," I said. "I can't stand it."

We felt our way out of the anchorage. It was still pitch dark, and the fog erased the meeting of boat and water. By the time we reached the mouth of Bull Harbour, the sky had begun to lighten, but our surroundings were still a uniform grey. We were almost at the northern tip of Vancouver Island. Somewhere in front of us was the Nahwitti Bar, the obstacle I'd been obsessing about for months. According to the chart, we were only a half mile away. Soon we would turn toward the shore, find the opening in the rocks that the locals swore by, and follow the edge of the kelp through this inside channel. This was the plan: we would bypass the bar and its multiple hazards altogether, then zip around photogenic Cape Scott, admire the surf exploding on the headlands, and congratulate ourselves for reaching the west coast at last. The home stretch. Nothing to it.

But following the inside route meant you had to see where you were going. I hadn't thought of that. GPS and radar couldn't see kelp, and kelp told you where the shallow spots were. I grabbed the binoculars and did a quick, frantic sweep where I thought the horizon should be. Nothing.

"We have to turn!" Hatsumi was inside, glued to the GPS screen. "We're running out of room."

"Keep going." I felt the Pacific swell lift us. "Don't turn."

"What?"

"I can't see the channel. I can't see anything." I grabbed the binoculars again, and for a moment, maybe five seconds at most, a hole in the fog revealed something. But it wasn't the inviting, kelp-fringed escape hatch I expected to see. It was a grey wall of water, smooth and undulating and evil-looking. The Nahwitti Bar, the thing we thought we were avoiding, was straight ahead.

This was the choice: go blind into confined waters or go blind into that wall. The third and most sensible choice, to turn around and go back, existed for about as long as it took me to hand the binoculars back to my wife. The wall was a lot closer than I thought.

"We'll just go through it," I said. "How bad can it be?"

In an instant, I'd done the equivalent of taking off my clothes in a snowstorm. Would Hatsumi have done it differently? For all my railing at Japanese inflexibility, this was one situation where Western-style improvisation was a mistake. We were entering the Nahwitti Bar at peak ebb tide, the worst possible time; behind that grey wall would be a field of standing waves that would take us, how long to get through? Ten minutes? An hour? I had no idea. And as *Vera* lifted into the first of them and I felt the weight and size of it, I knew that, once we were into that field, there was no way we could turn and run. If the engine stopped, if the blue goop I'd bunged into the leaking driveshaft two days earlier suddenly let go, if *Vera* reared so high the sludge at the bottom of the fuel tank got sucked into the fuel line, we would be driven, wallowing and helpless, onto invisible rocks.

These weren't ordinary waves. They weren't wind-driven and marching predictably at us; instead, they were gunmetal-glassy and weirdly stationary. *Vera* had to climb each one, and as we got deeper into the bar, I had to hold hard to the wheel to keep from slipping backward. Charley, clipped to a line that kept him on the cockpit seat and out from under Hatsumi's feet, cowered and scrabbled with me. Charley was a miniature schnauzer. He couldn't swim. *Vera* reared, climbed, and fell sickeningly into the next trough.

After a half-dozen waves, I gave up steering the course Hatsumi kept shouting to me and concentrated on keeping our bow more or less perpendicular to the crests. We were on a road, even if it led straight into the rocks, but I felt an overpowering need to just get through it. The worst part was the lack of a frame of reference. There was just enough visibility to see two or three waves ahead; everything else — land and sky — was greyed out. It was like being blindfolded and beaten in a locked room. All our planning, three years of progressively longer cruises, the courses, the reading, the conviction that circumnavigating Vancouver Island was the logical shakedown before a true offshore voyage — how did we end up in *this* mess?

"Are we okay?" Hatsumi kept asking. Where she was stationed, braced in the companionway, the view astern must have been just as bad. She wouldn't see the bow climbing to the sky and shedding sheets of water down the decks, but she would see me trying not to tumble backward off the stern. Every few minutes, she blew violently into the ancient brass foghorn I'd found in my father's effects and brought along as a memento. That was what you were supposed to do in fog, wasn't it?

"We're fine," I said. But I was seriously scared. When I suddenly found myself clutching a stanchion and vomiting violently over the side, I didn't know if it was seasickness or fear. I'd never been seasick before. I'd never been this frightened either. Except once — and that was a long time ago.

❧

I first saw Zero Rock on a summer weekend when I was eight years old. A number of things came together then, and because of those things, I was sure I was going to die. The things were: my father's impatience with the limitations on his time, his determination to learn new skills, a southwest gale, and a fishing fleet.

We had no business being anywhere near Zero Rock in *Frou-Frou*. She was a Lightning Class racing boat, nineteen feet long, open except for a few feet of foredeck under which you shoved spare life jackets, a paddle, lunch. The cockpit took up most of the boat: slat seats bracketed the centreboard box, a raised slot that penetrated the hull and through which the retractable keel protruded. With a good wind behind you and the centreboard pulled up, a Lightning planed like a surfboard. You raised and lowered the board by hauling on a block and tackle, an arrangement that allowed the racer to fine-tune lateral resistance and unfortunately allowed my father to conclude that a Lightning could be beached for a weekend's camping.

Our Lightning was painted a cheerful yellow. Her ridiculous name, which we never changed, was picked out in black plastic letters screwed to the transom, one "Frou" on either side of the rudder. That rudder is important to my story. It hung by two oddly named bits of hardware whose names I have never forgotten: the pintles, vertical pins attached to the rudder, and the gudgeons, two brackets like crooked fingers screwed into the transom. You lowered the pintles into the gudgeons, male meeting female with a solid bronze *thunk*, and there the rudder dangled and swung. What happened to this handy system was the first unravelling of my father's plan.

Zero Rock is in the middle of Haro Strait, a sizeable chunk of open water between the southern tip of Vancouver Island and the American Gulf Islands. Haro was Gonzalo López de Haro, a pilot on Manuel Quimper's *Princesa Real*, which passed through in 1790; his is one of the "Spanish names" on the coast of British Columbia, as opposed to the "British names." Two seafaring countries, two legacies. The actual mapping was done a few years later by the other team, led by the dour and dyspeptic George Vancouver, for whom the island and its largest city were named.

Haro Strait is a busy corridor. Freighters and bulk carriers trail mile-long smudges of diesel exhaust down its shipping lanes. Haro connects the Strait of Georgia with the larger Juan de Fuca Strait, which cups the southernmost end of Vancouver Island and connects to the open Pacific, where the really ugly weather comes from. But Haro Strait can be ugly enough; it's eight nautical miles at its widest point and wide open, north-south, for twenty — plenty of what sailors call "fetch," the open area required for a wind to really cock its fist and hammer you. Haro Strait is a complicated place for wind, fielding whatever comes from the Strait of Juan de Fuca, the Strait of Georgia, and Puget Sound and turning it into a baffling brew that can make for great sailing or chewed fingernails. The southwest is where the prevailing winds come from in summer, which means they're behind you going north and in your face heading south. A fine day in Victoria is a blue sky etched with mares' tails and a southwester steered in from Juan de Fuca doing its best to take the top off Haro Strait. On the day I thought I would die, this was how it looked.

My father was a neurosurgeon, and he didn't take holidays, not when I was eight. He was always on call. Evenings and weekends, the phone at home rang constantly because the hospital knew where he was. Most of the time, whatever he was doing when the phone rang — rewiring a light socket, knocking out a wall, developing a roll of photographic film, or varnishing a boat rail — simply stopped or went on without him while he went off to change out of his old clothes. But somehow, this weekend, he'd gotten free. Maybe he had an unprecedented opening in his schedule, maybe he just decided on the spur of the moment to make a run for it and hope nobody drove their motorcycle into a wall or had a massive aneurysm in the twenty-four hours our jaunt was supposed to take.

Our plan (*his* plan) was to spend Saturday night camped on Sidney Island, about fifteen miles north of Victoria. There were a number of problems with this plan — the wrong boat, no idea of the weather forecast, we knew almost nothing about sailing — none of them too surprising from a man whose previous experience with water was confined to the swimming hole by the railroad tracks in rural Alberta and a few lakes in Ontario. The really remarkable thing was that we were going at all. It wasn't even the entire family; my older brother and I got to go, but my mother and sister were stuck waiting at home. They ended up waiting for a lot longer than they'd expected.

The first thing I remember about the trip is the moment things started to go wrong. The north end of Sidney Island, where we intended to camp, is a long, curving spit of sand, an unmissable target. But it shallows abruptly, and we hit the bottom going fast, the southwester behind us, and the sails dropped too late. The centreboard swung up into its case, as it was designed to do, but the rudder, overlooked, caught the bottom and tore loose. The tiller must have leapt suddenly in my father's hand, and I can imagine his shock and the metaphoric slap to the forehead as he found himself suddenly dragging a floating rudder behind us. The gudgeons, of course, ripped out of the transom and slid silently into the sea.

The part of the story my father preferred to remember was how he actually found those two brass gudgeons at low tide the next morning; how he pounded bits of driftwood into the screw holes in the transom and reattached them; how we pushed off when the tide came back in and headed home. And it is a good story, especially the bit where he strode ashore after we'd crash-landed, emptied my army surplus knapsack, stuffed it with sand and pitched it out to where we'd hit the bottom. The bag was there when the tide went out, marking the spot where those gudgeons had to be.

But my own memory is uninterested in his quick thinking, preferring to jump forward to the point where I knew I would die. Here, in the southerly transit of Haro Strait, is where *my* details are.

I remember the sun. It was a beautiful day, cloudless from start to finish. But the wind that had sent us scooting up onto Sidney Spit was in our faces now. Poor *Frou-Frou*'s flat bottom slammed into the rapidly building seas with a sound you felt as much as heard. Voices were snatched away and blown astern. I heard my older brother, who was sailing the boat, yelling about the engine, but my father was bent over the lurching transom, fumbling with the thing, a surgeon trying to slap the machinery into life. Maybe he was checking those reattached gudgeons too, wondering when they would pop out of their new holes and the rudder would fly away astern and *Frou-Frou* would flounder and flip. When he turned and shouted at us, we heard nothing. "What?" he seemed to be saying. "*What?*" His mouth opened and closed silently, like a fish's.

My brother clutched the mainsheet in one hand and the tiller in the other and fought to spill the wind each time a gust threatened to slam us flat. The engine was useless. Our doughty British Seagull, all three horsepower of it, looked to have been the first of us to drown. Water spun off the drum when my father tried to start it, wrapping the cord again and again around the flywheel and yanking furiously with hands that would probably be navigating a hemostat through a tangle of cerebral blood vessels the next day. Finally, he decided to operate. We soldiered on while my father knelt on the pitching stern deck with pliers and wrench, one arm crooked around the wire backstay to keep him from falling off. I think he was trying to extract the spark plug.

By now Haro Strait was a field of beaten silver and white, a beautiful sight for anyone standing on the cliffs and taking in the view of the strait and the hills of San Juan Island and the distant peaks of the Olympic Mountains. We would have been a merry yellow dot. "Hell of a sail," they might have said, nodding in appreciation before ambling back to their cars. But for me, out there in the howling centre of things, it wasn't beautiful at all, just heaving green water that kept coming at our little boat, at my father, my brother, the British Seagull, me.

And so I concluded I was going to die. What was worse, I was going to die in a boat called *Frou-Frou*. I crawled forward, under the small shelter of the coaming, curled up and waited for the water to punch through the plywood next my ear and keep on coming. I prayed, for the first and (so far) the only time in my life.

Then I spotted the trollers. Back then, commercial salmon fishing was still thriving, there was good money in owning a boat and steaming out to meet the sockeye and the chinook as they zeroed in on their coastal rivers after four years getting fat in the North Pacific. There would be another two decades of good times before the only salmon fishermen in Haro Strait were weekend warriors in plastic speedboats. In the '60s, the fleet was still made from B.C. timber and the boats would move from one hot spot to another, racing for the next place where the Department of Fisheries had announced an opening.

And there they were! I could just see them between the boom and the heaving deck. They were big, thirty-five feet or longer, most of them a blinding white, forging unconcernedly through the whipped-up mess of Haro Strait. They were close enough that I could see the long trolling poles waving like insect antennae, and the occasional brilliant orange teardrop of a topside fender. I lifted my head just enough to keep them in view as they crawled past us, one every minute or so, each one, I felt certain, about to go hard to starboard and head for us.

"Good God," I imagined a skipper saying, peering through a spattered wheelhouse window. "Over by Zero Rock, it's a . . ." He reaches for binoculars, claps them to his eyes, whistles. His eyebrows go up under the hairy woollen watch cap. "It's a *kid* out there, hangin' on for dear life. Poor little guy. Hold on, we're goin' in!" Over the wheel would go and on she would come, the *Lucky Lady* or the *Pacific Marauder*, rolling wildly in the broadside swell with a white bone in her teeth, closing the gap, saving us.

But none of them broke ranks, and after an eternity, the procession was past, the transom of the last one vanishing but its long poles still visible, swaying mockingly above the tops of the whitecaps for at least another minute. Then we were alone again. I couldn't believe it. I went back into my hole and stared miserably at Zero Rock. It lurched past in slow motion, draped in shiny seals. How long had we been out there? To me, it felt like days; given the conditions, it was probably more like three hours. We were only halfway home.

My father went on with his futile dissection of the outboard, and my brother sailed the boat until the hand holding the sheet was a claw. The foresail exploded in Baynes Channel, the final gauntlet before Victoria. We coasted into a tiny cove near Ten Mile Point, a place of waterfront houses with kelp beds, not petunias, out front. I was sent ashore. It was almost dark. I remember slipping on seaweed-slick rocks and realizing

I couldn't get any wetter, making my way, still wearing my life jacket, up a pocket beach toward the lights of a house. A woman opened the door.

"Oh dear," she said. "You look like a drowned rat." I dripped onto her welcome mat.

"Can I please use the phone?" I said. "I'm supposed to call my mother."

After my father died, I spent an afternoon driving up the western shoreline of Haro Strait, nipping seaward whenever I saw the triangular "Beach Access" sign. Somewhere, I felt certain, there was a rock ledge or crescent of shingle where relatives could gather and release his ashes into the ocean. The cliffs near Cordova Bay (another of those Spanish names) would have been ideal. But the logistics of tide and wind were wrong, and although older relatives might have been able to scramble down to the water's edge, we would have had to winch them back up.

So I kept looking. Closer to Victoria, I took a turnoff I'd never noticed before and found myself in a pocket cove you could barely squeeze a boat into. There was a house on the rocks, looking out over Baynes Channel, and in the moment of realizing the place was too public for scattering a person's remains, I also realized I had been here before. As a drowned rat.

I really wished those fishing boats had stopped. One of them should have; even in the absence of a radio Mayday, maritime law dictates that a vessel in obvious distress be assisted. Somewhere on this coast there's at least one ninety-year-old ex-skipper mumbling and farting in front of his TV who remembers too. And don't tell me you couldn't see us; we were bright yellow.

I don't know what happened to *Frou-Frou*, except that she was replaced by a succession of larger boats as my parents struggled to figure out how to sail. I learned to sail too, but I stayed scared. Four hours hiding under the foredeck in Haro Strait, tossed around like a marble in a tin can and waiting for the end, left me with the kind of knee-jerk fear that a place like the Nahwitti Bar brought back with a vengeance.

My fear didn't keep me from sailing; as a teenager, when I was old enough to take the family boat out alone, I would push it to the limit, carrying too much sail and driving the rail down into green water. Rough sailing didn't bother me. But *deciding* to go out, watching those trees lash and sway and then stepping into the boat, that took me back under *Frou-Frou's* foredeck every time. It still does.

Leaving

After my father capsized once and for all on the bathroom floor with the last of the little strokes that had been ganging up on him for years, Hatsumi and I spent four years getting to know *Vera* before setting out to circumnavigate Vancouver Island. Every summer we took her farther north along its east, or inner, side. Each time, we stayed out longer: first days, then weeks, then months. A true offshore voyage — across the Pacific, or down to the Caribbean — was seriously discussed.

But wasn't there somewhere we could go to test ourselves in offshore waters without actually selling the house and leaving the country? Where the waves were bigger and the protection harder to find? We needed an offshore tryout — especially me, with my eight-year-old self running off to hide every time the wind rose. That's where the idea of circumnavigating Vancouver Island came from.

Getting ready for a long boat trip isn't much different from going camping. Lists proliferate, get lost, and are reconstructed; stores and suppliers are visited; tempers flare and fizzle;

arrangements for real-world responsibilities are cobbled together, collapse, and get rebuilt. All I can think about is what unobtainable item I've forgotten and when the engine will cough and die for want of a simple part I could easily have put in my spares kit.

A two-month trip, which was the time we figured we'd need to circumnavigate Vancouver Island, meant books, CDs, guitar and music, enough clothes to survive between laundromats, engine oil and the pump to change it with, spare filters and parts, dog food, toilet paper, and an astonishing amount of rice and dried seaweed. And the cargo I hadn't gotten around to telling my wife about yet: the yellowing transcripts and medical papers jammed into grocery bags and wrapped with duct tape. I had slid them into the dead pockets of space that exist even on a boat — behind the toilet pump-out hoses or wedged above the autopilot brain that hung over the spare berth. These were my father's things, the hard evidence of a calamity that had befallen him decades before the strokes finally ended his life. Sooner or later, I would start exhuming them, reading them, making sense of them.

I even tossed in a few fisheries books. It looked as though I was about to land a respectable contract that made use of my background as a biologist. The number of sockeye salmon returning to spawn in the Fraser River, once one of the biggest salmon producers on the planet, had collapsed. There hadn't been a commercial fishery for four years, and critics of the government's management of the resource were clamouring for change, explanations, blood.

A royal commission into the fate of the Fraser sockeye had been ordered by the prime minister, the costly legal machinery of a commission was being assembled, and the commission needed consultants to analyze the threats to Fraser sockeye — overfishing, climate change, pollution, the usual suspects. I had been asked to prepare a report on salmon farms. As far as I or any other fisheries biologist knew, linking the decline of Fraser sockeye with salmon farms was a stretch, but six months' work was six months' work.

"Call it the way you see it," the commission told me. "You'll have to testify, but that shouldn't be a problem. Should it?"

"I can't think why," I said. My father had handled lawyers, hadn't he? And in circumstances a lot more hostile than an inquiry into some missing fish. Maybe I'd even learn something that helped me understand the ordeal he'd gone through before he died.

"No hurry," they said. "Sign the contract when you get back."

So, happily betrothed but with the wedding and consummation safely in the future, I congratulated myself: not only would I test myself against the rapids and the rocks and finally unravel a family knot, our voyage would take us right along the juvenile sockeye's migratory route up the east coast of Vancouver Island, from their home river to the open ocean. We'd literally be swimming with the salmon. Whatever salmon farms they encountered on their way, we'd see them too; wherever we stopped for the night or for provisions, there would be people — commercial fishermen, aboriginal people, environmentalists, even salmon farmers — for whom the subject of salmon survival was an icebreaker second only to the weather. I couldn't lose. I just had to add my biologist's hat to the ones — sailor, husband, son — already on board.

To everyone who asked where we were off to, I said the same thing.

"Oh, as far as we can get, I guess. Might even go around the island."

"Good for you," they always said, as though they hadn't detected my indecision. By the time we were ready to push off, I knew the boat was ready, but I still wasn't, and that "might even" was still the best answer I could give. The previous year, we'd planned for a month exploring the Broughton Archipelago, but we bailed out on the doorstep, hiding from the Johnstone Strait gales for three days before admitting we were more comfortable in the benign waters of Desolation Sound. Turning back and sailing home the easy way had turned into an endless rationalization of what we both knew had been a bad case of nerves.

We'd had all winter to think about it. This trip would be a trial of sorts, making up for last year's failure. At least, that was the plan.

Most recreational boaters circumnavigate Vancouver Island counterclockwise: up the east coast and back down the west. The reasoning is this: even if the winds are on your nose all the way up the inside, those same northwesterlies will give you a sleigh ride back down the other side. That makes perfect sense for sailboats, which will theoretically have fifteen or twenty knots of wind right on the beam, where they like it the most, and the swell will just roll by beneath them. It's a little different for powerboats, which tend to be hard to steer going away from the wind, but most of the boats going around the island are sailboats.

So we would be fine. *Vera* was built to sail around the world. Instead of worrying about the boat, I concentrated on finding out what were the major hurdles on the west coast — beside the dreaded Nahwitti Bar that everyone had warned me about. A month or so before we were to leave, I unlocked *Vera*, went below, and lit the stove. The twenty new charts I had bought for the voyage were in a fat roll on one of the berths. While the water boiled, I untied them and began to fold them in quarters so they would fit inside the chart table. They were mostly charts for the west coast; we already had most of the east coast covered. I kept them in order so that by the time my coffee was ready, I had a neat, two-inch pile that started in Port Hardy, near the top of the island on the east side, then progressed around the top and back down the west coast all the way to Victoria.

Kyuquot Sound, Nootka Sound, Friendly Cove. The names I'd grown up with, from stories and news reports and history books, were suddenly in my hands. Towns like Winter Harbour and Tahsis, places whose names were familiar but I could never really pinpoint, well, now I would be locating them on a chart, navigating to them, tying up to their docks, and stepping into them. By the time I'd finished two cups of coffee and worked through the charts, my wife had joined me.

"There's nowhere to sit," Hatsumi said.

"True, but at least they're all in order. You'll like that. Now listen, I've figured out what we have to watch out for."

"Are you going to put all these charts away?"

"Of course I am. I always do. Now, the first obstacle is the rapids."

"We've done rapids."

"Right, so we do a few more. Then Johnstone Strait, which we mostly avoid, get an early start for the last bit, and bang, we're in Port McNeill."

"Can we go to Sointula?" Sointula was where we first got the idea of buying a sailboat; it's close to Port McNeill. I rummaged for the chart, making even more of a mess.

"Sointula's right across the strait, so yes. Two more short hops to Port Hardy, then Bull Harbour is the jumping off point for Cape Scott."

"What's Cape Scott?"

"The second obstacle. Here." I pulled out the right chart. "But I looked it up. You just have to hit it at slack tide." Slack tide is the moment when the sea takes a fleeting break between rising and falling. In places like Cape Scott, where wind and tide can gang up to confound the mariner, taking tide out of the equation makes life a lot easier. Hatsumi frowned at the chart.

"What about waves?" she said finally.

"Well, I guess we'll find out. Probably depends on the day. Oh, and wind. Apparently, it gets worse if it's windy."

"Oh."

"Or foggy. But look, after that, we're on our way south again! Although we do have to get around the Brooks Peninsula. This thing."

I pointed to an ugly stub of land a day south of Winter Harbour. It looked as though it had been glued onto the west coast.

"It's big," said Hatsumi.

"Yeah, but you just go well outside it." I tried to sound breezy and confident, as I generally do when something worries my wife. But there was no getting around the fact that Brooks Peninsula stuck out an awfully long way. I remembered reading about it in a little book called *Weather Hazards*; like all promontories, the Brooks Peninsula causes winds to speed up. It's the Venturi effect, the same phenomenon that provides lift for an aircraft wing. Brooks was notorious for nasty winds. I soldiered on.

"That's what the books say. Stay well offshore. Wait for a calm day. But hey, after that, it's a straight shot south."

"And this one?" Hatsumi's finger went unerringly to Estevan Point. It was, I had to admit, another promontory.

"Look, by the time we get there, we're pretty much home. A couple of days in Barkley Sound, soak in the hot springs, you're going to love it." Hatsumi was beginning to sound like all the other people who had tried to warn us off the circumnavigation. She looked closer at the chart.

"Where do we stop once we leave Barkley Sound?" She lifted the chart table lid to find her calipers, dislodging a few charts.

"Never mind, I already calculated it. It's ninety miles, Bamfield to Victoria."

"*Ninety* miles? With nowhere to stop?"

"Oh, there must be places. Look, we'll figure it out. It'll be a sleigh ride." Breezy again. That last day took us through the Strait of Juan de Fuca. When it got windy in Victoria, which it routinely did, Juan de Fuca was where the wind came from. And at the end of it was Race Passage, which I decided not even to mention. We would do it, somehow. Once we turned the corner at Cape Scott, we'd have to. I gathered the charts and clipped them together.

"See, all neat and tidy again."

But Hatsumi looked dubious. "What about Charley?"

Charley was a dog, not a human, but Hatsumi didn't really make the distinction.

"The waves, I'm worried about the waves. You don't know waves like that. I do. In Japan, the ocean is *all* offshore. What if he starts to freak out?"

Charley was outside in the cockpit, stationed in his usual crouch by the jib winch and staring down strangers. Schnauzers usually have their tails and the tips of their ears lopped off, but Charley still had all his appendages, and he used them like signal flags. His beard bristled.

"Look at him. He loves the boat. He'll be fine."

"And those are the only problems?" I could see she was still worried about those waves, and I didn't blame her. I'd been to Japan and stood on the shore; the place was a cauldron. I imagined her on an interisland ferry as a girl, puking and apologizing like everyone else.

"Well, yeah, there was this bar thing someone mentioned, Nahwitti something. But it doesn't seem like that big of a deal. Around Cape Scott somewhere. We'll figure it out."

Nahwitti Bar is right at the top of Vancouver Island, roughly at the halfway point, so we had plenty of time to solve whatever navigational conundrums it posed. By the time we reached it, we'd have planned our way through six sets of rapids and talked to the dozens of fellow cruisers I assumed would be going the same way. It was just another of those coastal hazards that everybody had to deal with. It didn't do to dwell on the risks; in that direction lay the unavoidable conclusion that *everywhere was dangerous.* The only detail that niggled at me from my study of the charts and guidebooks was that Nahwitti Bar and Cape Scott were awfully close together, and safe passage for both seemed to depend on tidal conditions.

"We'll figure it out," I said again and tried to put the Nahwitti Bar out of my head. We had a lot to do before we got anywhere near it.

By the end of June, tanks were filled with propane and diesel and water, bedding had been shoved into the V-berth in the bow, tools were stacked in plastic boxes in the spare berth. I set the battery-operated sprinkler timers to water the garden every three days and tried not to imagine them malfunctioning and firing random fountains at the neighbours for two months. Then we locked the house, put Charley on the leash, and walked the half hour to the marina. There was nothing left to carry.

A flat calm forced us to motor north all the way up Haro Strait, which was on its best behaviour. The sun dazzled on the mirrorlike surface, and I pulled on an old canvas hat salvaged from my father's closet. The brim kept flopping down into my field of view. As we chugged past Zero Rock, I had the disconcerting feeling that I was seeing this familiar place with his eyes. We passed a few commercial fishing boats going in the other direction, their long poles at forty-five degrees. But there weren't nearly so many of them as when I was a child, and my father's hat kept blocking the view. I skimmed it out over the calm waters and pulled on one of my own. His old one receded astern in *Vera*'s arrow-straight wake as the autopilot took us north. There wasn't much to do except watch out for logs and think about the past. I suddenly realized it was July 1, Canada Day. My father's birthday.

The Archive

My father's effects were like flotsam on a beach, each wave leaving something behind as he weakened and died, until the beach was littered with his life.

And there were so many John Harveys. The prairie kid who was happiest snaring gophers with his friends and crawling underneath the boardwalk on Main Street, who left home at sixteen and never came back, not even when his father died. The disillusioned high school teacher who borrowed money, went back to school, and became a doctor. The photographer who filled our house with the smell of developer and fixer and our family albums with images that were much more than snapshots. And the trophy-winning violinist and peripatetic physician who kept searching for the place where medicine was practised the way he thought it should be.

Getting a handle on a life like this one seemed impossible; there was always going to be something I couldn't quite grasp. After he died, I took a lot of that flotsam into my own home and went gamely through it, sometimes laughing, occasionally crying. I spent a month classifying, labelling, and judging, before distributing and disposing. Worst of all were the drop-offs at the Sally Ann, roaring away from the beaten chair and the obsolete stereo abandoned on a wet sidewalk.

In sheer tonnage, the photographs dominated the collection, and that seemed fitting. Photography and music had been the passions in my father's life that never faded, and he had left many pounds of meticulously labelled negatives and prints. Among the best were the black and white portraits of his fellow physicians, handmade sixteen-by-twenties he had shot in a hallway, or an operating room, or the smoke-laden doctors' lounge. My favourite bore a caption that typified the mordant sense of humour that my father tried to suppress but never really could: in this portrait, the doctor is grinning, a cigarette in one hand and the other hand aloft, the thumb and first finger measuring off an inch or so of air.

"Just a small one," the caption reads. "I have to operate."

He also left bits and pieces from most of our boats. I went through mountains of nautical detritus in the freezing-cold garden shed behind his house, high-stepping over rusting garden tools and reaching around scary bottles of thirty-year-old pesticide to get at the treasures. Rotting cardboard boxes rained hundreds of dollars' worth of bronze nuts and bolts on my shoes. I unearthed a priceless collection of teak scraps left over from the costly rebuilding of a doomed deck; cans of questionable kerosene and long-solidified spar varnish; the rope and wood boarding ladder he'd made during his fear-of-falling-overboard phase (this coincided with his fear-of-head-injury phase, when he wore a red motorcycle helmet while driving his convertible).

One boat in particular was responsible for much head-scratching and even the need for a German-English dictionary. From *Stortebeker III*, a classic beauty he'd bought from another doctor who'd finally given up on maintaining a seasoned wooden cruiser already well past middle age, I discovered old admiralty charts of Raoul Island, where HMS *Bounty*'s Captain Bligh and his men first made land after being cast adrift by the doomed Fletcher Christian; ceramic jars with cork-lined lids marked "Kaffee" and "Kakao" and even, stuffed into a black plastic bag that showered me with rat droppings when I tugged it out of a high-up cranny, a threadbare Nazi flag. *Stortebeker III* had been built in 1937 in Bremen; there was no lead in *her* keel.

But the boat stuff was not so difficult to deal with. A lot of it, like the screws and the teak, went directly into my own boat stores, with silent thanks that I would never have to buy it. The coffee and cocoa containers were washed out and refilled. The rest of the household goods found their way to new homes or to family shelves where they could bide their time for as long as it took for their new owners to die. I donated the doctors' portraits to the Victoria Medical Society.

That left the papers.

My father's papers (and there were a lot of them) were sealed in already-labelled cardboard boxes. I left those for last, finally working through them with a growing sense of dread. Most of them were no problem: letters, newspaper clippings about his early triumphs as a violinist, pristine instruction manuals for his many cameras, his own short stories and essays, and even a few tentative poems. But there was one box I didn't want to find. For a while, I thought it might not be there at all, that he might, in the final months before he was exiled to the nursing home and lost control over his own possessions, have managed to get down on his knees and enter the vile crawlspace beneath the kitchen, where I knew it was stored. I imagined him navigating shakily past the trap with the liquefying rat and the jumble of mouldy boat cushions, making it finally to the leaning pile of cardboard boxes to locate and destroy the one I feared.

I found it, of course. He could never have disposed of it even if he'd wanted to; it was too heavy. I shoved the box to one side, ignoring it until that's all there was on the workbench. It was labelled like all the rest (he was a labeller) but more carefully than the others. The word LEGAL was written on one of those white adhesive rectangles with a red border, then licked and smoothed hard onto the cardboard so there would be no mistake about what was inside. The pain its contents represented had been impossible to contain, but at least the evidence was secure. Until now.

The tape yielded after a short struggle and took some of the cardboard with it; he had sealed the box well. Inside were files, packed tightly, a solid cube of paper. I pulled them out in slippery handfuls, stacked them on the workbench, stomped the torn cardboard box flat — it was as frail, it turned out, as he was at the end. Then I began to go through the piles.

Work quickly, I told myself. Be ruthless. You owe it to him to see what's in here, but you don't have to read anything. If he would never explain it all to you before, why dig it up now?

The papers smelled of mould and neglect and, because I knew something of their story, of defeat. I began to go through them, quickly scanning each before they went into the recycling box. Files of patients long dead, each in its own named folder. Photocopies of scientific papers from medical journals, none of them more recent than the mid-1980s. Long and ominous-looking transcripts in vinyl 3-ring binders warped with age and a thick bundle of yellowed newspaper clippings that I tossed without even looking. Printouts of some kind of manuscript, the lettering faded, on side-punched computer paper. I glanced and tossed, as though washing my hands of a corpse. It looked like the whole story was here.

And then, after about twelve inches, I gave up and began to go in reverse. The discard pile got smaller again. I *couldn't* recycle or even shred this stuff. It was too sensitive. There were names. It must have taken him years to compile this dossier, with trips to the medical library, the archives, the stationery store for the recipe cards where every reference was recorded on its own little rectangle. "Hydrocephalus in Children." "Complications of Ventriculo-Atrial Shunts." "The Practice of Law and the Search for Truth." Most of the reprints were heavily annotated in orange highlighter or in his own neat hand; some of the notes were askew on the page. I imagined him, an unwilling student in his late seventies, cramming a heavy textbook over the photocopy machine, leaning on the cover, turning the page, and doing it all again. I couldn't throw this stuff away.

Pretty soon it was all back together again, a toxic little archive reconstructed. I grabbed a flattened U-Haul box, erected it, and shoe-horned the lot back in. Then I sealed it with packing tape, rather a lot of it, because I never intended to open the box again, and all it lacked was an unambiguous name. I took a felt pen and wrote the one he had already chosen for his own manuscript on the top and on each side for good measure so there'd be no mistaking it: THE TRIAL. Then I pushed it out of sight.

With that, the storm blew itself out. Successive waves had brought the flotsam of my parents' lives ashore, and I'd salvaged what I could. Now the final rogue wave, the one that had thrown up The Trial, had receded. As far as I was concerned, the box could sit in its dark corner forever. Trying to connect the dots between the handsome violin-playing medical resident and the querulous old man with the haunted eyes and the flyaway hair didn't enter my mind.

～

But I wasn't finished with The Trial, and it was all the fault of our new boat. Buying a boat had many unforeseen consequences; one was the change in character of the basement. Before the boat, it was a place for tools, workbenches, old furniture, warping LP collections. With the death of my parents, some of my own junk made way for their art collections, their drawings and photographs, their sheet music. Then, when *Vera* arrived, criteria for residence in the basement changed again. The ratio of boat junk to all other kinds began to shift in favour of utility — no matter how theoretical — on the water. Former tenants were replaced by extra life jackets, old mooring lines, miles of wiring ripped from *Vera*'s innards. Every week, something new needed a home, so something from a previous life had to be evicted.

One evening, I tugged a cardboard box out of a suitable-sized space, jammed a busted boat barbecue in the hole, and had a look at what I had extracted. Of course, it was The Trial. Maybe this was a sign. Should I refile this thing? Cart it around forever? Or deal with it? I knew I couldn't do any of these things until I had a real look at it.

I slit it open with a box cutter and pulled out a ring-bound sheaf of documents an inch thick. *Supreme Court of British Columbia*, it said across the top. *Proceedings of Trial.* I found another one, dated the following day, but that was all. So that was how long the trial had lasted: two days, and then the humiliating settlement, the lawyers paid off, and Dr. Harvey's accuser triumphant on the front page of the newspaper. The proceedings were date-stamped 1987; he had another twenty years to think about the trial before death called a halt to his brooding.

And all that thinking had just made things worse. Why had my father never recovered from whatever was described in the contents of this box? All doctors made mistakes. He had often entertained us with his blunders as a sleep-deprived intern: trying desperately to start an IV in an enormously overweight woman whose arms were "much bigger than most people's legs" or waking up in a cold sweat and realizing he had mismatched the blood that was to be used for an operation the next day (he got lucky on that one when the patient perked up and the operation was cancelled). Had more serious mistakes been made in the case contained in this box? If so, by whom?

So many perplexing aspects of those last two decades of his life related to this collection of documents that would still be on the shelf if I hadn't bought a boat and decided I needed the storage space. His horror of lawsuits was often extended to the actions of his children. "Don't do that. You'll be sued," he was always telling us. His determination to get his experiences onto paper, which resulted, near the end of his life, in a handsome memoir and a second, much thicker, manuscript about the trial, which he could never bring himself to complete. *The Game*, he called it.

I knew what his trial was about, more or less. There had been an infant, a neurosurgical emergency, an out-of-the-blue malpractice suit. I remembered the shock of the sheriff's knock on the door so many years after the events, and the stoic anguish in my parents' house when I came to visit. But "emergency" was a word I had heard so many times growing up, and my parents believed in suffering in silence. When the stories came out in the press, I read them, disbelieved them, and destroyed them.

But he hadn't. The press clippings were here, in this box, in their own neatly labelled folder next to all the other files that had survived my attempt at culling a year earlier. The headlines were familiar even after twenty years yellowing in the dark, and they still hurt and amazed.

"Doctor Offered Mother New Son to Replace Brain-Damaged Baby" was one. Like hell, I thought, exactly the same reaction I'd had twenty years ago. The other clipping was "$1.5 Million Offer Ends Lawsuit Over Brain Damage to Baby Boy." I didn't read either of them because I already knew the bones of the story, and the flesh that had been put on them for publication had been rancid even then. A hydrocephalic infant had received a shunt. The shunt had gotten infected, was taken out and replaced. Shunts were not something I knew much about; I thought they might be some kind of drain. Between the first and the second shunts, fluid pressure on the infant's brain had shot up, with effects that might be permanent. The plaintiff (the infant's mother) thought they were and that the defendants (my father, two other doctors, and the hospital where it all happened) were to blame. Tucked in behind the lurid newspaper reports was a photocopy of a cartoon in which a draped patient looks up at the surgeon. "Leave a clamp or something in me, Doc," he says. "I need the money." At least my father's morbid sense of humour seemed intact.

Then something else slid out from between the photocopies, as though it had chosen this moment to make up my mind for me. It was a black and white photograph — he had always worked in black and white — of an infant with its head almost concealed in bandages. This was no newspaper photo. A nurse in a rocking chair held the child on her knee, looking down on puffy, wrinkled-up eyes. It was a beautiful photograph; the light from some hidden window — a ward hallway? — fell softly on the two faces. The nurse looked serene, the way one wants nurses to look when they are holding your child. The child, as far as I could tell under all those bandages, just looked tired. There was a handwritten note stuck on the back, and I recognized the name written there: my father's lawyer, assigned by the Medical Protective Association to defend him in the suit.

That photograph, and the note on the back, said everything about my father. That he had taken the picture; that it was a good one; that he was so naïve, even in his seventies, to think its existence might somehow make a difference to the lawyer, to the case. That the trial had been about *him*, and that the more his lawyer knew about him as a person, the more it would be clear that he had done all anyone could have. In my parents' world, virtue was supposed to be its own reward. Hard work and excellence were your friends. Here was that belief, in this picture. Maybe the fact that the picture was filed with the sordid clippings meant he'd recognized how naïve it was. Maybe he'd never even sent it. But I had it now, and it triggered something.

How often can you hold in your hand something that represents a parent's life? This picture, which he had taken, developed, printed in the downstairs darkroom, was who my father *was*, or at least who he wanted to be seen as: the doctor-artist. Everything else in the box, including his own writings, represented the struggle between the way he saw himself and the way others saw and ultimately judged him. Now, stumbling on the offending box again, I found myself intensely curious about that struggle, because surely the image we have of ourselves, deep down, determines how we respond to others. What did he *really* think of himself? Here, with these official transcripts cheek by jowl with his innermost thoughts, was my chance to find out.

I wasn't interested in judgment — of him or his accusers — and I decided right then that if I looked any further into this story, it wouldn't be with any romantic idea of exoneration. There had been no findings in the hydrocephalus case, no assessment of fault, only accusations, discovery, a few days of trial, and the huge settlement. It was over a long time ago. Nobody cared about it anymore. But there was a detective story in this box, even if the only person interested in the outcome was me. Who was this man who came to the breakfast table with blood spatters on his glasses, who never took holidays, who lugged his camera into operating rooms, who exhorted his children in their projects, "Do a *job*!" (And, I have to add, who took his sons in a nineteen-foot sailboat to certain death in Haro Strait?) After death comes to me, will my own children unearth a summary of my life like this one? Not a chance. Most people, when their parents die, have to do their reconstructive work using letters, snapshots, mementoes. How many people get the chance to really understand what a parent actually did when they left the house each morning? How many people get the answers to family mysteries neatly packaged in a single cardboard box? Even if, as it turned out for me, it's not the answers they're expecting?

It wasn't that big a box. If I weeded out redundant files (I already knew there were multiple versions of his own writings, many fits and false starts), the whole lot would fit somewhere on *Vera*. Sailing around Vancouver Island would soak up two months of summer and demand plenty of reading material. Detective fiction was always a good choice for long evenings at anchor; now I would have detective fact, which was even better. Having my father along for the ride wouldn't be so bad; at least he wouldn't be able to talk. And anyway, he'd always liked cruising, or tried to.

～

What happens to people when they get stuck? When they can't go forward but they can't go back either? Of the thousands of photographs my father took, my favourite is of my mother poised at the end of a diving board. It's at a lake in Ontario; the board is long and high and sticks out from a wooden tower. She's facing the camera and the shore, toes on the board and heels on nothing, arms spread against a cloudless sky. Beneath the rubber cap, a look of serenity. It's more than a snapshot — my father rarely took those — and I imagine him kneeling on the dock, fiddling with the latest in photographic technology for 1946.

It takes courage to walk to the end of the board, grip the sandpapery plank with your toes, cancel out the shouts and splashes from below, and launch yourself backward into three seconds of nothing. Whenever I look at that picture, I think of the photographer forty years later, how he collected his courage and forced himself to walk further and further from the safety of a pleasant retirement, all the way to the courtroom in Vancouver where his accusers were waiting.

The horrible difference was that my mother dove, but my father never got to. For her, the shutter snapped and off she went, revolving briefly in the Ontario sun and then — I like to think — knifing neatly into the lake without so much as a droplet to hit the camera. And she kept on diving, metaphorically at least, all her life. When cancer finally took her, she was the one who decided when.

For my father, alone at the end of his own diving board, the voices stopped him at the last moment. "Come back," they told him. "It's over. Climb down the ladder, go home." But he couldn't, and that's where he froze, until the end of his life, unable to go forward or back. It nagged at me, seeing him out there, deaf to all entreaties. And when the end finally came, he didn't dive or climb back down — he just tumbled off. The best I could do now would be to understand why he decided to take that long walk to the edge, and why he was unable to return. Pride was something he had plenty of. But, unlike my mother, he wasn't fearless.

The accusations levelled at him consumed him until he died. He never closed the book.

He died lonely and unhappy, but he left me a lot of things. Some of them, like my love of boats and the sea, were intangibles that reflected his own interests. Others were very tangible indeed — like the "book" of the trial that he never really closed. If there was a story to be told about our circumnavigation, I realized, it would include both.

Stowaway

If you're heading north out of Victoria, up Haro Strait, there's not much mystery about where to spend the first night. The easiest place to stop is Sidney Spit, a marine park at the northern exit of the strait. But I don't like the anchorage there. It's shallow, and the sandy bottom shifts from year to year, building up here, eroding there so that even the latest chart is a work in progress. And I have a long memory: Sidney Spit was where the family sailboat blundered ashore all those years ago, where the famous gudgeons ripped off, the place I thought would be the last dry land I'd ever set foot on.

Today, between the effects of Canada Day and the American July 4 weekend, the spit was a zoo. I swore I could smell suntan oil as we motored past the rafted-together cruisers and dodged the big speedboats booming across from the town of Sidney on the opposite shore. No thanks.

Portland Island is the next marine park to the north. We puttered around the dogleg that hides the entrance to Princess Bay and let the anchor go near the cluster of fifteen or so boats that had arrived before us. It was only 3 p.m.; anchorages filled up early these days. With no wind to align them, the boats faced every which way, as though waiting for instructions.

Portland Island is perennially popular. It's close to several Canadian marinas and directly on the run north for boaters out of Seattle. A half-hour walk from the gentle crescent beach in Princess Bay takes you to the trickier anchorage on the other side of the island, at Royal Cove, past the arthritic apple and pear trees of a long-gone homestead. Charley would have given anything for a run around the stone foundations poking through the field like the stubs of long-gone teeth, but I had something else in mind.

We clambered into the dinghy and rowed away from *Vera* toward a small cut in the fringing rocks. A plastic screw-top container between my feet clunked back and forth with every stroke of the oars, and the late afternoon sun glanced off the glassy water and warmed our faces. The water was clear and shallow, maybe a dozen feet deep.

"Over there, I think. That little opening — there'll be some current. I think they should drift around a little, don't you?"

Hatsumi nodded and picked up the container of ashes. A cup or so from each of my parents, held back from the bulk of their remains after a struggle with the rightness of consigning my parents to two different deeps. Most of their ashes had already been released together into the ocean near Victoria. Oceanographically speaking, I told myself, the two locations were all part of the same basin; theoretically, some microscopic part of their ashes could even travel from one place to the other. Less scientifically, I figured that my parents simply wouldn't mind, and Portland Island had special meaning because it was the last place they had travelled to together by boat. Among their papers I'd found the record my mother had kept.

"Powered to Portland Island," it said in her microscopic handwriting. "Tide in Baynes Channel too strong." They only stayed a day, but my mother, finding the silver lining as usual, called it "hot and heavenly." She rowed around and sketched. My father apparently slept a lot. Then they powered back home. It was July 1982; the visit from the sheriff was still five years away.

I could picture her rowing to the spot where we were now. It felt right. I shipped the oars, and we both peered down at a dense bed of eelgrass, a forest of green ribbons leaning gently shoreward as Princess Bay filled on the rising tide. We sat there, going imperceptibly up, the water licking higher on the pebbly beach and *Vera* slowly rising behind us, pulling sand-shedding loops of chain off the bottom.

Hatsumi handed me the open jar. We leaned over as far as we dared and I submerged the container. A representative sample of my parents slid out and into the current, the two handfuls of ashes fanning into a twinkling curtain that drifted down to settle on the eelgrass. For a minute or so, the emerald fronds were white, and then the ashes were gone, washed away by the currents and my own tears.

⤳

Sitting in a busy anchorage is usually social. Most of the other boaters, even the annoying ones, have interesting stories, and it usually takes no more than a "Nice evening!" from the dinghy to initiate a conversation that can easily turn into days spent together exploring the next fifty miles of coastline. But this night was different. We ate late, sitting in the cockpit with a bottle of wine and listening to the mutter of small outboards propelling dinghies back and forth. When the trees began to merge with the darkening sky, we went to bed, and I lay listening to the anchor chain grumbling against the bottom. I'd forgotten the night noises a boat makes at anchor even when there's no wind to push you around: the tick-tock of a bowl rolling in its cradle, squeaks from the dinghy tethered along-side, the pops and bubblings that herald a tide change.

I awoke the next morning to two loud noises. The first was a sort of *whap*, like someone snapping an enormous towel. The noise was quite loud, as though the towel were right outside the boat and whoever was doing it would wait a minute or so between whaps, just enough time for me to start the slide back into sleep. Finally, I got up on one elbow and peered out the porthole. Two boat lengths away, a seal flipper rose from the water, flexed, and descended, spinning off a crescent of spar-kling water beads and coming down with an extra-loud clap that probably woke up half the anchorage. If he was trying to warn boats away from Princess Bay, he'd picked an odd time to do it; more likely the flipper-slap was meant to get the attention of an attractive female. If she was there, I couldn't see her.

I lay back and began a satisfying early morning reverie about all the harbour seals undoubtedly cruising around the boats anchored in Princess Bay, what a spectacular view they had of all the things that caused the owners to lose sleep — rusty chain, anchors clinging by their fingernails, corroded thru-hull fittings about to cave in and let the ocean inside in a silent, insidious rush.

Then I heard the second sound. It wasn't another seal. It was a sneeze. A human sneeze, loud enough and so much like a roar you might think the flipper-slapper had a terrible cold. The problem was, I knew the sneezer.

"I'm *freezing*," said a voice from the cockpit.

"Well, I can't do anything about that," I said.

"*Wha* . . . ?" said Hatsumi. "What time?"

"Go back to sleep," I said. "I'll deal with it." My feet hit the cold cabin sole, and I rummaged around for clothes. I always leave my clothes within easy reach in case I have to get up in the middle of the night and do something heroic.

"It's warmer down here, you know," I called up to the cockpit.

"I don't want to come down," said my father. "I like it fine up here." He sneezed again. The sound bounced off the rocks at the head of the bay, as though there was some kind of early-morning sneezing contest going on.

"Except for it being freezing," I said and started up the steps.

He was tucked in behind the steering wheel, under the dew-soaked Canadian ensign hanging limply from the backstay.

"You know you're supposed to take the flag in at dusk," he said. He was wearing the vile brown acrylic pants we'd tried so hard to steal and replace and the oversized fuzzy slippers we'd bought to keep his edematous feet warm in the care home. He clutched a blue hospital blanket around his small shoulders; peeking out from underneath was his favourite red-and-white woollen jacket. It went with the flag.

"Nobody seems to do that anymore," I said, waving at the rest of the boats. Sodden flags were everywhere, a mass affront to nautical etiquette. "Things have changed since you were here last. Look at all those inflatable dinghies. Like bagels."

"We never had an inflatable dinghy," he said. "Or an outboard motor." He ran his bony fingers through white hair that obviously hadn't been cut since I'd seen him last.

"Sure we did," I said. "Not that it ever seemed to work. *Frou-Frou*, remember? Sidney Spit? Near-death out by Zero Rock?"

"I have no idea what you're talking about." He began to pick slowly at the skin on the back of one hand. A few flakes drifted onto the cockpit floor. "How did you know we came here, your mother and I?" he asked finally.

"Because she wrote it up in a notebook. Apparently, you slept all day. And some people kept you awake at night, singing. It must have been awful."

"I warned you about going through my things."

"You *died*," I reminded him. "What did you expect me to do, shred it all? Believe me, that would have taken weeks. And if you pay someone to do it, they read the stuff as they go."

"Mm." He picked some more at the hand holding the blanket.

"I've got some skin cream down below, you know. Do you want me to ask Hatsumi to dig it out?"

"Who are you talking to?" My wife was up now, puttering in the galley at the bottom of the steps.

"Just my dad," I said.

"Say hi to him for me. And turn on the propane, okay?" She went back to fiddling with the stove.

"It's horribly cold here," said my father. "I can't stand it much longer. What else did you find in my papers?"

"Oh . . . you know. Some letters. Your old LeCoultre watch. About a million boxes of negatives."

"That's it?"

"Maybe some stuff about, you know, the thing that happened."

He stopped picking at his hand and looked at me hard. I thought his eyes looked a little red. He'd missed some places shaving. "That's not your business," he said.

"It is now." I thought about all the times we could have talked about the trial and didn't. But that was the way he'd wanted it. "You might as well know," I said. "I kept the lot. Not just the manuscript you wrote, but the hospital records, the examinations, the trial, everything." I waited for the explosion, but he just stared at his hands and then slowly began picking at the dry spots again.

Finally, he said, "I helped a lot of people."

"I know that. Maybe now you can help *me*. You're the expert. I'm just a fish biologist. All that technical stuff — I'd hate to get it wrong."

"I'll need to think about it." I could smell eggs frying and coffee. He was right, it *was* chilly out here with the seals and the dew. On the neighbouring boat, a hatch squeaked open, and my father turned sharply.

"I want to go," he said.

"Well, you know where to find me."

I peered over the side, where a school of young salmon was making its way past *Vera*'s mothering hull. I wondered if they were the Fraser River sockeye whose troubles would be keeping me solvent once this trip was over. The school moved in a series of shuffles, like an uncoordinated robot. But finally, it was gone. And so was my visitor.

"Breakfast," said Hatsumi.

Vera

My wife and I got serious about buying a sailboat after we showed up to visit my father at the care home one afternoon and found him on the floor, his torso in the hallway but his legs still stubbornly in the bathroom. Another stroke, another nasty irony: his Ph.D., at the University of Chicago almost sixty years before, had been on blood flow in the brain, exactly the thing that had gone wonky and put him on the floor. Watching your father learning to crawl is a powerful argument for starting on your personal list of things to do before you die. It wasn't his first fall; as it turned out, it was actually his last.

We bought *Vera* only partially because of my father's decline and the warning it carried; the other reason was an exhausted border collie in Sointula, on Malcolm Island. This place lies a few miles off Port McNeill, at the northern end of the tricky passage between Vancouver Island and mainland British Columbia. Hatsumi and I had crossed on the car ferry from Port McNeill on a whim during a mid-summer week negotiated away from responsibilities in Victoria, where my father was now a tottering time bomb.

The border collie found us on the beach below the lighthouse at Pulteney Point, a crushed-shell spit where the wind that had barrelled up Johnstone Strait tore at your hat and whipped the sea white. Just looking at the water made my heart turn over. *I'd* never go out there. The dog ran a perfunctory circle around our feet, flopped down in the sand, and hung its tongue out. His owners waved at us and started walking over.

"I don't know how to ask you this," the man said. Curly hair stuck out from beneath a blue ball cap. "Is that by any chance your car in the parking lot?"

His name was Scott, his wife was Debbie, and they had walked all the way from Sointula, a distance of ten miles. We loaded the dog into the back. They were embarrassed and apologetic. The dog began to snore.

They had sailed up from Seattle. Today was too windy to leave Malcolm Island; a walk had been the obvious diversion. We fishtailed around a gravelly corner. I had no idea how windy was too windy. One look at Johnstone Strait from the lighthouse had been enough. I might as well have been out there under *Frou-Frou*'s foredeck.

"Can we see your boat?" I asked.

Their boat, *Viva*, was tied up at the marina, one of only a few pleasure craft, even at the height of summer. The dog woke up long enough to jump gracefully aboard and into the cockpit, where he curled up and went back to sleep. I wondered if I should take my shoes off. I hadn't been on a sailboat for twenty-five years.

"Glass of wine?" Debbie asked. She went down below, and I looked around the cockpit.

Sailboats had changed. What on earth were all those gauges? Even the old-fashioned things, like the winches, looked different from the ones I had used to wrestle in the jib sheets on the family boat: they were bigger and shinier, with a crown of grooved teeth that completely baffled me. (I later learned they were self-tailing winches, a wonderful invention that lets you crank with both hands while the toothy bit grabs the rope.) When I peered below, I could see teak woodwork, carpet, an inviting settee, and a light-flooded galley where Debbie was doing something with cheeses. We sat in the cockpit and ate off a varnished table that folded out across from the enormous steering wheel. I had never touched a steering wheel in a sailboat; in my experience, sailboats had tillers. A tiller was the essence of sailing, the varnished wooden wand that connected you straight to the rudder and thus to the water. A tug on the tiller was like a tug to a horse's reins, a communication with something living. What would a wheel feel like — driving a truck?

Outside the marina, the wind whipped Johnstone Strait, but you couldn't feel much where we were sitting. I liked Scott and Debbie, their openness and the way they didn't allow the grandness of their boat to rub off on them. They gave us a business card with their names and a little picture of their boat, a practice I would later learn was *de rigueur* among serious cruisers. The dog didn't look up when we left. When we got to the top of the ramp, I caught Hatsumi's sleeve, and we turned to look out over the marina.

"We should get a boat too," I said. "To go with all my dad's stuff."

"Sure," she said.

Neither of us dreamed we would be back — in our own boat.

Hatsumi grew up in Tokyo, in what she calls her "hometown" of Kugayama. As far as I can make out, there are about a thousand of these hometowns in the city. If you walk one train stop from

Kugayama, dodging bicycles on the path that follows the con-cretized banks of the Kandagawa River, you come to Inokashira Park. It's one of the livelier parks in Tokyo, especially in the spring when people line up hours in advance to claim a spot to spread their blankets, open hampers, and consume staggering amounts of alcohol to welcome the *sakura* — Japan's spectac-ular cherry trees — back into bloom. Inokashira is one of the best places in Tokyo to get sozzled and serenade the cherry blossoms. If you're watching a movie filmed in Tokyo, chances are pretty good there'll be a scene in Inokashira Park.

The closest ocean is Tokyo Bay, another hour by train. There are few pleasure boats in Tokyo Bay, but Inokashira Park has two kinds on its little manmade lake. Courting couples gig-gle and flail in clunky rowboats, occasionally colliding beneath the overhanging branches of willows, and the dock at one end of the elegant curved bridge corrals a gaggle of blinding white pedal boats in the shape of swans. You and your partner sit in the swan's fat body and pedal like maniacs, as though climbing an impossibly steep hill, and the swan goes around in slow cir-cles, an icebreaker in a sea of cherry petals.

So, my wife's entire nautical experience, until our glass of wine on Scott and Debbie's yacht, was aboard a large mechan-ical bird.

"Don't worry," I told her, "in our family, we boated. I know all about sailing."

A few months after our visit to Sointula, I called Hatsumi over to my computer. "Look at this,"

She glanced at the screen. "It's a boat," she said. "So?"

"You agreed. That we should buy one. You don't remember?"

"I thought you were kidding."

"So did I," I said. "Until I saw this one."

We drove out to the sales dock the next day. It was raining and cold and *Jade Myst* looked miserable, the lines led aft along her deck gone green with algae and a deflating rubber dinghy draped over the dock like a Dali watch. But even neglected and in the drizzle, she was beautiful: dark green with massive bronze portholes, lots of teak, and a serious, seagoing flare to her bows.

"Big," said Hatsumi.

"Thirty-four feet," I read off the description printed on the brokerage card that dangled crookedly from a lifeline. "Same size as our family's last boat. No problem. But that name has to go. *Jade Myst*? Sounds like a stripper." The broker's write-up trumpeted the name of the boat's designer and builder but neither meant any more to me than the white radar dome twenty feet above my head. *Everything* was above my head. The asking price was astronomical, which probably explained the algae on the deck.

"I'm cold," said Hatsumi. A seagull landed on the radar dome and went "*Buk-buk-buk.*"

We remortgaged our home and made an offer. "Subject to survey," the broker, Allan James, had insisted. "And sea trial, of course." Allan was about my age, a worried-looking New Zealander in sweatpants, running shoes, and a blue toque. I liked him; his black humour and perpetual air of martyrdom over the inanities of the boat-buying public appealed to me immediately.

We walked down to the sales dock for the short trip across the harbour to the "travel lift," a monstrous wheeled gallows which would pluck *Jade Myst* out of the water so that the marine surveyor could do what he had to do. I had no idea what he had to do.

"Sailing all my life," I mentioned as we walked down the ramp. It was still raining. Allan hopped into the cockpit and did things to the engine. "I'll take her," he said. We were already moving by the time I jumped on. Allan brought the boat smoothly to the dock at the marine yard, working levers and spinning the big stainless steering wheel so that the boat seemed to levitate sideways into the tight space. I really wanted to ask Allan how he did that thing with the engine and the steering wheel, but he was gone already, up the ramp to the yard office, and someone else was holding out a wet hand.

"Bob Whyte," said a tall, bookish-looking man with a neat grey moustache. He held a clipboard. "Can we get out of the rain?"

"Be my guest," I said to the surveyor. That moustache was a good sign. Only anal-retentive people wore moustaches like that. If anything was wrong with *Jade Myst*, Bob would find it. We clambered down slippery wooden steps and looked around. *Jade Myst* smelled musty, a house from which the family had long departed. Everything was teak; it was like descending into a showroom for Scandinavian furniture. Daunting-looking electronics were recessed neatly into bulkheads.

"Bigger than my last boat," I said.

Bob Whyte pulled out a pocket flashlight, clamped it in his teeth, and dropped to his knees. He yanked out a trapdoor. "Might as well start in the bilge," he said and stuck his head in like an ostrich. I looked at his thin buttocks and the soles of his oxfords for a while and then went back out into the cockpit and started pulling things out of the lockers: half-empty engine oil containers, a dampish pair of blue coveralls, stained life jackets, and assorted lengths of hose. I rejoined Bob and found a wobbling bead of water hanging to the underside of the plexiglass hatch in the cabin roof.

"Got a leak here," I said.

Bob's checklist had begun to accumulate ticks. He snorted. "You're lucky. Usually, those ones are right over your berth." He didn't make a tick.

After that, I kept my mouth shut while Bob methodically

sounded the rest of the boat, inching along the deck like a man checking for mines, tapping the fibreglass with a rubber mallet and cocking his head to listen for the telltale sound of delaminated layers. Allan rematerialized, untied the boat, and eased her between the two canvas slings that dangled from the travel lift like enormous rubber bands. One went under the bow, the other was tugged beneath the stern, then a cautious revving of the travel lift's diesel and *Jade Myst* exited the water vertically to hang, dripping, in the frame of the huge machine. There was much more of her underwater than I had imagined.

Bob went over all of her considerable underbelly with his little hammer. I took out a credit card and began chipping at the barnacles on her propeller until Allan nudged me aside to screw a shiny new zinc anode onto the shaft. Bob peered around the curve of the hull, still tapping. "Don't forget to paint it," he said.

Did one paint zincs?

"You bet," I said.

"I was kidding," he said.

It started to hail. I ducked beneath the curve of the hull and stood next to the propeller as the concrete slowly whitened to outline the shape of our new boat.

Bob gave *Jade Myst* a clean bill of health, but there were more hoops to jump through. The next was the sea trial, when the prospective owners get to try the boat out on the water, just to be sure. Ours was no more than a slow loop around the bay in a dead calm, during which I was mostly concerned with hiding how much of sailing I'd forgotten. That was farcical, I thought, not knowing that the real sea trial would come four years later.

Boat names are important. I was sure *Jade Myst* should be renamed *Ima Kara*, an expression I first heard when I was hiking up a mountain in the Japan Alps, before Hatsumi, before boating. It was cold. I was labouring. A middle-aged man wearing spotless white gloves and wielding hiking poles appeared out of the mist. I stood aside to let him pass. But he stopped and grinned.

"*Ima kara,*" he said. Which means "this is just the beginning."

But *ima kara* would be useless for radio communication in Canada. I'd have to spell it out every time, I imagined the Coast Guard operator pushing the headphone harder into his ear and waving his hand for silence, writing it down and scratching his head: India-Mike-Alpha-Kilo . . . it would never work. One day, my wife announced the problem was solved.

"Your mother spoke to me last night," Hatsumi said. My mother had been dead for five years. "She asked if we would name the boat after her."

"Sounds right to me," I said.

But when we called on the Register of Vessels, "*Vera*" turned out to be a popular boat name; *Vera II* and *Vera III* were already bobbing around out there somewhere. Cathy Kimoto in the registry office shook her head as she went through the list. It began to look like we were back to *Ima Kara*.

"Wait," she said suddenly, flipping back a page. "*Vera*, just plain *Vera*. Here it is, but it's reserved." She ran her finger down the fine print. "Aha. The guy's time ran out. You can have it if you take it now." She dug under the counter for a form.

When Allan called and said he needed a certified cheque, we finally realized that we very nearly owned a large boat. We went to see the notary. Her office was a chaos of papers, piled, peeking out from folders, settled in uncertain stacks on the floor. She sifted through them, clucking. "You know what 'boat' stands for, of course?" she said, her head between her knees.

Hatsumi and I looked at each other and a small dog wandered in to sniff at our feet.

"Bring On Another Thousand." The notary surfaced, red-faced, and waved a document at us. "Sign here."

The next day was moving day, to the permanent space we'd reserved ten miles south, down Haro Strait. The first thing I did when we stepped aboard our new boat was hang over the side and laboriously scrape off four vinyl Jade Mysts with a putty knife. She was *Vera* now. I dug out the key, opened the engine seacock the way I'd seen the broker do, switched on the batteries, and pushed the starter. Hatsumi seemed frozen on the dock, and when the engine fired and cooling water shot out the stern, she jumped back.

"Sailing all my life, remember?" I looked up encouragingly and wrestled with dock lines that were stiff as boards. "Although Sidney *has* changed a bit since I was here last."

In thirty years, the foreshore around Sidney had become a nautical parking lot. The chart looked like a map for a new subdivision. I hadn't looked at a chart for a long time, and I turned it this way and that while the Yanmar diesel hawked and spat against the wharf. "Quit dithering," it seemed to be saying. "Can't you even find your way out of a marina?"

When we finally pushed off, the channels on the chart were replaced by a maze of navigational spars and buoys. "Red right returning" was all I could remember: keep the red marker on your right when entering a harbour. But there were many harbours here. Within seconds, the depth sounder showed five feet. Five feet was exactly *Vera*'s draft. I threw the engine into reverse and sand clouds boiled up around the stern, as though we had disturbed a sleeping sea monster. I headed straight for the fuel dock, channels and charts be damned.

"Stand on the bow," I told Hatsumi. "With the line, the *line*." She glared and shrugged. What was a "line" to her? It was what anybody else would sensibly call a rope.

"One of *these*," I yelled, waving the stern line at her. By the simple act of taking the wheel of a boat, I seemed to have become my father. A teenager on the fuel dock watched us come on, expressionless. As we nosed in, I tried what Allan had so effortlessly done: put the engine into reverse. The stern walked rapidly away from the dock. We hurled the lines at the kid and let him reel us in. When I jammed the fuel nozzle into the filler hole and pulled the trigger, *Vera* burped a foul splash of diesel into my face.

We passed Zero Rock on the trip down Haro Strait. It was a glorious, calm spring day, and we broke out the sandwiches as a colony of seals watched us chug past. I suppose they were the great-great-great-grandchildren of the ones who had peered indifferently at *Frou-Frou* and her frightened crew. I decided not to tell Hatsumi about the time I had been here forty years before.

Oak Bay, our destination, was another two hours down the road. When we began our way through the maze of rock and kelp beds outside the marina, *Vera* seemed to expand, her keel lengthening as the depth sounder's little grey numbers clicked backward. Docking and undocking, I'd read somewhere, were considered the most stressful part of boating. Now my bladder was confirming it. I wanted desperately to pee, but I hadn't figured out the marine toilet yet.

The boat slips, from water level, didn't look anything like the neat diagram in the marina office where we'd put down our deposit a week before. I'd overshot the Sidney fuel dock completely — how was I ever going to turn *Vera* up one of these tiny cul-de-sacs and bring her to a safe stop? As we closed in, I could see movement. One man got slowly out of his own boat and began to stroll with us, keeping pace. Two docks over, a heavyset fellow in shorts had begun to run, his sandals flapping. *Vera* and her petrified crew came on. A kneeling woman dropped her paintbrush and took off like a sprinter. By the time *Vera* had more or less turned the corner into her new slip, the three Samaritans were waiting for us, breathing heavily, arms outstretched.

"Just throw us your lines," they said.

And that was the easy part.

Travels with Lolita

After the unexpected meeting with my father at Portland Island, we sailed an unambitious few hours further north to Genoa Bay. With all the scramble of planning and packing, we needed a few lazy days before the jump across Georgia Strait to Desolation Sound. Genoa Bay was familiar and predictable, a notch in the southeast shore of Vancouver Island with a marina and plenty of anchoring space — a good place for Charley to work on his sea legs. We dropped anchor in mid-afternoon and were immediately surrounded by a flotilla of Canada geese. They paddled around *Vera*, muttering, while Charley vibrated and sniffed. One of them, apart and alone, was crippled, a leg twisted up and out of the water so that the bird advanced erratically, like one of the mechanical swans in Inokashira Park. I wondered how long it would last.

The sun sank behind its hill, Charley paced, and the water calmed and turned a muddy emerald. The geese had left; now we were surrounded by a constellation of floating seaweed, arbutus leaves, a paper plate. I decided to wash away the scramble and stress of leaving with something clear and sparkling.

"Hand me *Lolita*, would you?" I called down.

"Excuse me?"

I kept forgetting, Hatsumi's cultural legacy was as far away from mine, as though we were raised on separate planets.

"That book, the one with the ankles in bobby sox on the cover."

I like to reread Nabokov every few years — *Lolita, Pale Fire, Pnin* — for the sheer sensual pleasure of his prose. I didn't need much this time, just a quick hit. By page thirty-five, I had found Humbert Humbert's description of his mother's demise: "She died in a freak accident (picnic, lightning) when I was three."

"And English wasn't even his first language!" I said to Charley. I put *Lolita* down. Charley was starting to look longingly at a scruffy pocket of beach. Almost overnight, the transporting of our dog from boat to beach and back, a chore I'd watched other boaters submit to for years and sworn I would never, *ever* consent to, had become my new job. Maybe it was because the crunching sound of a boat on the gravel of a new beach seemed hard-wired into me, or just that I was a better rower than my wife. Two days into the trip, and Charley's bladder and bowels had slotted into my routine.

"Let's do it," I said, pulling the dinghy alongside, lowering myself in, holding out my arms. "Come on, jump, I've seen you go twice this far." But I still had to lift him, grabbing the handle on his life jacket and swinging him down like a flailing fluorescent briefcase. Charley's back legs were catapults, the thigh muscles like drumsticks on a Thanksgiving turkey. His default behaviour when lifted was to jump free. Carrying Charley up a few steps usually meant being kicked in the testicles. This time, he treaded air until landing in the dinghy, then scrambled to the bow and stood precariously balanced on the stem, a hairy figurehead with eyebrows. The closer the beach came, the more he wriggled; halfway there, he toppled over the side and began to swim in outraged circles, his front legs pawing at the water like a boxer working a punching bag. I yarded him back in, and he shot back to the bow, dripping but defiant. As soon as the boat touched the shore, he sproinged off vertically, like a kangaroo.

The only beach in Genoa Bay had an abandoned look, muddy and littered with ghostly crab moults and shreds of blue fibreglass encrusted in mussels. A rotting dock had come to rest under the trees, draped in rusted cables and carpeted in moss. I found a dryish spot and sat down while Charley raced around on the mud, looking for the perfect spot to urinate. When he was finished, he tried to sneak a fish head into the dinghy.

"She'll kill you," I said, flinging the thing away and shoving off.

We spent an uneventful night at anchor, the boat at rest in its allotted position in the bay as though we were curled up in one of those sailing-book diagrams of the yacht at rest, tethered to the elegant swoop of chain that led to the neatly buried anchor. I knew it couldn't last and found myself recalling an anchoring story I'd heard from David Bruce, a complicated man who dives under people's boats to replace the zinc anodes that corrode and fall off twice a year. I think he collects stories down there too. He was standing on the dock in his diving suit, dripping, when he told me this one.

"You remember those kerosene lamps we used to hang on the forestay as anchor lights at night?"

I did. As a child, it had been my job to light the sooty clunking thing at dusk, snap it to the jib halyard (the rope you pulled on to raise the foresail), and pull it up twenty feet or so. The lamp would bang around all night, keeping everyone awake.

"Well, this guy decided to put a really long shock cord on his lamp so it would stay quiet."

Good idea, I thought. Why didn't we think of that?

"Anyway, the wind got up that night, the boat started to rock, and suddenly the halyard chafed through and the lantern came down onto the deck. *Smash!* Unzip me?"

David turned around and I yanked on the big zipper that held his dry suit together across the shoulders. It was heavy and stiff, and he had to brace his feet against my tugs. I imagined the lake of burning kerosene running down the deck, the howls as the owner rounded the cabin corner in his pyjamas.

"What'd he do?"

"This is the best part. He sees all that burning kerosene, freaks out, grabs the lamp, and throws it as far as he can. But it's still attached by that shock cord. He said it came back at him like a comet!"

We both laughed, but afterward I kept imagining those seconds: the fireball hurtling into the night, diminishing, then suddenly expanding again, like a burning boomerang. It could so easily have been me.

⌐

When we got underway the next morning, the anchor came up pasted with mud and grit; the bottom we had swung over for the night was just an extension of the slimy beach Hatsumi had sluiced off Charley the night before. Mud bottoms are bliss for boaters, holding an anchor like glue. But they tend to come aboard when you leave.

Sailing was impossible along the sinuous channel of Sansum Narrows that separates Saltspring, the largest of the Canadian Gulf Islands, from Vancouver Island. Both the current and the wind were against us, so we motored through, finally raising the sails after exiting the narrows into the more open waters of Stuart Channel. Dodging a tug towing two barges kept us on our toes; although sailboats have the right of way over power-boats in most cases, tugs are one of the frightening exceptions.

Tugs look slow, but to a sailboat trying to make the most of a fitful wind, they're anything but. They can't stop and they would rather not turn. In these waters, tugs had a way of showing up everywhere, dragging barges piled with containers, or vehicles, or booms of fresh-cut logs. They frightened me.

Our next stop, Clam Bay, was as unambitious as Genoa Bay, but there was a tidal rapid coming up, and the next convenient opening was early morning. Dodd Narrows, between Gabriola (the northernmost Gulf Island) and Vancouver Island, is narrow and crowded in summer, so any attempt to "cheat" it — to go through much before or after slack water — meant going against a substantial stream of boats. If something went wrong, you wouldn't have much room to manoeuvre. Spending the night in Clam Bay would make it easy to hit Dodd Narrows at just the right time.

So we stopped there in mid-afternoon, after picking our way through a scattering of widely spaced navigational buoys, like the last pieces in a chess endgame. Clam Bay fronts the shallow corridor between Thetis and Penelakut Islands. They're really the same island, separated by a dredged channel through mud-flats called The Cut.

The two "islands" are geologically identical, but culturally they are worlds apart. Thetis is privately owned, chopped up into small waterfront lots and larger, interior acreages. Several of the bays are dominated by Christian summer camps. Penelakut Island, a bridge and literally a stone's throw away, is a reserve for the Penelakut First Nation, who were confronted by a British naval expedition a decade or so after British surveyors named the island Kuper (after the captain of the surveying ship *Thetis*). By the final decade of the nineteenth century, "Kuper" Island had its own Catholic residential school, a holding pen for First Nations children removed from their homes throughout the Cowichan Valley. You can still see the ruins of the school from the water; it closed, to universal shame, in 1975. Penelakut Island finally got its name back in 2010.

Clam Bay is on Penelakut territory, so most people who anchor there don't go ashore. The bay is guarded by a sandy spit and a marked shoal, between which you have to insert yourself, and I cut it too close. Eight feet, the sounder suddenly read (*eight feet!* Only three feet of water under the keel!), and I had to crank an embarrassing hard right to clear the unseen mound of sand. But there was plenty of room to anchor, and I curled up for an hour inside the mind of Nabokov's monstrous anti-hero. Teenagers cannon-balled off a power cruiser across the bay, whooping and hollering, while Humbert Humbert quietly plotted his campaign for literature's most famous bobbysoxer. The constriction of the channel we would need to negotiate our way through tomorrow, the unforgiving headlong rush of water from one basin to another, faded from my mind. But constrictions of another sort were at the heart of all those medical and legal records I was ignoring in favour of a novel I'd already read.

The Sea Inside Us

By the time we had set out in *Vera*, I already knew at least as much medicine as the lawyers who had made the deal my father had had to live with for twenty years. I had to: if I was really going to read his detective story, one document at a time, at anchor somewhere, or sitting on a log in some remote cove, I needed to understand the technical basics. If I did, the two months our trip would take might be enough time to get to the bottom of the person who'd been a puzzle to me for fifty years.

I hadn't brought any medical textbooks though. *Vera* had bookshelves, but those were needed for all the tables and guides and how-to books that made up our floating library. In a choice between *Principles of Neurological Surgery* and the shop manual for the Yanmar diesel engine, engine maintenance won out. What I didn't know yet was how close engine maintenance was to surgery. And I would never have guessed how the currents and constrictions we would navigate in *Vera* were mirrored, in miniature, by an aquatic labyrinth inside the brain, where my father did so much of his travelling.

He got his first look at the human brain when he was eleven. An "unknown man" (as his hometown *Killam News* put it) had fallen asleep across the railroad tracks that led to the swimming hole. "Not a little excitement" ensued when the poor man was discovered decapitated. In his memoir written seventy-five years later, my father picked up the story:

"The men who were responsible for overseeing the remains informed me that they were going home to lunch, and it would be my job to watch over the deceased. I remember my feeling of pride; I had been given a very important assignment! It was a hot day; flies covered the stump of the neck and the smashed-in head, and the man's brain was scattered about like spilled porridge."

I've always wondered how it fell to him to guard the corpse and whether his sang-froid in the presence of all that grey matter was real or just a convenient memory. Either way, twenty-five years later he was struggling to become a brain surgeon. That brain surgeon's nemesis was a disease called hydrocephalus, "water on the brain." If I could get my own head around hydrocephalus, its treatment, maybe even something of its history, then I could make sense of the rest of the stuff I had squirrelled aboard *Vera* — and of him. Without putting in the time to learn about this disease, whatever I wrote about my father would be as worthless as those newspaper articles from twenty years before. And if I could figure out what made my father tick, it wasn't too late for me to learn a few lessons myself. Never a bad thing at a time when people start commenting on your resemblance to your parents.

Conveniently, there was a medical library right across the street from my house. A few months before leaving on our trip, I had given the librarian a short list of topics I was interested in. A week later, I walked down the street and across the road to the Royal Jubilee Hospital to pick up the results. The last time I'd been there was to take my father to Emergency after finding him on the kitchen floor next to a puddle of melting chocolate ice cream. His bewilderment and rage at having to spend the night on a gurney in the hallway, for lack of bed space, had been hard to watch. Thirty years before, he could make beds materialize with a snap of his fingers.

The Victoria Medical Society maintained a brave little museum of old textbooks and instruments in a corner of the psychiatric ward. I passed the loading bay with its smell of soiled sheets. A scarecrow figure with exploding hair stared wordlessly at me as I struggled with the heavy door. He was wrapped head to toe in a blue hospital blanket. One side of his face seemed lower than the other, like a comic-book villain's. Whatever his condition, it was entirely possible that somewhere in the materials I'd requested there was an article that described it. We could sit down together, the sagging man and I, on one of the green vinyl sofas and pass an instructive hour looking for similar cases. An attendant took his elbow, and I escaped to the medical library.

To get around the cost of purchasing scientific articles online, I had used a subterfuge when filling out the request that would put the librarian to work downloading and printing out the twenty or so I'd asked for. Where it said, "Requesting Physician," I wrote "Dr. Harvey." It was true, in a way, and it worked, although the librarian gave me a searching look when I picked up the fat envelope.

"This will mean a lot to him," I said, taking a surreptitious peek at the contents. The papers I'd requested were all here, even the ones on the historical treatment of hydrocephalus, going back to the Middle Ages. But before I did any reading on history or treatment, I needed a road map. If I was to understand the disease, I had to know the terrain, and that meant textbooks. I extracted an up-to-date *Clinical Neuroanatomy for Medical Students* and the latest edition (the thirty-eighth) of *Gray's Anatomy*, a good fifteen pounds between them. Then I lugged my treasures to a table, along with a book I'd brought from home, my father's own copy of *Gray's*.

I started with that one. The leather-bound *Gray's Anatomy* had been my great-grandfather's, and it looked its age, stained and beaten. When I opened it, some dried petals drifted out, brown, veined, and paper-thin, like the wings of a moth. They fell apart in my fingers. Leander Harvey's signature on the inside cover was dated 1862; he must have bought the book the year it came out. The oval business stamp next to his signature proclaimed him "Surgeon, Accoucheur and Coroner, Watford, Ontario." "Charges Moderate," it said too, and "Attendance on the Destitute Free of Charge." An accoucheur was an obstetrician, so my great-grandfather must have done a bit of everything.

My father's signature, dated ninety years later, was the latest in a list of four medical Harveys, a streak that ended when none of his children offered to pick up the scalpel. His own father, in fact, had been a druggist and optician, and the closest my father got to a "medical upbringing" was the hours he spent hand-filling gelatin capsules with the concoctions his father had mixed. Still, some cabal of genes must have called to him across the generations; if anybody had asked me, right then, why my father had quit his job as a high school teacher and enrolled in medical school, I would simply have pointed to all those signatures in *Gray's Anatomy*. For him, the years as a medical student were years of hope and discovery — the best years of his life.

Gray's Anatomy, like all early anatomies, was the product of innumerable dissections of cadavers, accompanied by meticulous note-taking. This battered original was his ancestors' working manual: parts of the text were heavily marked up with pencil or green crayon. What I needed to know — the basic architecture of the brain and spinal cord, and especially the system of channels and ducts and reservoirs for the fluid that was at the core of hydrocephalus — was all there.

Modern editions are still called *Gray's Anatomy* but are the product of a committee. Comparing the two as I sat in the medical library, I saw that the modern version wasn't *all* new; a few of the original diagrams lingered on, a testament to how good those early anatomists had been. But the progress in imaging techniques was extraordinary. Now, the anatomist's eyes and simple light microscope were augmented by electron micrographs and magnetic resonance imaging (MRI) scans that allowed anatomists finally to observe and take measurements from a living subject. The MRI pictures of the brain in the new *Gray's* were so clear they could have been, well, diagrams.

～

It only took me an afternoon to get my bearings. The new anatomies were that good, allowing me to leapfrog a thousand years of medical observation and trial and error. I learned that our central nervous system contained an aquatic labyrinth and that I was going to have to navigate it. Like a nautical chart, the map of the cerebrospinal system was three-dimensional, and it depicted a tiny ocean within the globe of the skull. And, as I soon learned, these waters of the brain ebbed and flowed just like the waters of the ocean.

For the mariner, the greatest problems usually occur at constrictions, where water squeezes through narrow openings and the resulting buildup in pressure creates rapids as fast-running and dangerous as any river. It was the same in the sinuous channels of the brain; there were constrictions everywhere. To me, the generations of anatomists and physicians who had charted this inner ocean seemed to have something in common with their seafaring contemporaries. The great anatomist Giovanni Battista Morgagni opening the brain of a cadaver in Padua, the mapmaker George Vancouver creeping farther and farther up the forbidding fjords of Desolation Sound: both were explorers.

But there was too much terminology for me. I needed a way of seeing the cerebrospinal system in a practical light. I decided to think of it as the solution to a problem in engineering design and add the fancy names later. Here is what I came up with.

The brain and spinal cord comprise a single mass of neural tissue (imagine a pudding with a long tail). If you had to design a way to nourish and protect this delicate system, you might bathe it in fluid because fluids absorb shock and transport nutrients and wastes. Why not give the brain its own fluid-creating engine? Set it for continuous operation and attach a system of reservoirs and you've made a good start.

But you need to get that fluid *outside* the brain and spinal cord if it's going to act as a shock absorber. You also have to find a way to return the overflow to general circulation. So you do two things: perforate the inner network near the base of the brain, allowing fluid to leak out, and capture what comes out by wrapping the whole brain and cord in a membrane. Most importantly, you make that outer membrane a leaky one: tight enough to cushion the brain, but porous enough for the overflow to seep into the blood circulation.

Problem solved, in a way that's beautiful and mind-boggling. You now have *two* fluid spaces, two seas, one inside the brain and cord and another bathing them. Fluid is produced in the inner system, enters the outer system through a few critical one-way drains, and escapes through selective pores through the membrane that wraps everything together.

Here are a few critical names.

The fluid is called cerebrospinal fluid. All the authorities abbreviate to CSF, and so will I. There are about 130 millilitres of it — a cappuccino's worth — filling the spaces in and around the brain and spinal cord. The whole system is renewed four to five times a day. It's made in four cavities in the brain that look like a three-dimensional version of the Great Lakes. Those cavities, which will appear again and again in my story about hydrocephalus, are called ventricles (think "vent" and "trickle"), and they form a cascading system that's a prime candidate for blockages and obstructions. Eventually, the CSF escapes out the fourth ventricle to collect in that cushioning outer sea which encapsulates the brain and spinal cord. Things are crammed in here: that envelope also surrounds the optic nerve, an arrangement that can have unpleasant consequences if CSF pressure increases. Pressure on the optic nerve was at the heart of the plaintiff's case against my father.

Pressure is normally kept constant, however, and we know the entire fluid volume turns over every five hours, but *how*? The heart doesn't push it around. How does it get from the ventricles, down around the spinal cord, around the brain and out?

This is the part that made me sit back in my chair in the medical library, look up from the shiny colour diagrams, and shake my head. Because circulation of the CSF is *passive*. Fluid moves because of the beating of a million hair-like cilia that line the ventricles like microscopic oars, because of the flexing of the spine, because of respirations, coughs, and changing body position. Even the far-off beating of the heart is tapped. It was like my father's self-winding LeCoultre wristwatch that fascinated me as a child; I would pick it up from his bedside table and tilt it back and forth in my palm just to feel the mysterious internal clunk of the tiny weight inside, rolling around and somehow keeping the watch ticking.

And I had all this in my brain! No wonder he'd had such a horror of the head injuries we might suffer if we swung from a tree, played football, rode a motorcycle. This microcosm of pulsations and membranes and imperceptible internal tides had been his universe, and he knew from daily experience that a blow to the head could easily overwhelm the shock-absorbing capacity of the CSF. His warnings to us were fifty years ahead of today's vigilance about concussions. What I was finding in my reading was mechanisms upon mechanisms, checks and balances, an exquisite homeostasis of the kind that nature is so profligate with, from the microscopic world to the planet we live on. I gave my head an experimental little shake, in case my own cerebrospinal fluid needed a nudge, like my father's ancient watch.

Unfortunately, a tiny failure somewhere in the chain can crash the whole system, as surely as a single submerged rock can hole a ship and sink it. In the human brain, the consequences of failure in the CSF circulatory system can be spectacular. The best known is hydrocephalus. The name means, roughly, "water on the brain," although really that should be "too much water on the brain." Hydrocephalus is a nightmare, and for over a thousand years, physicians stood and watched while children died from it. Hydrocephalus had been the gremlin riding on my father's shoulder in 1976, looking down while he performed the simple operation all neurosurgeons did to put the brain's plumbing back in order.

Relearning is a second chance. What I learned about the workings of the CSF system in an afternoon at the library was wondrous and felt new, but it wasn't really. I had studied these things before, as an undergraduate in biology, but the learning then had been unengaged and impermanent. I had no reason to care about the human brain, not then. This time around, though, the cerebrospinal system went from being just a diagram to be memorized to a small universe populated with the ghosts of ancient anatomists and my own family's skeletons. The novelty, the complexity, the history — it was irresistible.

Learning to Sail (Again)

I also had to relearn how to sail. I had learned the hard way, my father lowering me into an eight-foot sailing dinghy and pushing me away from the dock to fend for myself while he tried to get some varnishing done. I wound up jammed against the side of a tug anchored in the bay. Most horrifying were the white roman numerals painted on the stem, like a ladder into the depths.

The last sailboat I had owned was a twenty-foot daysailer that was little more than a big dinghy. *Vera* was almost twice as long, and a sailboat's volume and complexity don't increase with length in a linear way; they metastasize. Here was novelty, here was an embarrassment of complexity, and mastering it would all be very public.

Sailing would be relearning for me, and my wife's maritime experience with the pedal-driven swans in Inokashira Park wasn't going to be much use in Haro Strait. From the moment we took possession of *Vera*, Hatsumi and I would be partners in a three-legged race with plenty of spectators. For the first few years, it felt as though we had opened the wrong door and stumbled into the Olympics.

The first lesson we learned about sailing was that it's ruinously expensive. I already expected this, although I soon realized it was mostly non-boaters who, when I told them what we'd just done, brightened and said, "A boat! You know what a boat is, right?"

"No. What is it?"

"A hole in the water into which you throw money. Har! Har!"

I've always thought this a feeble image; in my imagination, the bills simply float around until you reach in and retrieve them. I prefer "Boating is like standing in the shower and tearing up dollar bills," because it better captures the masochism of it all. But both adages claim the same thing: boating is a waste of money.

This tearing up and flushing of currency refers mostly to parts and maintenance. When you buy a boat, you meet a lot of men in coveralls (and a few women). The silver lining of inflated marine prices is that they establish a dividing line between two kinds of boater: those who pay the professionals and those who are prepared to put themselves through all manner of contortions in order to avoid shelling out. If you pay, boating really is ludicrously expensive. If you don't, and you learn how to fix things yourself, it's almost affordable.

The water pump on *Vera*'s Yanmar diesel engine, for example, would cost me nearly a thousand dollars to buy new and another couple of hundred to have installed. It's a critical component, even though all it's asked to do is sit on the end of the engine and be spun by the alternator belt so that it sucks in seawater to cool the engine. Is that so hard? There's nothing to the thing: a cast-metal body the size of a baseball, a pulley, a shaft that spins a rubber impeller inside like a miniature water wheel. It only costs a thousand dollars because people are willing to pay that much for it.

By the time *Vera*'s water pump began to weep and accumulate an unsettling crust of verdigris and salt crystals, I had already been a boat owner long enough to know where to go for help. I pulled the pump off the engine, took it apart in my basement, put all the cruddy corroded bits in a plastic bag, and drove out to Willi Fahning's shop. The plastic bag told Willi instantly what kind of boater I was: a cheap one.

"You got a crack here or two." Willi bent one of the impeller vanes back. He was right, the rubber was split. I'd missed that.

"Hard as hell to get it out," I said, fishing for information. "I read you could get a special tool, a what-do-you-call-it, a puller?"

"Forget about that," said Willi. "Two screwdrivers, like this." He stuck imaginary blades into the impeller's body and made vigorous prying motions, like a duck taking off. "When you put the new one in, put some of this on the shaft." He handed me a free tube of KY lubricant. "Or you can spit on it."

"That's it?"

"Mit one of these gaskets, that's it." He handed me a circle of punched paper in a plastic sleeve. "If you don't have one, maybe you just cut one out of a shopping bag. Shaft is okay?" He wiggled the pump shaft.

"It has seals, right?" I said. "I could put in new ones, maybe?"

Willi frowned under his toque. It was winter outside. I was the only person in the shop, which was papered in photographs and articles about its owner: Willi twenty years ago, riding one of his own handmade racing bicycles in a South American race; Willi ten years before that, beside a freighter propeller four times his height. There were testimonials from competitive cyclists and faded photographs of Argentina. Tomorrow, Willi would leave for a month in Patagonia.

"New ones? What for? You don't got leaks with the old ones. New ones gonna cost you."

I followed Willi into his work area. Piano music came from a portable stereo perched above the solvent bath, below pictures of friendly looking naked women. I recognized middle-period Beethoven.

"Impeller's forty-five dollars," Willi said, handing me another baggie. "You're lucky, this one's still marked with the old price."

I managed to cram the new impeller in after coating it with the lubricant, then bolted the pump back together and repainted it shiny white for good measure. In all, sixty dollars, a little of my time, a lot of freely given advice, and a chance to meet somebody interesting.

This leads to the second lesson about boating: everything you do is for the first time. The third lesson follows: there are no teachers. Or, more accurately, there are no courses where you can learn more than the rudiments of things that can be covered in a classroom: navigation, safety, weather patterns. But when you head into a well-marked channel for the very first time, that "north cardinal" buoy, so easy to distinguish from the east, west, and south cardinal buoys because of the arrangement of black spheres and triangles on top, now just looks like another chess piece. You have no idea what to do. Rocks materialize and grow inexorably as you scramble for handbooks, rack your brain, argue.

~

Our first summer of actual sailing in *Vera* was an excruciating cram course on fluid mechanics involving current, wind, and lateral resistance. These things are the basis of sailing: you try to use resistance and airflow to your advantage and try to cancel them when you can't.

Each lesson began and ended with the dreaded docking. The first complication was the current, which had to be checked religiously, before untying anything, by dropping to your knees and peering at the seaweed streaming away from the underside of the dock like underwater windsocks. If they pointed north, that's the way the boat would take off, the moment you untied. Whatever you did.

The second problem was wind. Sailboats under power at low speed react more to the wind than to the helm; the bow thinks it's a sail. The third problem was reverse gear because the turning of the propeller drags the stern sideways. Boat shape matters profoundly: a narrow fin keel makes for a sailboat that can spin on a dime, while a full keel produces a stately, stable craft that needs a *Queen Elizabeth*'s worth of turning room. *Vera* was one of those. Docking *Vera*, that first year, was like trying to back a semi-trailer into a parking spot — on a slope, on ice, and with a crowd watching. It literally scared the pee out of me. The nerves would creep up on me two miles from home, with physiological consequences.

"Take her for a second?" Hatsumi would be on the fore-deck, staying out of my way, when I asked her this.

"Didn't you just *go*?"

"It's the coffee, okay? It goes right through me. Just keep the cardinal buoy to port." And down below I would go, to crouch again over the toilet.

"What *kind* of cardinal buoy?"

Hatsumi came occasionally unglued at the disorder so common on deck. The raising and lowering of sails became a flashpoint. When a sail needs to come down, I want it *down*; for my wife, the collapse of the mainsail in chaotic folds was very un-Japanese. Flaking the main, something I thought people only did in books, became an obsession for her, two hundred fifty square feet of heavy Dacron wrenched and patted into neat, accordion folds on the boom. It took a long time.

"My shoulder hurts," she might say after one of these flake-a-thons.

"Then don't flake the main."

"Why don't *you* flake the main?"

"Because I can't do it *nearly* as well as you."

Tantrums were common, on both sides. My face, Hatsumi informed me, was perpetually "difficult." *Vera* felt as big as a ferry. A routine sailing manoeuvre like "going about," where you shift the wind from one side of the boat to the other in order to make forward progress against it, felt as though we were sailing in glue. The sails snapped sullenly. I lost a thumbnail in a winch. Even when things were going well, they went badly. Once, going full tilt into a fresh breeze, water foaming at the lee rail and everything singing — finally! — I misremembered the rules of the road, shaking my fist at an onrushing sailboat until I realized why they weren't going to turn. *They* had the right of way. We were an embarrassment.

⌇

With a start like this, what happened to us in Baynes Channel our first year was inevitable. Baynes is a notorious constriction at the south end of Haro Strait where currents can reach eight knots. This may not sound like much, but it is the equivalent of the entire body of water moving at a brisk walk. *Vera*'s top speed under power is six knots, so we would go backward. The combination of wind against tide creates waves and whorls that snatch at your keel and make the wheel jump in your hands. Even on a relatively calm day, Baynes Channel sounds like a river.

"We'll go out through Baynes," I said. "It'll be a good experience."

"I trust you," said Hatsumi.

It was a warm, early summer evening, with just enough breeze for getting to know *Vera* better. We squirted easily through Baynes Channel with the current behind us, and Haro Strait broadened to include the distant cliffs of Sidney Island and the closer, greener shapes of the American Gulf Islands. We coasted back and forth, getting the feel of the boat in the warm evening breeze while Hatsumi went below and boiled water for coffee. Then we dropped the sails and starting the engine to make it home through the remaining turbulence.

"See that little bay?" I pointed to an indentation in the Vancouver Island shore. "Right there, me and my brother and my dad, that's where we ended up."

"What are you talking about?"

"I guess I never told you. It was forty years ago. Don't worry, *Vera*'s a lot more boat."

Then the engine stopped. *Vera* coasted a few lengths, then began to drift backward. Instead of the drone of the engine, I now heard seabirds and the rushing of a tidal river.

"I *know* we have fuel," I said. Hatsumi looked stricken. "There's still some wind. We'll sail back." We got Hatsumi's impeccably flaked mainsail back up, unrolled the jib, and caught the remaining breeze, nosing *Vera* as close into the wind as I could, trying to make headway upstream. Finally, the little bay was visible again. But the wind was just a cat's paw now, toying with us. To one of the lucky homeowners on shore, we must have made a pretty picture as we ghosted along, the kind of image that causes people to go out and buy boats.

"Take her," I said. "I'm going down to look in the tank."

"I wouldn't bother if I were you," said a voice. I looked back up the companionway; Hatsumi had a death grip on the wheel and was staring fixedly ahead.

"Did you say something?" I asked.

"What?" She kept staring, as though she could will the wind to come.

"Never mind. I must be hearing things. I'm opening up the tank."

It was the only thing I could do. I didn't know my engine at all, but I could at least look in the tank, a stinking wedge-shaped aluminum coffin beneath the cabin floorboards. Even down below, on my hands and knees, I could tell *Vera* wasn't moving on her own anymore.

"Got it," I yelled up, pulling the hatch off and peering down at what I already knew I would find: a lake of fresh diesel fuel, the level unchanged from when we had filled it a week ago.

"What should I *do*?" said Hatsumi. I dropped the screwdriver and emerged to see a tug bearing down on us. A log boom the size of a football field stretched astern. The tug operator leaned on his horn, an outraged *blatt* that rolled over us and must have brought the homeowners upright in their chairs on shore. The log boom swept by twenty feet from us, most of the logs rough-cuts, with untrimmed branches grabbing crazily at the sky as though the trees were trying to right themselves and escape. An eagle perched on one. It looked disgusted.

And so the sun set as we drifted toward the shipping lanes and the state of Washington. After an hour, my pride faltered, and I reached for the cellphone. In the logbook I'd started, there was a short list of numbers, one of them a boat owner named Stuart, who kept his forty-footer across from us. In the few weeks we'd owned *Vera*, Stuart had become a friend, popping up with invaluable advice ("You will always need an extremely long-handled screwdriver") and commiserating over the flaws all boats have.

"We're in the middle of Baynes Channel," I said.

"I'm in the middle of dinner," Stuart said.

"There's no wind and our engine is out and we're heading toward San Juan Island."

"It'll take me an hour to get there." We turned the running lights on and sailed aimlessly back and forth along a wall of moving water that repelled *Vera* like some malignant, charged curtain. Finally, Hatsumi spotted Stuart's boat, and I joined three docklines, praying that I'd remembered the special knot correctly, and soon we were under way behind him, sails down and with a reassuring view of Stuart's transom and the forceful jet of cooling water spurting out of it.

"You know," I said to Hatsumi, "I could have sworn I heard my father when I was down there taking the tank apart."

"Your father's dead."

"I know that. But does it mean we can't communicate?"

"What did he say?"

"Nothing special. Basically that I didn't know what I was doing."

Two Faces of an Island

Quite apart from the "offshore trial run" argument for going around Vancouver Island, there was also the desire to find a little more space to yourself. On the eastern, and much more popular, side, especially its southern portion, you were constantly cheek by jowl with everybody else who could afford a boat.

To get an idea of the historic expansion of pleasure boating around Vancouver Island, imagine taking a nautical chart of the coastline between Seattle and Alaska and dipping it in the sea. The first place to submerge is the U.S. Gulf Islands, clogged with yachts by the 1980s. The Canadian Gulf islands, which were relatively empty when I was cruising as a child, filled up soon after so that by the early 1990s — lower the chart a little — boaters were passing straight through the arbutus-fringed coves and lichen-spattered rocks of the southern Gulf Islands and flooding up the Strait of Georgia. They were headed for Desolation Sound, a paradise of sheltered anchorages roughly bounded by the city of Parksville and the Sunshine Coast to the south and the gauntlet of rapids north of Quadra Island to the north. Desolation Sound, once you got past the slightly worrying transit of Georgia Strait, meant short trips between anchorages, oysters so thick you could sit in your dinghy and chip them off the rocks, and alpine peaks that seemed to shoot straight up from the ocean. And warm water: you can swim every day in Desolation Sound.

Of course, Desolation Sound filled up too. Lower the chart a bit more, and the water level rises into the Broughton Archipelago. Yes, navigation is trickier up there; yes, the temperature drops, but by the mid-'90s, everybody had GPS and on-board heaters and computer programs that told them how to get past the rapids. So, on they came. The worst obstacle was getting through Johnstone Strait, fifty miles of frequent wind-tunnel mayhem between the top of Quadra Island and the town of Port McNeill, but boaters figured out how to dart around the back alleys for most of it. The Broughtons haven't filled up yet, but they're starting to.

What's north of the Broughton Archipelago? If you stick to what locals call "the mainland," meaning the coasts of northern B.C. and Alaska, there are plenty of fjords and fishing communities, and all you have to do to explore literally thousands of miles of coastline is to pick a good moment to cross the one unprotected section of Queen Charlotte Strait. You can even opt for Haida Gwaii (the former Queen Charlotte Islands) if the mainland doesn't appeal, as long as you stick to the relatively protected eastern side. You need a bigger boat to go north, but plenty of people have big boats now. Slowly, the northern coast will fill up too. You might as well let that sodden chart float away; what used to be the haunts of commercial fishermen, Indigenous peoples, and hardy settler families are now the summer homes of fifty-footers from as far south as Portland, Oregon.

But what about the rest of Vancouver Island? In the case of a long, thin island like Vancouver, why concentrate on one side? The reason is the same as for the Haida Gwaii: the east side is protected, while the west shore takes the full pounding of the open Pacific. So while the west side of Vancouver Island is well known as a place of extraordinary natural beauty — a lot of it is national or provincial parkland, and parts of Clayoquot Sound comprise a UNESCO Biosphere Reserve — most people will admire those sandy beaches, those jagged black reefs, that pounding surf, and the frequent enveloping mists from somewhere safe. They'll be on land.

Because once you step off land, you're entering a place where bad things converge: oceanic waves from Pacific storms a thousand miles away, high local winds (or quixotic calms, which can be almost as bad), impenetrable fogs, and many, many rocks. The rocks are very different from the ones on the east coast, not only in their shape (they tend to be pinnacles) but most horribly in their number and placement. There are an awful lot of them, and some are more than a mile offshore. When I first saw the paper chart for Kyuquot Sound, about a third of the way down the western coast, the "open" waters off the coast were speckled with tiny black crosses.

There isn't much protection. You hide where the natives and the early settlers hid, built their villages and trading centres, lost their sons and fathers to the storms and shoals. The towns that have survived are small and tough and widely spaced. If you need a dozen eggs or shelter from a building westerly, you'd better plan ahead.

For all these reasons, the west coast of Vancouver Island will always be a challenge. People with a taste for adventure, plenty of time, a good boat, and a low tolerance for crowded anchorages *do* circumnavigate the island, and the numbers have been rising steadily ever since satellite-based navigation systems have taken the edge off some of the white-knuckle passages through reefs and around headlands. But when you hear about someone having gone around the island, it's still a "wow" moment, and few boats head out alone.

A lot of boaters see circumnavigating Vancouver Island as a test, especially people who, like us, were dreaming about sailing their boats offshore to somewhere warm, like Mexico or Tahiti. There are (of course!) two schools of thought here.

"Once you've gone around the island," a speaker at the Bluewater Cruising Association once lectured us, "you're ready." But when I mentioned circumnavigation to Allan, the broker from whom we bought *Vera*, he didn't even look up from the cat's cradle of docking lines he was trying to sort out. Dock space at his small brokerage was limited, so Allan often had two or three sailboats mysteriously tethered, like flies caught in a spider's web, where there was really only room for one.

"Why would anyone want to do that?" He tugged on a line and a thirty-five footer two boats away turned slightly.

"They say it's a good tune-up for going offshore," I said.

"It's nothing like going offshore. Going offshore is pointing your boat west, sailing a hundred miles out, and turning left. Long ocean swells, hit the trades, keep going until you reach the Marquesas."

"And the west coast of Vancouver Island is . . . what?"

"Fog. Wind. A rockpile."

"Did you ever do it?"

Like many other long-distance sailors, Allan seemed to have fallen into boat-selling after washing up in Victoria. He looked up from his knots.

"What would I want to do that for?" he said. "But if you're set on it, watch out for the Nahwitti Bar."

"Sure," I said. There it was again. I was starting to worry about this place. "What exactly should I watch out for?"

"Don't cross it at the wrong time, when the current's running. Don't go if the wind's blowing the dog off the chain. And once you head into it, remember, there's no turning back."

Water on the Brain

My father once had a wooden boat that began to leak after we'd had it on dry land to paint the bottom. The planks had shrunk enough for water to fill the bilge in minutes once we'd put the boat back in. He sat in the boat all night, pumping the ocean out and waiting for the wood to swell enough to stop the bleeding. I wonder if, during those long, lonely hours, the analogy with hydrocephalus occurred to him.

I began to visit the medical library more often after my father died (or, as he might have put it, finally fell completely apart). I spent much of one winter there trying to understand the thing that happened when the currents in our inner ocean became backed up or reversed: hydrocephalus. Hippocrates appears to have coined the name. For him, hydrocephalus meant a collection of fluid *outside* the brain — what we would now call a hematoma. Because autopsies were then considered an impiety, there was never any link made between cerebrospinal fluid (CSF) and the ventricles, those four cavities in the brain in which the CSF pools. The ancient Greeks and Romans knew about the ventricles all right, but for them their function was to house the soul.

Hydrocephalus was well known throughout the Dark Ages, a six-hundred-year stretch in Europe when "Western" science was kept alive by the Arabs and Turks. Avicenna's *The Canon of Medicine* was one of many learned treatises from the flowering of the Moslem Empire, and the English version of Avicenna's book that I found in the Victoria Medical Library was based on Latin ones that were in use all the way to the nineteenth century. What better illustration of how slowly science moved in those times: a text with an eight-hundred-year shelf life!

Islamic cultures shared the distaste for dissection, so Avicenna's writings are probably based on clinical notes alone, which explains why he could not identify the exact location of the cerebrospinal fluid. Avicenna knew there was no hope for true, intracranial hydrocephalus, the kind I was most interested in. The treatments available to him for *any* disease seem depressingly wrong-headed: blood-letting, leeches, cupping (in which a candle was burned in an inverted glass, to create a slight vacuum). I thanked my lucky stars and moved on.

Four hundred years after Avicenna, Şerefeddin Sabuncuoğlu was a surgeon who wrote one of the earliest Turkish medical texts. Hydrocephalus is largely a disease of children, and it was Sabuncuoğlu who made the first pediatric neurosurgical drawings. For him as for Avicenna, hydrocephalus seems to have meant the external type of the disease. One of his exquisite miniatures shows a female physician extracting a dead hydrocephalic fetus from a seated mother.

These were Dark Ages indeed. Physicians and frightened parents knew about early childhood hydrocephalus, the most common form of the disease, but they were powerless to cure it. Its appearance in the weeks after birth must have been appalling: the bulging anterior fontanel (soft spot); the splitting cranial sutures; the telltale resonance when the skull was rapped (still called, quaintly, "MacEwan's crackpot sound"); the downward gaze ("setting sun eyes") from compression of the bony plates. The infant's scalp became shiny, the veins bulged, and the rapidly enlarging head was hard to hold up. Something was going horribly wrong, the child's cranium blowing up like an overfilled wineskin. In these times, the physician was as much a spectator to hydrocephalus as were the parents; his treatments, as with so many in the history of medicine, proved spectacularly irrelevant. In a few cases, the disease arrested spontaneously, but usually the head just kept expanding. Then came the seizures, merciful unconsciousness, death. From the Romans to the Renaissance, a period of recorded medical experience and opinion of more than eight hundred years, this was how it was.

This shouldn't be a surprise, because medicine has always moved slowly. My father used to relate how, in the mid-1940s, he worked on what he called an "assembly line" for electroshock therapy in a Toronto psychiatric hospital (he was in the Army Medical Corps). When the convulsions had subsided and the patient began to breathe again, "every breath was a screaming gale, and foaming saliva poured from his mouth, and sometimes the foam was mixed with blood. The attendants wheeled him out and brought in another." That sounded pretty medieval to me.

⌇

Hydrocephalus remained misunderstood and untreatable until the anatomists came along. These men went in with saw and scalpel and prising fingers to see what made the human body tick, falter, collapse into entropy-filled chaos. For the anatomists, if there really was a "*spiritus animus*," it had to fit in with the plumbing, the ducts and valves and cavities they sliced open, traced, measured, and drew. It was like going inside the black box.

The shift in treatment of hydrocephalus wasn't sudden — the disease remained virtually a death sentence until the early twentieth century — but it did follow the leads uncovered on those dissecting tables. The Renaissance anatomist Vesalius was the first to describe internal hydrocephalus in a scientific way. His report on a two-year-old hydrocephalic girl he dissected in Augsburg, Mozart's birthplace, convinced him finally to break with the Hippocratic concept of the disease: fluid *could* be found in the ventricles. The poor girl's brain had become all ventricle; what was left was like the rind of a grapefruit.

But progress was agonizingly slow, as it had to be in a field where experimentation was near-impossible and inferences could be made only after dismantling dead people. So there was still no hope for famous hydrocephalus sufferers like William Henry, Duke of Gloucester, next in line as ruler of Great Britain. Hope for continuing the Stuart dynasty died with William in 1700. He had mild hydrocephalus. At age five, "his hat was big enough for most men." A generation later, Jonathan Swift may also have suffered from hydrocephalus. By 1740, the author of *A Modest Proposal* and *Gulliver's Travels* had lost most of his memory. He died at age seventy-eight after three days of convulsions; the post-mortem found "much water on the brain."

After a week or so in the library, I knew this: by the close of the eighteenth century, childhood hydrocephalus was known to involve accumulation of cerebrospinal fluid in the ventricles. It would be another hundred years before physicians could do much about it, but they'd made a start. The turning point came with the dissections of Giovanni Battista Morgagni, the young professor of anatomy at the University of Padua. Morgagni's work marked the birth of the "anatomical concept," in which disease and symptoms are correlated with observable changes in an organ — in other words, the beginnings of pathology.

On hydrocephalus, Morgagni writes about the dissection of a baby girl in whom there was "no cerebrum, but only a kind of bladder, in which nothing was contained but a kind of yellowish water." Another infant's brain was "hollowed out after the manner of a species of cabbage." And another where "a portion of its substance remained, so small as scarcely to equal a little egg in bulk." As to cause, he speculates that the "pituitary gland may be obstructed, or other passages, which serve to carry off the water collected in the brain" — so he wasn't far off.

But really, the message I took from Morgagni was still the wretched slowness of it all. Another two hundred years after Vesalius, and we're still describing swollen heads in terms of garden produce? Sitting in the library surrounded by the accumulated medical wisdom of two and a half thousand years, I found it hard not to think about the past — and not just the flash and sizzle of my father's life and career, no more than a mosquito caught in the bug zapper on a hot summer night, but the drawn-out, deeper drone of ghosts long past.

I found myself conjuring the scene in Morgagni's time: the anatomists bent over the small body on the table, the saws and knives and bowls, the oil lamp brought closer. For me, his most appalling description is of opening up a *living* infant in whom the bones of the skull had been "drawn asunder" by the pressure from accumulated cerebrospinal fluid. Morgagni found, with successive cuts (between convulsions), that the brain was "extended almost to the thinness of a membrane." Medicine advanced; the child died. It was a gory business, and I wondered how my father had stood it for so long.

⁓

By 1808, the surgeon John Cheyne was able to write his long *Essay on Hydrocephalus Acutus, or Dropsy in the Brain*. The title alone tells us how far we still had to go: *dropsy* is the old word for *edema*, and in those days it meant cathartic medicines were in order. So Cheyne's poor patients vomited out emetics and voided the ghastly stools he characterized as oily-looking, glazed, tremulous, or glairy (which means, I found out, "covered with glair"). Cheyne ignored intracranial pressure. For him, hydrocephalus *had* to be dropsy. So his harrowing treatments continued: the leeches, the foul-smelling poultices, the blisters to the stomach and head that only acted, like Vicks VapoRub, as counterirritants.

The last great contribution from the anatomists was by the protean Swede Gustaf Retzius. Until him, people still believed the fluid was only present as a result of hydrocephalus, not in healthy people. His monumental neuroanatomy text of 1875, written with Axel Key, contained many illustrations of the crucial dye-injection experiments that finally mapped the cerebrospinal circulation. Retzius and Key's exquisite engravings became the road map for neurosurgical advances in the next century.

But the new chart of the cerebrospinal fluid system did not prevent L. Emmett Holt, in his 1897 textbook *The Diseases of Infancy and Childhood*, from believing it better to refrain from any treatment at all "unless rupture seems likely." Most of the twentieth-century writers like Holt were practising physicians, and their texts read like how-to books. In the 1912 edition of Cheyne and Burghard's *Manual of Surgical Treatment*, I learned how to insert a crude permanent spigot into the lateral ventricle, to drain off excess CSF. This was the first time I came across anything that resembled the modern shunt, the mainstay of treatment until just recently. Sometimes it worked. In a few cases, skull size diminished dramatically, the edges actually overlapping to produce "a most curiously deformed small skull," a description that brought to my mind a curled-up woodbug.

W.W. Keen, in *Surgery, Its Principles and Practice* (1919), went one better with a bypass that drained CSF from the lower back to the peritoneal (abdominal) cavity. This required a tricky laminectomy (removing part of a vertebra) to get the fluid out through the lower spine. It was daring surgery, a kind of permanent lumbar puncture or spinal tap.

Once I encountered terms like "laminectomy" and "lumbar puncture," I began to feel on oddly familiar ground. Not because I knew what the words meant, but because they had been a subliminal part of my upbringing. At the breakfast table, other children might have heard about politics or the weather or perhaps the hockey scores; for us, it was my father's offhand, "I have to do a laminectomy today," or my mother's anxious, "Keep it down. Your father was up all night doing a craniotomy." I had no idea what these words meant, but I never forgot them, and it was when I began to meet them again, in the library, that I realized I was enjoying myself. Nosing around in the classics of medicine, finally finding out what a ventriculogram was (another of those breakfast-table words), reading about glairy stools and exploding heads — this stuff was *interesting*.

But I was still stuck in 1919. Neurosurgery, the specialty my father trained so hard for and, at the end, likened to "just being a cobbler," hadn't even been invented yet. I needed someone to get me from W.W. Keen to the treatment for hydrocephalus that my father first learned at the University of Chicago in 1949. There was only one person who could do that, and his name was Walter Dandy.

～

The history of the treatment of hydrocephalus is all about getting rid of fluid. All those surgeons bent over swollen-headed infants seemed to me like sailors struggling to keep a leaking boat afloat — except that, for the surgeons, the boat was producing its own water. The child was drowning in its own ocean. But the solution was the same: man the pumps.

The terrible prognosis for children with true intracranial hydrocephalus stayed unchanged until the 1940s and the ultra-competitive American surgeon Walter Dandy. Dandy was *the* authority on hydrocephalus. My father's copy of Dandy's

1945 *Surgery of the Brain* is inscribed "Chicago, August 1947," where he was completing his Ph.D. in neurosurgery. The pages are shiny and yellowed and well thumbed.

Much of Dandy's information came from experiments on dogs, and reading his book brought back uncomfortable memories. Even as a child, the little I knew about my father's research included the use of dogs and monkeys, and it troubled me then. There was no CT or MRI in those days; if you wanted to learn about the cerebral circulation (which was why my father was in Chicago), you did things to monkeys and dogs. I still have a cardboard box in the basement with his collection of monkey skulls; in many, the top half has been neatly severed, like an ostrich egg cup.

Dandy and his colleague Blackfan went through a lot of dogs, and what they did was this: inject the animal with a dye, engineer a blockage in the CSF system, then wait to see where the dye did or didn't go. Tracing the plumbing, that's what it was. Long before our trip with *Vera*, I remembered leafing through Dandy in my living room and listening to the nighttime snuffles and sighs of my own dog. Charley was the perfect size for advancing medical knowledge. His cranium fit nicely into the palm in my hand. But he wouldn't go quietly: the Colonel Blimp eyebrows would shoot up and the facial fur erect like a bottle brush and Charley would be a salt-and-pepper blur. The doctor would be lucky to escape, lab coat flapping, before Charley got the syringe away from him and jammed it into a calf.

But it was no good romanticizing; I didn't have a hydrocephalic child. The deaths of Dandy's dogs, while conclusively mapping out the canals and spaces, still hadn't offered much in the way of treatment for hydrocephalus. There's a picture in Dandy's book of a three-year-old boy lying against the pillow and gazing expectantly at the photographer. He has lovely eyes, a button nose, an alert expression — but above the eyebrows his head balloons like a cartoon Martian's. I flashed back to my only experience of hydrocephalus, on a clogged, malodorous sidewalk in Bangkok where the competition for alms was so fierce, the beggars outdid each other with sympathy-inducing props. A hydrocephalic kid lay uncovered on the pavement next to someone who was presumably a parent but might just as easily have rented the boy for the day. The skin of the youngster's head was taut, like a grape on a stick. The boy stared wordlessly at me; I dug in a pocket for damp, soiled *baht*.

For the hydrocephalic child of Dandy's time, the surgeons could do little. Repeated ventricular and lumbar punctures, used to reduce pressure since the time of Hippocrates, could still end in meningitis and death. Artificial bypass drains or "shunts" got clogged and infected. So Dandy's book offered only ten pages on treatment, and he devoted them to the then-unpopular method of puncturing the third ventricle. Here he was ahead of his time, and his operation is only now coming into its own with the advent of endoscopes that actually let you see what you're perforating.

Dandy's biggest practical contribution may in fact have been the procedure he pioneered called the ventriculogram. Dandy knew his ventricles, and he developed a way of visualizing them long before we had CAT scans. It was brilliant: he drained the CSF out of the ventricular system and replaced it with air so that an X-ray would show the size, shape, and any defects in those cavities. His procedure became a mainstay of diagnosis.

The cerebral ventriculogram (there is also a cardiac ventriculogram, done on the heart) is important to my father's story. It was just about the only imaging tool he had. I remember watching him do one. As teenagers, my brother and I once gowned up and followed him into the operating room. Nobody batted an eye; in those days, the neurosurgeon was top dog. When he pierced the ventricle, CSF spurted like water from a squirt gun. Once air was injected and the patient's head rebandaged, we all rode the freight elevator down to X-ray in the basement of the old Victoria General. The air-filled patient snored lightly on the stretcher.

Now, of course, a neurosurgeon would no more think of doing a ventriculogram than he would order up a few leeches to slap on the patient's head. CT scans and MRIs reveal a galaxy where a ventriculogram might have shown a few dim stars. But in my father's time, the neurosurgeon confronted by a hydrocephalic child did a ventriculogram. That was all there was.

Regarding the causes of hydrocephalus, what have we learned since Dandy? Most childhood hydrocephalus is caused by impaired CSF absorption or by blockages. Other common causes are cysts, tumours, and meningitis. When there's no blockage, hydrocephalus is called "communicating," and its main causes are intraventricular hemorrhage (the most common) and meningitis. Hemorrhage is especially common in premature infants, so prematurity and hydrocephalus often go together, a terrible double whammy. This is also important to my story, because the case for which my father was sued involved a premature infant with hydrocephalus. Nowadays, an ultrasound shortly after birth can tell doctors if there's been an intraventricular hemorrhage; if there has, there are some newer treatment options to prevent hydrocephalus developing in very small preterm infants, or at least to keep it in check. In my father's time, hemorrhage couldn't be detected in the premature infant, so the temporary fixes didn't exist.

What about modern treatments for hydrocephalus? We still deal only with the symptoms. While advances in medicine might eventually produce a real cure, pediatric neurosurgeons will probably continue to do the plumbing work-around, as they have since the 1960s. In other words, most kids will still be "shunted." By the early 1990s, the prognosis for most hydrocephalic children was to develop with relatively normal intelligence at the cost of a lifelong shunt. All that matters to my story is that, at the time my father was operating, shunts ruled, and the cascade of events that brought him down all started with an infected shunt. So shunts deserve a little more attention here.

The first shunt was done in 1908, a rubber tube that led from the brain to the peritoneal cavity (the space around the abdominal organs), not very different from today's preferred route. Many variants were tried over the years. Other overflow destinations included the heart, the jugular vein, the gallbladder, and even the salivary ducts — a destination I imagine is especially unpleasant, the patient having a permanent mouthful of cerebrospinal fluid. The earliest shunts my father did were connected, amazingly, to the middle ear, which in turn drained into the throat.

In the 1950s, John Holter, an engineer and father of a hydrocephalic child, worked with surgeons to develop a shunt with a valve. There are now hundreds of valves, catheters, and anti-siphons for surgeons to choose from, including programmable valves that let you fine-tune your own CSF flow. Survival of shunted children has reached 95 percent, although 30 percent end up intellectually impaired.

Shunt insertion is still the most common neurosurgical procedure; for pediatric neurosurgeons, shunting is a large part of their business. I found a 2004 paper that provided a step-by-step method for inserting a shunt, and it made me marvel at the trust we put in surgeons, especially when we hand over a months-old infant with an inflated head and say, "Fix this, please."

In one picture, the tiny child is arched backward over a rolled towel, the gourd-like head lolling to one side; the marking of the two incisions, in scalp and abdomen, demonstrates how thoroughly the child will be plumbed. Of course, the article doesn't say plumbed. It refers instead to "tunnelling," the gentle passing of the tube under the skin, mindful of wrong turns, all the way from the abdomen to the valve waiting under the scalp.

Many things can go wrong. Sometimes the tube gets plugged. Some shunts overdrain and collapse the ventricle. In the old days of spring-loaded tubing coiled in the peritoneal cavity, other weird things could happen — the tubing eroding into the intestine, bladder, vagina, even out the anus. If you combine complications mechanical and infectious, the numbers aren't great: even now, 30 to 40 percent of all shunts will have problems in the first year.

Infection is the second most common problem (after obstruction), and it happens in 5 to 15 percent of cases, usually within six months of surgery. The younger the child, the higher the risk. Often there's no option but to take out the hardware. But the safest time to reinsert a new shunt is still a big judgment call for the surgeon. The infection *has* to clear up before the shunt is replaced — or you're back where you started. The big question is how to deal with increasing pressure in the meantime because once you remove the drain, the clock starts ticking. The lawsuit against my father was all about that ticking clock.

Within the fifty-odd years of shunting, my father's surgical experience of hydrocephalic patients fell into the early stages; he was already in mid-career by the time the kinks were being worked out (this was in the mid-'60s). In 1976, when he operated on an eight-month-old premie called Billy, it was a straightforward business of "shunt first and be prepared to remove the shunt if it gets infected." If it *did*, you pulled the damn shunt out and hoped for the best, which is what he did for Billy. It was a bit like the decision many a sailor would make when faced with a sudden and savagely rising wind: shorten sail and keep slogging toward your destination. It's going to be nasty for a while, but sooner or later the wind has to ease up.

But what if it doesn't?

Herring Town

But we weren't trapped in a rising gale, we were comfortably anchored in Clam Bay, where it had turned into a lovely evening. The cannon-balling teenagers had worn themselves out, and I heard a new, more welcome sound, the rhythmic chanting of the coxswain in an eight-person canoe.

The long cedar dugout emerged out of the setting sun behind The Cut, making straight for us across the darkening water. I shaded my eyes; there were eight paddlers, and the man urging them on from the raised stern seat wore a traditional woven cedar hat. Hatsumi and Charley joined me, and we all watched the canoe sweep past a boat's length away, paddles glinting in the fierce late-afternoon sun. Charley growled softly, way back in his throat, like a distant Harley-Davidson. Incongruously, all the First Nations paddlers wore bright yellow life jackets, and I wondered, is that what it's come to? Do they have to carry flares and plastic emergency whistles too? On a trip like the one we were starting out on, there would be a strong Indigenous presence, and the absurdity I sensed at seeing those paddlers cutting a hard and fast line through the anchored yachts would be repeated time and again over the next two months. From masters of their own land to families blown to dust by nearly a century of residential schools, and now to paddlers in Transport Canada–approved life jackets — whose idea of progress was this?

It was high tide when we left the next morning, so there was only a sliver of pebble beach for Charley to defecate on, crouched like a sumo wrestler beneath overhanging cedars. We left in time to catch the eleven o'clock slack current at Dodd Narrows, raising the sails once we were past the shoals and tacking into a freshening northwest wind. We fell into the routine of upwind sailing: maintain a course roughly forty-five degrees off your intended destination until you run out of sea room; spin the boat ninety degrees by steering through the eye of the wind; sail the new leg of the zigzag until you run out of sea room; repeat. It can get boring.

"I had a weird dream last night," said Hatsumi after an hour or so of this. "A dead person on the floor of the cabin."

"Man or woman?"

"Man. I had to step around him."

"Were you frightened?"

"No. But when I woke up this morning, I thought somebody will die."

We turned *Vera* again. Convulsing sails, whiplashing ropes, immovable winch handles.

"Well, somebody *did* die, you know," I said. "Maybe it was just him."

"Maybe."

I said what I generally say. "Let me know if it happens again."

Even with the wind on the nose, we made decent progress, and by ten we were only a half mile south of the narrows. We dropped the sails and started the engine.

"You're always too early," said Hatsumi, as I put *Vera* in a holding pattern of slow circles. To the south, boats began to appear behind us. On every one of them, the same conversation was probably happening.

"*I'm* too early? I thought there were two of us making these decisions."

"Let's just go."

"An hour before slack? Come on, we only make six knots, the current'll still be running at, what, four?"

"You worry too much."

In the end, we went through thirty minutes early, merging into a parade of hell-bent pleasure boats like a squabbling family entering an on-ramp. Dodd Narrows seems to bring out the worst in boaters, some of whom will churn past you in their rush to be through it, even though, at its narrowest, there's barely room for two vessels. The waning current spat us into Northumberland Channel, a five-mile industrialized stretch that leads to the port city of Nanaimo. Northumberland Channel is a wind funnel, gathering the prevailing northwesterly and stuffing it into the hourglass that ends at Dodd Narrows. We abandoned the idea of sailing, hunkered down, and pounded into it under power, an hour and a half of substantial seas on the nose, sheeting the windows, coursing down the decks.

It seemed to take forever to crawl past the log booms and the red-and-white barges of wood chips tethered along Gabriola Island. I kept the binoculars on the huge ferry docked at Duke Point and breathed a sigh of relief when it separated from the land and, accelerating smoothly, plowed across our bows and into the Strait of Georgia. One more obstacle avoided.

And a good thing, because Charley was letting us know what he thought of his first taste of rough weather. He cowered on a cockpit seat, shivering rhythmically, as though some fiend were zapping him with electricity. Hatsumi wrapped him in blankets and winced along with him as *Vera* punched through the whitecaps.

"Should I take him down below?" she said.

"Don't even think about it. You'll both get sick." As dogs, I might have added. "Tough it out, we're almost there." She and Charley stayed in the cockpit that time; two days later we would find out what happened when they didn't.

Finally, we rounded Protection Island and followed the channel markers into the relative calm of Mark Bay, on Newcastle Island. Everybody stops in Mark Bay; it's across the harbour from the best provisioning city on the coast and minutes from the extraordinary marine park at Saysutshun, the Indigenous name for Newcastle Island. It's usually jammed with boats of every size and description, from derelict local liveaboards to gleaming sixty-footers. And the skill level of the boaters in Mark Bay is similarly all over the chart. Part of the evening entertainment is watching boats back slowly through the anchorage, husbands at the wheel and wives standing forlornly on the foredeck, towing a too-shallow anchor along the bottom and wondering why it won't dig in.

We found a spot at the head of the bay, near the public wharf, and launched Charley into the dinghy. He was vibrating with anticipation, and he urinated ecstatically as soon as his feet touched the dock. We hurried along the wharves and up the trembling ramp to Newcastle Island. Charley broke free, grabbed a four-foot branch better suited to an Afghan, and began to cut delirious circles in the grassy meadow that looks east across Georgia Strait to Vancouver. He even ignored the goose droppings that speckled the grass like thousands of thick green worms. If ever there were such a thing as pure joy, here it was doing rings around me.

The history of Newcastle Island, however, was more complicated. Joy there must have been, but hard work and sorrow were here too. Newcastle sat upon a fortune in coal (the name given it by British colonists was no accident), and you had only to walk ten minutes from where Charley was now savaging his stick, and scuff the trail with your shoe, to uncover the black grit of Nanaimo's past. A trail ran all the way around the island, and at one point, fenced-off concrete platforms, moss-covered and crumbling at the edges, marked the walled-off openings to the ventilation shafts that kept the miners alive.

Beginning with the ubiquitous Hudson's Bay Company and continuing at the hands of a succession of coal barons, companies pulled coal out of a half-dozen mines around Nanaimo into the 1950s. In coal's heyday, shafts criss-crossed beneath the city, even across the harbour to Protection Island. Today, home buyers in some parts of the city are still advised to check with city hall before plunking down their money.

There were quarries here too, where the unique sandstone of the island was sawn out in disks by huge rotating cookie cutters that now sat rusting in the pit beside a monolithic jumble of rejects. The discs became millstones for grinding wood in pulp mills. Other chunks of Newcastle sandstone were shipped as far afield as San Francisco as building material.

Beyond the quarries, along the narrow passage that separates Newcastle Island from the City of Nanaimo, the Japanese families who were so much a part of the commercial fishing industry in B.C. before the Second World War built salteries for the salmon and herring that they shipped back to Japan and the Far East. By the 1920s, Nanaimo, which had been known as "Coal Town," had forty-three Japanese salteries and was now known as "Herring Town." The Japanese lost it all, along with their boats and everything else they owned, when the xenophobic wartime government banished them to internment camps.

Of the Indigenous people who were there first, there are few artifacts beyond the mounds of shells in Midden Bay, a seasonal encampment for harvesting the herring that used to mass near Protection Island. They got their first taste of the white man's progress by digging coal shoulder to shoulder with Chinese miners, for half the wage of the whites. Now the Snuneymuxw First Nation manages the park, which is part of their traditional territory, offering cultural tours and interpretation on Saysutshun. Every evening we watched their aluminum scow depart for Nanaimo, piled high with the white man's garbage.

Nanaimo is a good place to contemplate human nature; like every place we stopped in the two months it took to go around Vancouver Island, the sense of past lives was overwhelming. You never had to look far — there was usually an abandoned log skid or a drunken length of cedar fence to remind you that families had been here. Sometimes you even brought up the evidence on your anchor. The bottoms of many bays were criss-crossed with old tackle, and remote beaches were often littered with what, at first sight, looked like sizeable brown turds. They turned out to be fragments of two-inch cable so rusted you could shatter them against a rock.

The hot wind blew all night, carrying snatches of music from a wedding being celebrated in the nineteenth-century pavilion on the island. Hatsumi steamed the two barely legal crabs I had managed to entice into our trap, and we ate them in the cockpit while *Vera* swung uneasily on her chain. I wondered if we'd make it through the night without bumping into our next-door neighbour, the *James Island Belle*, an ancient liveaboard with a dinghy whose sails hung, algae-slimed, in the water. A young guy and a mutt came and left in a decrepit runabout, and the whistle of his windmill generator rose and fell in the gusts fanning across Mark Bay. A dirty rope at the bow led to something on the bottom; I hoped it was an anchor.

Winnowing

When I'd confessed to my father that I'd kept all his papers, I hadn't gone into detail. But before we actually detached *Vera* from the dock and pointed her north, there was one last thing I'd had to check off my list: "sort F's records." The cardboard box marked The Trial was too big to stow on *Vera*. We needed every available nook and cranny for legitimate provisions.

So I had to winnow. I was interested in the effect the experience had had on my father — on all of his family — not in establishing right or wrong, fairness or injustice. That would be the criterion. I decided to begin at the end. After all, that's why the story was in a box: it had ended badly. This wasn't a whodunit. I already knew *how* the story ended; what I desperately wanted to find out was *why* it had ended that way, and why my father had never recovered.

A single photocopy said it all: the order in the Supreme Court of British Columbia, dated 1987, for a settlement of $1.5 million. Liability was not admitted by any of the defendants, who were never heard in court. Attached to the order with a rusted paper clip was a nice letter from the Canadian Medical Protective Association — my father's insurers — wishing him "many pleasant retirement years." End of story . . . except that it wasn't.

I spent a few minutes with the clutch of newspaper stories that came out during the trial itself, but the idea of my father not responding to phone calls about a patient, of offering to "find another baby" for the distraught mother seemed as ridiculous as it had in 1987. Facts were what I needed, not newspaper stories. Having reasoned my way soberly to this point, I took the media stuff on the trip anyway; those articles were like the gory illustrations in a book that you just couldn't help looking at.

Next came the "patient records." There were several slim folders, one to a patient, and then Billy's gargantuan file. I knew why Billy's file was there, but who were those others? So many people had passed through my father's hands, but for some reason, I had seven of them in front of me — a curious little collection of hangers-on. I had no idea who most of these people were, but I figured they might tell me something about Dr. Harvey. Welcome aboard.

That left Billy. What I did with his file was up to me, but I knew I had to watch myself. Condemnation or vindication were not only irrelevant, they were probably risky as well; if I wasn't careful, I'd be looking at a lawsuit of my own.

Billy's file could be subdivided into categories, which I arranged more or less on a scale of believability. If one assumed that things written on a form were believable, then the six inches of "hospital records" had to come first. Here was the official record of every encounter between Billy and the medical system in British Columbia, from the moment of his birth to the trial almost ten years later. Of those hospital records, nursing records took up the most space. Each day of Billy's life presented a cluster of boxes to be filled in, for intake and output, temperature, blood pressure, medications. Many had sections for the nurse's comments, and these were often filled in by two or three different people. This child passed through many hands. The doctors themselves contributed history sheets, consultation records, and progress notes. Laboratory reports summarized tests on blood, urine, and cerebrospinal fluid. Actual operations were described in consent to operation forms, the doctor's own report of operation, and anaesthesia records. Much of the doctors' reports was narrative, and they ran to several pages, often in the dry, laconic style of an airline pilot. Most were in the first person, perhaps because they were dictated into a machine. "I presume this is a hydrocephalus," said my father to his Dictaphone, right at the start.

Once out of the hospital, Billy moved to a special-needs clinic, yielding five years' worth of psychological evaluations, physiotherapy, and social work notes. The sense of urgency running through the hospital records was gone now; instead, it looked like a methodical charting of one boy's progress through a smoothly running system.

All in all, the official records comprised a formidable brick of paper. Some poor soul had spent hours over a photocopying machine, dizzy with ozone, hand-feeding flimsy pink carbons. Without knowing anything about the case, you could start at one end and emerge, days later, at the other, cross-eyed but theoretically knowing as much as anybody about what happened to Billy. You could also come to about a hundred different conclusions as to *why*, and I imagined the legal staff for the plaintiff and for my father doing just that, forcing themselves through the smudgy, often illegible pages, staggering out for coffee breaks, then diving back in to look for weaknesses. Bulky or not, the records had to come along on *Vera*.

Next, and decidedly lower on the believability scale, were the expert opinions. The opinions were also written by doctors, but they were based not on their own actions, but on the pile of photocopied hospital records I'd just gone through.

The doctors who wrote these opinions had read exactly the same material I would read on *Vera*, except that they had been paid for it. Some, it turned out, had been selective; one hadn't bothered with the nurses' records at all. All the opinions were written long after the events took place. I decided, after a quick look, that the six expert opinions about Billy (three on each side of the case) would be an interesting read, like one of those novels where the events are retold through several points of view.

The opinions fed into the next category, the "examinations for discovery." These are when plaintiff and defendant sit down with the opposing lawyer for a good grilling while their own lawyer hovers, ready to dart to the rescue at the first sign of weakness. Finding weakness is what examinations are about, and cases are won or lost in discovery. There were six examinations in the pile. My father's was by far the thickest. I packed them all.

Next were the trial transcripts. What people said in the trial was probably even less believable than the examinations, and these records were a long way from the black and white of the hospital records. Thinner too, because this trial only lasted a few days before a deal was struck and everyone went home. I could bring the trial transcripts along without sinking *Vera*.

The final category was my father's writings about the trial. Unlike all the others, this one was open-ended. It started soon after the writ of summons was served, and he added to it until he could no longer operate a computer or even a pen. It was to be the story of his experience, a diary expanded into a book, a "stream of thought record" describing his encounter with what he called "the armoured tanks of the law." The project was never finished, fading out like his handwriting and finally wandering off the page. I selected the latest draft and added it to the "take" pile which, I now realized, dwarfed what I would leave behind.

In all, I had about ten inches of paper to go cruising with us. My father's life, wedged under the floorboards. But there was one folder that didn't seem to sort with anything else, portentously labelled "Truth." I decided to get truth out of the way before we left. There was only one thing in there, but it said everything about my father's values. It was a long essay called "The Search for Truth," by Justice Marvin E. Frankel, a bulldog who seized truth in his jaws and never let go. It must have been heady reading for my father, and his orange highlighter had squeaked across nearly every page. Here was the way to trump incompetence, criticism, and calumny: truth was what mattered!

Except that, according to Justice Frankel, an advocate's main loyalty was not to truth but to his client. So, the conventional skills of adversaries include the techniques of truth-bending. Few lawyers, Frankel wrote, believe their clients tell them the unvarnished truth.

For my father, this was just what the doctor ordered. Frankel's description of judges as "passive moderators" viewing the case from a "peak of Olympian ignorance" must have made his heart turn; it certainly brought his orange highlighter out. Maybe this was what he had been up to, all those bleak years after the trial, downstairs in his study with the curtains drawn and the heat cranked up, pouncing on high-minded sentiments as though they could somehow justify what had happened to him. Psychologists talk about "confirmation bias" when people seek out information that confirms what they already believe. Well, here was the textbook example, and it didn't do him much good.

Hospital records, media stories, expert opinions, and the unimportance of truth: these were the murky waters that closed over my father's head. All that was left of his naïveté was a page of Four Seasons Hotel notepaper floating on the surface. On it was written, "Did A.T. believe me? Would anyone have believed me?" A.T. was Allan Thackray, his lawyer, who we will meet later. My father probably wrote these words on the way back to Victoria, while the skyline of Vancouver and his aborted trial receded in the widening *V* of the ferry's wake. They weren't the words of someone who had been planning to lie.

The Lasqueti Triangle

It was still windy in Mark Bay the next morning, but the wind now came from the southeast. When I poked my head through the companionway, everything had changed, as though a completely new fleet had snuck into the anchorage in the dead of night. The *James Island Belle* and its banshee windmill hung way off in the other direction; now we threatened to tangle anchors with a forty-foot powerboat I had hardly noticed the day before. A wind shift had rearranged everything. Southeasters were a mixed blessing: going north, as we were, they came from behind and made for easy sailing, but they could also be storm winds, accompanied by several days of blustery, rainy weather.

But we weren't going to get to the Nahwitti Bar by sitting in Mark Bay and fretting about a southeaster. I listened to the weather forecast while Hatsumi made breakfast.

"Looks like a couple days of this," I said, scribbling down the long-range prognosis.

"Uh-huh."

"Twenty-five knots late this afternoon."

"Charley needs to be fed."

"And Whiskey Golf is active today."

That got her attention.

"*Today?*"

Whiskey Golf (Area WG, on the chart) is a modified parallelogram dropped over a ten-by-fifteen mile stretch of the Strait of Georgia, like a haphazardly surveyed building lot in the middle of an uninhabited forest. It's one of two military exercise areas off Vancouver Island — the other one, Whiskey Hotel, on the west coast not far from Victoria, was almost two months away. By some arcane political arrangement I couldn't even begin to fathom, both were shared with the United States. Whiskey Golf, the bigger of the two, is used by the U.S. Navy for testing torpedoes, which could be fired from submarines, airplanes, or boats, and whose movements were tracked by an underwater cat's cradle of sensors. When Whiskey Golf was active, you had to go around it.

And that wasn't always easy, especially in a sailboat. I imagine the joint committee who decided the boundary of Whiskey Golf where it runs close to the shore, defining what the Canadian Department of National Defence calls the "transit area." Uniformed men circle a chart table, pondering the route *Vera* will have to take. Ash drops from cigarettes glued between thin lips, and the harsh overhead glare bounces off crewcut scalps. Finally, a retired U.S. admiral leans forward, brushing cookie crumbs off the coffee-stained chart. He taps the chain of nasty reefs that follows the Vancouver Island shoreline for five miles north of Nanoose Bay, where the naval base is.

"How about right here, gentlemen?" He inks a wavering line, following the prickly shore. "Send 'em past those big ol' rocks, turn 'em up here, past those, whaddaya call them, Ballenas Islands. Let's leave those boaters, what, a thousand yards of sea room? Hell, that's ten football fields! Whadda y'all think?"

"Sounds good to us," say the Canadians, in unison.

And it is, on a fine day, but today might be ugly.

"*Shikata ga nai*," said Hatsumi. It can't be helped.

The wind rounded in after us as soon as we cleared Departure Bay. We got the jib out with a minimum of clattering and cursing and settled into the long downwind run.

"Not so bad," I said. "We'll be at Lasqueti Island in four hours."

But I was wrong. We made good time along the western edge of Whiskey Golf under jib alone, passing the surveillance dishes and domes that encrust Winchelsea Island by noon. But the southeaster behaved as advertised, building under darkening skies until, by the time we were nearing the final turn at Ballenas Island, where my resentment toward all that military hardware whirring and clicking deep inside Whiskey Golf builds to a peak, the incessant roll and lurch of a downwind passage was turning Charley green.

"I'm taking him below," said Hatsumi. "He's scared, look."

"Don't do it." Charley did look miserable, wedged in a corner, his ears laid back. "You'll get sick. Really." *Vera* slewed violently, Charley scrabbled at the seat, and Hatsumi scooped him up and disappeared with him down the companionway. I brought *Vera* around ninety degrees just as Lasqueti and Texada Islands, the landmarks that mattered, began to dissolve behind curtains of rain. The change in course brought the wind onto our beam, and it felt twice as strong as it did when it was behind us. We started to roll, a slovenly wallow that put one rail in the water and then the other. I heard a bang from below, followed by a moan: a cabin locker had burst open, dumping shoes and bottles over the two forms curled up on the floor.

"Gotta get the main up," I called down. "We're going sideways." By then it was clear that whatever could go wrong, would. The main halyard got away from me just enough to snag around one of the steps that run up the mast. I managed to get twenty feet of sail up before it refused to move further in either direction. I secured what I could, and *Vera* began to move forward again, but by now the rain had arrived in earnest. The coast of Lasqueti Island, which I knew had only one opening where we could find shelter, became a grey blur. My glasses misted over.

"Where are we?" When I peered below, all I could see of Hatsumi was the soles of her shoes, poking through the bathroom door. Small bottles of Japanese cosmetics rolled past her. As I watched, the rest of my wife emerged. She was clutching Charley, still in his orange life jacket, and her face was white.

"Sorry to bother you, but I really need a position. I can't see the opening to Bull Channel."

"Can't look at the computer," she croaked. "Get sick."

This was the first year we had used electronic charts. We had them on a laptop and were still getting used to the seductive belief that you knew exactly where you were. But the laptop was jammed somewhere secure now, so we were back to the old system of paper charts. I took a quick look at the radar, which confirmed that the shore of Lasqueti was only a half mile away, before my own gorge rose.

"Well, use the old GPS then, just get me a fix, a lat-long. Come on, I can't leave the wheel."

More heaving.

"We're on a fucking lee shore!" I reminded myself that alarm in my voice would only increase hers. "Honey."

The lee shore is, or should be, very high on the sailor's list of to-avoids. A lee shore is a shore you're being blown onto; a lee shore you couldn't even see, I was finding out, was extra frightening. In a westerly wind, the entire west coast of Vancouver Island is the ultimate lee shore. That's why it's called the Graveyard of the Pacific. And that's where we were going.

"I'm trying," I heard faintly from below, and she was, on her knees and clawing at the chart table where the elderly GPS was fixed. Finally, a shaking hand fluttered a hastily folded chart at me; I grabbed it, found Hatsumi's weakly pencilled dot-and-circle that represented our position.

"Holy shit."

I spun the wheel. If we hadn't been socked in, I would be seeing breaking waves on the island's distinctive black cliffs. Any closer, I might soon be hearing them. I started the engine and put the bow back into the waves, on a course that should take us clear of the rocks even as we went sideways. We settled in for more uncomfortable slogging. It was pouring now. It took another hour, and several more nauseating fixes, before I finally saw the entrance to Bull Passage. It really was framed in surf.

"Just a little longer," I said to Hatsumi, who had finally rejoined me in the cockpit. She was still white as the sail I couldn't get down. We went wide around the corner, then hard over into Bull Passage. The rolling ceased, the engine stopped gulping, and, by bringing the main in tight, I was finally able to wrestle it down. Even the rain stopped. Just like that, the coast proved, once again, that your punishment can end abruptly, leaving you wondering what just happened. I shut down the engine, let the jib out again, and went below to put on some cobweb-blowing music. The life-affirming, C major blast of the opening of Beethoven's Emperor Concerto poured out of the cabin, bounced off the straining jib, and ascended to the heavens.

"Hah!" I said. "Whiskey Golf, but still. We made it. I hope the guys cleared a space for us at the dock." *Vera* surged ahead, steam rose from the drying decks, and Beethoven caromed off the cliffs on either side.

❧

"The guys" were Gordon and Bruce Jones — the Jones Boys — brothers who had operated a shellfish hatchery and farm in Skerry Bay on Lasqueti Island for thirty-five years. Both were stocky, eccentric, generous, and ferociously strong. Although I had known them for twenty years, I still found them impossible to categorize, and I won't attempt it here. For the four years we'd been cruising these waters, we'd shown up at the farm in *Vera*, and every year, it became harder to untie and continue on our way. Bruce Jones's explanation for this was always delivered with widespread arms that took in the cluttered docks, the mussel rafts, a boat they'd salvaged off a rock, Bruce's house perched on the cliff above with its hot tub that had been empty for twenty years — and the explanation was always the same.

"It's the Lasqueti Triangle!"

"We'll stay a few more days this time," I said.

Skerry means *rocky* in Gaelic, and the Jones Boys' shellfish operation filled half of Skerry Bay with a jumble of outbuildings and floating structures that reminded me of the floathouse communities I'd visited in Thailand. "Whatever worked" seemed to be the principle here, and whatever didn't work was stored somewhere on the theory that, someday, it could be made to. I say *floating structures* because sometimes it was hard to tell what you were stepping on: it might well be a dock, but it could also be a barge that, through disuse, had turned into a sort of dock, or a workshop so full of spare parts you couldn't actually work in it. Lines of demarcation were indistinct, so watching your step was important. Most of the floating space that wasn't actually being used to process shellfish or raise their feed was simply another place to store whatever drifted in from where we'd just been. I wasn't in the least surprised when, one year, I found the fuselage of a small yellow airplane tucked in behind a shed. The wings, I noticed later, were leaning against the side of Bruce's house. They didn't seem out of place.

We slid past the black turtle-humps of Rabbit and Bull islands, turned left into Bull Harbour, and motored down into Skerry Bay. Through the binoculars, the farm looked as cluttered as ever. A few sailboats were anchored outside the bay, and I wondered what their owners made of the scene inside, the sudden, high-speed comings and goings of workboats, the dogs barking, the diesel generator in its shaking shed on the point, grinding away until ten o'clock at night. In addition to caretaking the nearby provincial park on Jedediah Island and running a full-time shellfish hatchery, Gordon and Bruce were the local responders for the Canadian Coast Guard, so people anchored off the farm had to be prepared for the sudden middle of the night throat-clearing of the *Pac 1*'s twin diesels, the firefly pinpoints of the Jones Boys' headlamps as they jumped aboard, the dazzling eye of the searchlight, and the unapologetic wake of the big workboat churning through a sleeping anchorage.

We managed to avoid the two horrifying rocks in Skerry Bay (Bruce: "Why should we mark them? They're so obvious!") and nosed in between a work launch and what looked like an aluminum party boat, twenty-five feet long, with a cabin and wide decks for lounging around on a lake and drinking. This one seemed to have sat on the bottom for a year or so; there would be another Jones story there, I knew. The dogs reached us first, and Charley was off before we had even tied up, racing up the dock with Fergie, a rangy and limping part-coyote somebody had dragged out of a ditch near Calgary. The last I saw of Charley was his orange life jacket disappearing up the ramp. Next was the barrel-shaped Simba, a crumbling, waist-high senior citizen with a grey muzzle, friendly, exhausted eyes, and a lump the size of a grapefruit hanging from his abdomen. Last year, there'd been one of those lumps on his shoulder. Maybe it had migrated. Simba let out some face-saving foghorn sounds, then began the painful process of subsiding on the dock while Bruce brought up the rear.

"What took you so long?" he said. "Look, we even cleared a special space for you."

"It was nasty," I said. The southeaster had followed us into Skerry Bay, but the sun was out now. *Vera* sparkled with salt.

Tied up snugly to the dock, with the cliffs breaking much of the wind, it seemed like a nice day again.

"You're a *sailboat*. You *love* wind!"

Bruce and Gordon had pulled so many sailboats off the rocks that their opinion of recreational sailors was somewhere down around kayakers, which they called "speed bumps." I didn't take any of it seriously; I knew they had grown up cruising Desolation Sound in their parents' sailboat, and there were two bright red Jones-made fibreglass kayaks on the roof of the shed next to me. I joined Bruce on a wooden park bench (where had *that* come from?) while Simba completed the operation of lying down at our feet, keeling over like a collapsing tripod. As if to confirm Bruce's low opinion, a sailboat puttered down one side of Skerry Bay and up the other, miraculously missing both rocks.

"He better not try anchoring down there," said Bruce. "The end of the bay is planted in geoducks." Geoducks (pronounced *gooeyducks*) were enormous clams, I knew that much. But despite many visits, I still understood little of what was going on here. What I saw above sea level made a kind of sense, but so much of it was underwater. The mussels hanging from their rafts, the vast, bubbling, sunken swimming pools of green stuff tethered below Gordon's "apartment" at the top of the hill, the circular cages farther out in the bay that might once have belonged in a salmon farm, that might contain something alive and needing feeding, or that might just be gathering weed. And now geoduck clams. I rowed out to them later and found myself gliding over a small city of geoduck-houses, each one a length of white PVC pipe jammed into the sand.

Bruce stretched his legs in the sun while we caught up, though he jumped up briefly to give Hatsumi a hug. He wore shorts and a frayed sailor's hat that had long ago lost its shape.

"You can just leave her here, you know," he said, holding on. Hatsumi put her head on his shoulder. Within fifty feet of where they stood were plastic barrels, rusted chain, a coil of frayed and faded ship's hawser, and a salvaged yellow weather buoy with what looked like a perfectly good strobe light fixed to the top. The dock was so untidy you needed a map, or the feet of a dancer, to negotiate it. Yet here was my clutter-abhorring Japanese wife, clutching the proprietor.

"Hey, don't I get one of those?" Gordon appeared, dressed in filthy jeans, a plaid shirt, and an Innovative Aquaculture baseball cap, incongruously bearing a pitcher of lemonade and a stack of disposable plastic glasses. Where Bruce is voluble (his conversation has been called "the Bruce-wind"), Gordon is self-deprecating and ironic. Bruce's humour is broad; Gordon's draws blood. Their banter is unrelenting. Apart from the separate skiing holidays they take when the hatchery slows down in the winter, the brothers are inseparable. They both got long hugs.

"We have mussels to set," said Gordon, draining his glass.

"I know, I know," said Bruce.

Gordon and Bruce went off to prepare the mussel rope for planting, a baffling procedure that involved pulling what looked like an endless roll of narrow cotton pantyhose over a length of thin plastic pipe as it spat out a slurry of mussel larvae, then attaching the string to hundreds of feet of hairy plastic rope.

"It's therapy," said Bruce, slicking the cotton sock off the plastic tube like a jaded Casanova. While they worked, I passed an hour making a detailed inventory of the back-from-the-deep party boat tied up next to *Vera*. The whole place reeked of mould. I wondered how long it would sit here before Gordon and Bruce towed it around the corner to join the seaplane and the rest of the abandoned reclamation projects.

When I emerged, they were attaching the seeded mussel rope, now coiled in the bottom of a workboat like an enormous chain of sausage links, to the underside of a floating raft made of thirty-foot lengths of black plastic sewer tube. Gordon straddled two of these barely floating logs, reeling in the sausage Bruce fed to him and suspending it from hooks so that it fell in gentle underwater loops, beneath a trapped scum of twigs, crab moults, and weed. In a few months, the whole thing would be dragged up again, foot by slippery foot, the sock rotted away and the baby mussels firmly attached. Back it would go for stripping and sorting by a mechanical grader, and then the brothers would go through the whole pantyhose-therapy business again before retrieving the mussel-garlands a final time, tearing the finished shellfish off the plastic rope before grading, power-washing, bagging, and shipping them. If anyone wondered why *moules marinière* cost more than steak, here was a tiny part of the answer.

Aided by their long-time business partner Cathy (a.k.a. the Algae Queen), Gordon and Bruce had been growing oysters, clams, and mussels for decades. In a barnacle-like warren attached to the cliffs above the docks, Cathy maintained thirty-foot fibreglass tanks for coddling the baby molluscs until they were ready to set and an entire room of ten-foot-high circular algae tanks that would feed the larvae. Each translucent silo looked like a core taken out of the ocean. Tethered just off the point, more algae multiplied in swimming-pool-sized vinyl tanks held up by a ring of floats. The Joneses even processed algae into a vile green toothpaste, packaged it, and marketed it to other growers. There really wasn't anything they couldn't do.

"Except, maybe, get a life," said Gordon later that evening. The dogs had collapsed in malodorous heaps. From the upper "boardroom" lined with books and hung with Bruce's paintings, where we'd just finished a gargantuan pot of mussels, you could see the sailboats anchored in Bull Harbour and just make out the black cliffs behind them. The VHF Coast Guard channel muttered in the background.

"He sleeps with it under his pillow," said Gordon. I could believe it: Bruce could be in full rhetorical flow, hands chopping the air, then suddenly halt, alert as a hound catching a scent, and dart for the radio.

I reached down to squash a mosquito on an unprotected ankle. "Any problem if we stay another day?"

"Another *day*? Why not a week? Better still, just leave your wife—" The VHF burbled. Bruce jumped up and disappeared in mid-sentence. When he reappeared, he was putting on his floater coat.

"Some guy drifting out in Bull Passage. If you want to come, we have to go *now*."

This was a Bruce I hadn't seen before. The bonhomie and bad puns were replaced by a headlamp vanishing down the path. The southeaster was still blowing. Even in Skerry Bay, the dark water was ruffled and uneasy. Out in Bull Passage, a disabled boat would drift quickly, and there was nowhere to go but rocks.

I picked my way after him, back down the treacherous path to the *Pac 1*, the aluminum landing craft used for transporting supplies, hosting parties, and rescuing feckless mariners. We hurriedly off-loaded an orange sofa, some white plastic lawn chairs, and a barbecue. I cast off the lines and hunkered down on the huge foredeck as the twin diesels erupted under my feet. In the raised wheelhouse aft, I could see the ghostly green faces of Gordon and Bruce, illuminated by the radar screen. Within seconds, the big boat was at top speed, cutting a foaming wake between the anchored sailboats. I imagined the owners clawing their way into their suddenly rocking cockpits and going "What the . . . ?"

There was enough of a moon to pick out the sixty-foot cruiser rolling in the slop from what was now a more serious fifteen knots of wind blowing their baby toward Jedediah Island. A searchlight played briefly over the little knot of anxious-looking people on her foredeck. We came alongside and made fast under the great flaring bow, the two boats jostling while I scrambled around trying to insert fenders between them without losing a finger. The owner shouted down, Bruce shouted up, and we pieced the story together while Gordon slowly backed the joined boats away from the rocks: their anchor windlass had jammed with sixty feet of chain out. Part of it hung in a loop from the bow.

"I keep resetting the circuit breakers!" said the owner. "Is there some way to get this thing up manually?"

"Shouldn't *you* know that?" said Bruce under his breath. He was struggling to pull the vinyl cover off a hydraulic crane. This wasn't life-threatening, simply absurd: *Charlie's Charm* couldn't go very far with an anchor ready to snag anything shallower than sixty feet. Bruce rigged a length of elderly polypropylene line to the dangling chain, pushed the button to withdraw five feet of chain from the waters of Bull Passage, and went back for more. The anchor itself finally emerged, to nervous clapping from above. I felt cautiously superior; we'd never done anything quite this dumb.

We returned sedately through the anchored yachtsmen, who were probably just getting back to sleep. Gordon brought the *Pac 1* to the dock with the kind of seamanship that takes a lifetime to acquire, shuttling in and out of gear so that the twin screws fired bursts of blue-green bioluminescence. Beside *Vera*, the weather buoy that had drifted into Skerry Bay was blinking serenely. Hundreds of miles from where it was supposed to be, it seemed perfectly at home here.

"Maybe we will stay another day," I said.

We hung around, firmly in the clutches of the Lasqueti Triangle, while the weather improved and the long dock filled up with the next shift of summer visitors. With each boat that came in, we untied *Vera* and shifted her back, until there was only six inches of water under her keel and I could count the furred-over bottles on the bottom.

But I didn't spend long chatting with the latest arrivals. Instead, I decided to ease into my father's story by having a look at those intriguing "other patient" files he'd held onto for so long. Who were they? Why had he kept them? Maybe there was something revealing mixed up in all those carbons and onion skins and yellowing envelopes.

A Hole in the Head

My father had been sixty-four when Billy came along, near the end of his career as a surgeon but still playing the violin he had begged his father for lessons on and had practised every day in the woodshed for exactly an hour. He was still taking photographs too, still sailing. In his fifties, he made two more attempts to leave his practice in Victoria for situations in the United States where he could spend more time doing medical research and less time dissecting out brain tumours and operating on bad backs. But neurosurgery in California had struck him as mercenary, and neurological consulting in Baltimore bored him. Maybe he missed his leaking boats and his darkroom. In his sixties, he ground it out back in British Columbia. The years of wandering were over.

"I'm a cobbler," he told me then. "People bring me stuff; I mend it." It was a long way from the young doctor whose early cases had been fodder for the stories I grew up with. The strangest were from his wartime years as a psychiatrist. One patient was a physician with acute schizophrenia who endlessly pencilled perfectly round breasts on reams of toilet paper. My father tried to get the attendants to give the artist some decent paper and a set of coloured pens.

"No pens," they said.

"Why?"

"They always end up in his rectum."

That was all I had on the crazy physician, but the other patient files I'd brought along on *Vera* were different because they told stories that actually involved my father as a surgeon. Occasionally, while I was growing up, he had talked about cases he was especially proud of, or especially upset by. Jimmy Ho, I thought, he never forgot about Jimmy Ho. I bet he's in this bunch of files — and he was. I started to read.

Jimmy was four when he fell out of bed. Not much happened for a month or so, then he started falling again. His hands shook. He listed to one side, a small sinking ship. My father's notes were, as always, colourful, and as I read them I began to notice the little things that showed how he felt about his patients.

"We find a four-year-old Chinese male sitting at the desk looking quite well," he began of the initial examination. But then, "He appeared quite frightened . . . and he could not co-operate in testing the sensory system." Not "would not," but "could not." The narrative of that first visit ends, "I think he has a left cerebellar tumour."

Remember, this was long before CAT scans. Symptoms were all you had to go on. But my father's in-office diagnosis was correct: Jimmy did have a tumour. It took more than four hours to tease out a growth the size of a lacrosse ball. Jimmy's heart stopped on the operating table and his lungs filled with fluid; the surgeons massaged and intubated. His heart stopped again; they restarted it with adrenaline. It was the worst tumour my father had ever seen.

"The post-operative course was stormy," he wrote years later to an insurance company needing a statement on Jimmy's condition. He charged the company $15 for the report, which probably gave him some pleasure to write, because Jimmy Ho did recover, and his family never forgot. They moved to Hawaii and began to send letters and photographs. My father's collection was fat with invitations to Jimmy's high school graduation in San Francisco, letters of gratitude and career updates from his parents, and from Jimmy himself a record of his grades, his new Schwinn bicycle, and a succession of school photos featuring gigantic horn-rimmed glasses. A wispy moustache appeared, then a wife, a child, a better job. The last letter in the file, more than thirty years after the operation, ended, "All my love through the years."

The next patient I finally got to meet was known as "The Korean Seaman," a 21-year-old "struck by a pipe onboard ship in the right parietal region in a way which he finds difficult to describe accurately due to his language difficulty." Seaman Park had staggered into my father's office. His head hurt. My father found that "a circle eight centimetres in diameter was completely punched out and a great deal of hair driven into the wound. A fragment of bone was driven in 15 millimetres, pushing the derma before it." The pipe had struck end-on, like a javelin, cookie-cutting the scalp and creating a mess of buried bone shards. On top of the fracture was a hematoma that needed to be sucked out. When a second operation was needed two weeks later, the young man produced this handwritten note: "I am sorry to give you trouble again. I am not worry about this operation. I trust you. Do my operation please with peace of mind."

The bill was sent to the shipping agents in Victoria. There is no record that it was paid; many bills weren't. My father asked for $969, not bad for saving a life. A month later, another Victoria doctor and his wife escorted the refurbished seaman back to Korea. A Christmas card came the next year, with a picture of a delicate painted vase that made me think of the frailty of the human head.

Beside me in the cockpit, Charley lifted his own head and

made a sound I hadn't heard before, a kind of whimper. His ears stood out like wings.

"He kept writing to me, you know."

Despite the heat in Skerry Bay, my father was still wearing the checked wool jacket. Charley turned three rapid circles and went back to sleep.

"He wanted advice on his condition, but he didn't want his physician to know. Dr. Lee, I think it was."

"What did you tell him?"

He looked at me sternly. "The only thing I *could* tell him. That there were many good doctors in Korea."

"So you actually remember this Korean guy? The details, I mean? The hematoma, all that stuff?"

"Was there a hematoma?" He pulled the folder out of my hands and leafed shakily through it. "Oh yeah, there was. But no, I don't remember it. Details like that, you don't. Nobody could."

"So you just kept the file because it turned out well?"

"Most of them turned out well."

But not all, even in this tiny sample he'd left. One was a two-year-old Indigenous boy, whose folder was marked "subdural; child abuse." The notes said, "I saw this little boy shortly after his admission to Emergency with the story of having been spanked by his mother and subsequently losing consciousness." He had a subdural hematoma, a dangerous, pressure-producing bleed, which was removed. But, "in the Recovery Room the boy went quite flat. We took him back to the operating room because it seemed likely he was bleeding again. This was true. By the time I had lifted out the bone flap, the child had died."

Why did he keep this file? It was the briefest of histories and the sorriest. Was he especially moved by the child's case? Why did he add, in his notes, "It should be specifically noted that at no time was any sign of external injury to the head present"? There was an autopsy, which found some bruising on both legs, but nothing in the file suggested charges had been laid. Maybe he simply feared legal complications down the road. I knew better than to ask him about this one.

My father surely had mixed reasons for hanging onto Sergeant Maxwell's file. *His* interminable handwritten letters were always addressed to "Dr. John Edgar Harvey B.A., M.A., M.D., Ph.D." — I could practically taste the bile. "Possibly it would have been better if the scalpel had slipped in 1966. NO — that is not fair to say — you are so skilled!"

Sergeant Maxwell had an aneurysm — a burst vessel in the brain — which my father repaired in 1966. But the sergeant had a mental problem that couldn't be surgically removed: he refused to accept repeated rejection from the Canadian Pension Commission. Once, he left a demand that my father write to the commission stating that he was "invalided out of the Royal Canadian Mounted Police due to service conditions causing an aneurysm to rupture." That particular letter went on for nine pages, alternately fawning and berating. The letter ends, "I really feel I was summarily dismissed from your office today!"

"A nutcase," muttered my father, still perched behind *Vera*'s wheel. "I should have climbed out the window when I heard him coming."

"Did you help him out with his pension problem?"

"Of course not! If that's the kind of conclusion you're going to draw from my stuff, I want it back."

Sergeant Maxwell's letter was written two weeks after the fateful operation on Billy. Charley yipped in his sleep, and I was alone again in Skerry Bay.

⌇

High standards to the end; no fudging with the truth. That was my father all right, and those patient files had just confirmed it. Where had those traits come from? His upbringing in a small Alberta town may have accounted for some of it, but all I knew of those few years (he left home at sixteen) was the relentlessly rosy picture he painted in his own memoir. The bigger influence was almost certainly a role model, and for him that could only be one person: Dr. Harvey Cushing. Cushing was my father's hero. My father even had a copy of Cushing's first biography, by the surgeon-historian John F. Fulton.

Fulton's biography was clearly the "official" one, written shortly after its subject's 1939 death of lung cancer at age seventy (like so many doctors of my father's time, Cushing was a chain smoker). Here was the saintly if prickly Cushing. Even so, it was easy to understand why my father had idolized the man. They were peas in a pod: multitalented, peripatetic, indefatigable, authoritarian. Cushing's biographer described him as a perfectionist with the temperament of an artist and the enduring patience of a scientist; that sounded like someone I knew.

Both men had interests far beyond neurosurgery, and Fulton's book includes lengthy extracts from Cushing's diaries and letters, revealing a note-taker and observer with a dry, naturalistic style. It was easy enough to find similarities. Art, for instance. Cushing sketched prolifically: he drew fellow surgeons, a country inn, the preferred route into the third ventricle. My father's artistic side, apart from the sheaves of unpublished essays I found on side-punched computer paper, was best expressed through his violin and his photography. And lineage: both men came from a long line of physicians. Both were formidable workers who rarely took holidays, both were popular with their patients, and both were feared but respected by nurses, who may be the best judges. It was an O.R. nurse who wrote the following poem about Cushing, and the doggerel could easily have described my father:

C is for Cushing
So cleverly cursed
If he ever gets sick
He will never be nursed.

Cushing was a details man who took every aspect of his patients' care personally. Sleep and holidays were well down the list, and he got the same dedication out of his assistants. But when Cushing lost a patient, he was hardest on himself. When I read this stuff, I sometimes had to remind myself it was written about another man, not my father. I did once ask a local doctor, who had worked with my father, what he was like in the O.R. "No comment," he'd said.

The Great War of 1914–1918 produced the biggest explosion in head trauma the surgical world had ever seen. Harvey Cushing did two tours in Europe, one of them in a casualty clearing station behind the lines at Passchendaele. Neurosurgery took a bloody leap forward in those years, and the slippery operating tables behind the trenches became a sort of high-speed testing ground for surgical treatment of head wounds.

So much could go wrong with the brain: fractures, infections, growths, and the awful squeezing that destroyed the central nervous system so that people lost their senses, endured unimaginable pain, went mad. At first, surgeons were lucky if they got out before the patient bled to death; bulging of the brain often meant you couldn't even close the skull up again. Cushing's first foray "inside the box" was to relieve a former sea captain of the coruscating pain of trigeminal neuralgia (*tic douloureux*), a disorder of the largest facial nerve. He chloroformed the man in 1899, trephined his cranium with hammer and chisel, and dissected out the bundle of nerves connecting the brain to the trigeminal nerve. The captain lived another forty years, pain-free, while his surgeon built brilliantly and relentlessly on that first great success. And despite the extraordinary advances since Cushing's time, brain surgery still means opening up the box with burrs and saws, clamping off pulsating forests of blood vessels that insist on obliterating the field, finding your way through a blancmange of neurons that control everything from a wiggle of a toe to the wink of an eye, then accomplishing what you came to do and getting the hell out.

Outside the hospital, Cushing was revered, admired, emulated — but it doesn't appear that he was much liked. He turned on the charm when it suited him, apologized strategically, and intrigued with the best of them. He was the prototype of the egotistical, imperious surgeon. He often shamed his assistants into doing things they felt were beneath them, like emptying bedpans or cleaning up vomit.

A much more recent biography by Michael Bliss is less sparing of Cushing's defects than Fulton's, but more illuminating for me. Bliss's book recreates not only the man but his times as well, so I understood that it wasn't simply that my father regarded Harvey Cushing as the role model for a caring, competent surgeon, he also revered the system that had produced Cushing, that Cushing had perpetuated and changed, and that had taken root from New England to the Midwest and produced an unbroken line of surgeons who thought like Cushing, acted like Cushing, and took their inspiration from him. It was virtually guaranteed that anyone who came out of that system, for generations after Cushing, had it firmly in mind that they were leaders.

My father was one of those. In the late 1940s, when he was studying for his Ph.D. in neurosurgery in Chicago, Cushing had been dead ten years, but his legacy was alive and well. Cushing began the tradition of the neurosurgeon as the star of the hospital, something my father picked up in Chicago and imported, for a while, to Vancouver and Victoria. When I was growing up, this role was well entrenched in the public mind; having a father who was a "brain surgeon" — well, what could have topped that?

Going in Backward

The next day, we tore ourselves free of the Lasqueti Triangle, determined to make up for lost time. We had to stop acting like a couple planning a leisurely visit to Desolation Sound because we had a lot farther to go. Cape Scott, the turning point, was still many days ahead. We hadn't even finished crossing the Strait of Georgia. The forecast was for — well, it wasn't for much of anything. The southeaster had blown itself out, and it would be another day before the wind did a 180 and returned from the "real" summer direction, northwest. When that started, we might have the wind on the nose for weeks.

Once clear of Lasqueti, we followed a long, angling course up the eastern side of Texada, a thirty-mile-long lozenge I call the never-ending island because it seems to take forever to get past. After rounding the southern end of Texada, you're technically out of the Strait of Georgia and into Malaspina Strait, which, if you ignore all the right-hand off-lanes that lead up the spectacular mainland inlets ("Not this time!"), eventually deposits you in the town of Powell River, on the doorstep of Desolation Sound. That's where we would spend the night.

Nobody seems to pay much attention to Texada, and the 1,200 or so residents may like it that way. The most press the island had attracted in the last decade was outrage over the proposal, a few years earlier, for a liquid natural gas terminal at the north end of the island. Nobody was thrilled at the prospect of gas tankers in Georgia Strait.

Now, Malaspina was glassy. It was like motoring across a mirror. The only landmark on Texada, at least on the east side, is the limestone quarries to the north, not far from the terminal for the small ferry that shuttles to Powell River. The hillside is excavated in great shelves that look like the entrance to a giant's castle that never got built. At six knots, it would take hours even to reach the quarries. I put *Vera* on autopilot and went forward to sit on the foredeck. The Yanmar droned comfortingly behind me, and *Vera* cut her silver path. For anyone sitting on shore, we would be a stationary speck. We were weirdly alone, not even a tug to worry about, never mind a hypothetical tanker, and I had to fight to keep a lookout for floating logs. I tried the meditation technique I'd been reading about in my father's book on Buddhism: breathe in, breathe out, concentrate on the act itself to the exclusion of everything else. But it only made me drowsier. Meditation and watching for flotsam didn't seem to be compatible.

So I thought about my friend Chris, who in two months had gone from helping me tear out my rotted exhaust system to submitting to a surgical operation that left him without an esophagus. It was cancer; the odds were discouraging. We had thought a lot about cancelling the trip, but he wouldn't hear of it. What business did I have being out here, when things like that could happen out of the blue? For that matter, what was waiting out there for me? I decided to ask my father about Chris. After all, if he was able to pop up on *Vera* without warning, why couldn't I summon him when *I* felt like talking?

"Trust the surgeons," he said.

My father wore the same checkered flannel jacket he'd had on in Skerry Bay and was perched on the pulpit, gripping the stainless tubing with both hands like a child banished to a corner. His slippered feet dangled over the glassy water, and he rose and subsided gently against the unmoving green backdrop of Texada Island. I noticed he was now wearing the white floppy hat I'd tossed into Haro Strait days ago. I decided his wardrobe was beyond my influence.

"The surgeons know what they're doing. Anyway, what choice has he got?"

"Get a second opinion?"

"Oh, yes. I would." He frowned. "You know, Chris never invited me to see my boat after he made all those changes to it."

"That was twenty-five years ago! You sold it to him, remember? Anyway, he was probably afraid you wouldn't have approved."

"Well, maybe I wouldn't have."

A chunk of waterlogged driftwood thunked into the bow, right below my father, and tumbled the length of *Vera*'s hull making bass-drum noises. I watched it bob in our wake: a couple of feet long, too small to cause any damage, but what if it had been the top of a deadhead? I got to my feet and went back to the cockpit. Hatsumi looked annoyed.

"I think I was dreaming," I said. Like many Japanese people, she believed in ghosts, but I didn't think I could get away with blaming the collision on one.

"How much longer until we get to Powell River?"

It took us another three hours, and by the time the wind finally arrived, predictably from straight in front of us, I'd lost interest in sailing. The wind increased alarmingly as we rounded Grief Point, a notorious shoulder on the mainland side that sticks out into Malaspina Strait just enough to force the wind to accelerate as it follows the shore. Grief Point is a kind of mini

Brooks Peninsula, which would kill four men this year; they both work the same way. People with homes on Grief Point, and there are some beautiful ones, are in prime storm-watching territory, even in mid-summer. We rocked and rolled past Grief Point, then ducked in behind the breakwater at Westview, which is where the Powell River ferry dock and boat harbour are.

I like Westview. You can't see the clouds from the pulp mill in Powell River, and the people are so welcoming, I only had to stroll through once to decide I would be perfectly happy living there. It's just that — not to put too fine a point on it — Westview Harbour is hell to dock your boat in. The wind is one thing; even behind the breakwater, Malaspina Strait makes its presence known. But the real challenge is the way the harbour master, who is actually two or three people with handheld VHF radios and seen-it-all expressions, packs the visiting boats into the available space.

Westview is really there for the fishing fleet. It's a work-ing harbour, not a manicured grid of pressure-washed concrete wharves with nightlights that actually work and kiosks for shore power and water. At Westview, visiting yachtsmen are asked to back their boats down between the slips, where you either form a raft with several other boats, or moor stern-in so that you have to get off your boat by clambering over your own safety lines and jumping off the back end. You don't get a choice: the harbour master radios your slot to you, you some-how turn your boat around in ten feet of water without hitting the breakwater, and back you go, trying to control an object that was never designed to go backward. I've seen people lose it in Westview, husbands yelling at wives standing petrified on the foredeck ("The pole! Get the *pole!*"), wives imploring the con-verging attendants, off-duty fishermen, *anyone* to somehow help the maniac at the controls bring their twenty-thousand-pound whale to a stop without taking out the dock. Backing into Westview is the kind of situation where people get so flustered they grab the wrong engine control, hurl too-short docklines into the water, take flying leaps.

My father's ghost would fit right in at Westview, but he wisely chose not to show his face this time. Somehow the wind co-operated, *Vera* responded to my puppet-master routine with throttle and shifter, the dinghy didn't get cracked like a sunflower seed between two boats. Or maybe we actually finally knew what we were doing. We tied off to a small gillnetter, exchanged a surreptitious high five, and set off for a late-afternoon walk to Willingdon Beach Park. When we reached the top of the gang-plank and looked back, *Vera* had been swallowed, a green stitch in a carpet of boats.

Willingdon Park was a gem, a sandy crescent of beach with a long fishing jetty backed by green lawns, a kid's play pool and swings, the Forestry Museum, a cedar band shell. The Beach Hut sold burgers and oysters, and we lined up behind a motorcycling couple in their sixties; they both wore Doc Martens shoes, blue shades, and leather jackets with "Powell River Harley Owners" across the back. We ate an early dinner off paper plates the wind kept trying to spin out over Malaspina Strait, then walked back along the main street to the docks.

Powell River would be the last sizeable town for us before Port McNeill and Port Hardy, near the top of Vancouver Island; after that, only Tofino and Ucluelet, two-thirds of the way back down the west coast, would have much in the way of services and communications. I noticed a few new businesses — an espresso bar, a bistro, a curry hut — that seemed to confirm an influx of retired city-dwellers, but Westview didn't seem in danger of losing its small-town flavour. The sign at the Legion Hall still advertised "Saturday and Sunday Meat Draws," and Ace Auto Marine, with its window full of rebuilt alternators and starter motors, was still there between the barber shop and an accountant's office.

Vera was thoroughly hemmed in when we got back. A

small tug had tied up nearby, stern-in, two lines compressing the multiple layers of old auto tires that made up its aft fender. "Japanese style," Hatsumi called it. Japanese harbours look a bit like Westview, with the fishing boats stacked, stern-in. In the low sun, the mundane became beautiful: the fuel dock, a row of orange fenders tied to a trawler, a frayed flag snapping in the wind. The whole assemblage rocked and creaked. Charley was in heaven, lapping at oily blotches on the dock and urinating every few feet.

There was a new arrival across from us, a forty-five-foot white ketch that seemed to be crewed by middle-aged women — eight of them, it turned out, signed on for an adventure circumnavigating Vancouver Island. And the skipper in charge of this group of neophytes turned out to be the wife of a biologist I'd known decades before. Valma Brenton looked like she was up to the task: weathered and deeply tanned, with short blonde hair caught behind a band. She had dirt under her fingernails and didn't bother with shoes.

"I'm teaching them yoga, mindfulness, and offshore sailing," she told me, grinning. "And it's not even my boat. The engine broke down as soon as we left Nanaimo, so we're here until the parts come."

"So — you've gone around the island before?"

"Lots of times."

Valma might be useful. "What about the Nahwitti Bar?" I asked.

"Slack tide," Valma said. "Don't go any other time."

"Unless we take the inside route, right? Through the kelp?" Finally, I thought, someone who's actually been there, and more than once.

"Never heard of it," said Valma.

The Man I Never Expected to Meet

Valma Brenton seemed like an interesting person. You meet a lot of interesting people when you travel by boat, but I was already finding out that you meet just as many when you decide to tackle a medical detective story. Allan Thackray, for example. His name was everywhere in my father's files. It was as though this one man had taken it upon himself to infiltrate every hole, however small, in the great smelly cheese that was the case against my father. Mr. Thackray was, strictly speaking, the Canadian Medical Protective Association's lawyer, but my father thought of him as his. Very soon, so did I.

I wasn't prepared to cut Mr. Thackray much slack at first, not when all I knew of the case was its out-of-court outcome that I couldn't help thinking of as capitulation. If anything, the Allan Thackray I had in my mind as I began to trawl through the files was the generic barrister, an argument for hire, the kind my father habitually railed at. But there was way too much of Allan Thackray here for anyone to maintain that kind of image for long. His letters to my father were unfailingly respectful, but this was clearly the kind of respect that reflects immediately upon itself; it was obvious to anyone reading the letters, and especially to my father, that Thackray had done his medical homework on every relevant aspect of the case. He knew where the strengths and weaknesses lay, and he expected my father to grasp their significance. And so the two men developed a correspondence of careful camaraderie, at first only by letter but later, when the examination for discovery rolled around, in person.

I began to form my own image. The preliminary letters I imagined written by a big man, suited, in a corner office high above Vancouver's photogenic harbour, aware of his power yet careful with his wording, the way a big man is careful of his bulk. When they met, I imagined, the lawyer would have towered over his client, and it was easy to picture him covering the room where the examination for discovery was held, a football lineman ready to protect his quarterback with a lightning dive for the knees of the opposition.

When Thackray went into court alone on the first day of the trial, the transcripts only strengthened that impression: clearing the way, sizing up tacklers in an instant, derailing or demolishing them, and then offering a sportsmanlike hand to get them back on their feet. And when it suddenly became clear that the star player would never take the field, my imaginary Thackray played the part of the benched player to perfection. In the final exchange of letters to my father, he produced a good impersonation of an athlete being interviewed after a loss: we gave it a 110 percent, the coach did what he thought best, time to move on.

It took me the better part of a fine afternoon in Westview to get through everything with Mr. Thackray's name on it. When I'd finished, I knew that his neat summing-up couldn't be the end of the story. The greatest athlete-diplomats leave you marvelling at their restraint while more than ever convinced that the real story is more complicated, and so it was with Thackray's exit from the case and from our lives. When I closed the last file folders of his correspondence, I resolved to track Mr. Thackray down.

What prodded me to do this was the thorn of a single sentence buried in a spiral-bound exercise book containing twenty pages of my father's handwritten account of the trial, all of it struck through with thick pencil, as though he had opened it one day, shaken his head, and leafed methodically from beginning to end, slashing diagonally as he went. Bottom left to top right, a backhanding of bad memories, like shooing a persistent fly. The sentence that sent me looking for Mr. Thackray was this: "My lawyer's letters do not reflect his warm personality; they are polite, brief, cold, and to the point."

Warm personality? I *knew* it! I had to wait until our trip was over to follow up on my hunch, but this is how it turned out.

Allan Thackray wasn't hard to find. He was still in Vancouver, a retired judge. We met at a cavernous Japanese restaurant across from the Vancouver courthouse. I was early and nervous. Stuffed in my back pocket was a five-page memo Thackray had sent me a week or so before. He'd written thirty-two numbered paragraphs, starting with Billy's birth records and ending with a reminder that settlements do not constitute an admission of liability ("Indeed, to the contrary"). Here was the case in thirty-two devastating nutshells, which I suppose I could simply have asked for before I dove into the mass of records and testimony. Here were the first stirrings of fear for a gravely disadvantaged child; the first operation; the infection; the second operation; the emergency procedure to reduce pressure on the child's brain; the final operation; the gradual dying down of incident and record until the knock on the seventy-four-year-old surgeon's door so many years later.

It was a hell of a story, and I wanted more than ever to meet its author. But there were no lineman-sized retired barristers standing to attention in front of the garish colour photos of sushi and donburi, so I did a quick circuit of the block, teeming at the noon-hour with men and women in suits. One of them *had* to be Thackray, look for a big guy, perhaps moving slowly from an old rugby injury. But when I re-approached the restaurant ten minutes later, there was still nobody there — unless you counted the little man in a moss-coloured suit who'd been there the first time. This time, he stuck out a hand and grinned.

So much for imagination. Allan Thackray would not have towered over my father; he was even shorter than me. The green suit had a stain or two on the lapels, and the purple tie might have been chosen by someone who was colour-blind, the way my father was.

"My wife insisted I dress properly," he laughed, pumping my right hand with short, knobby fingers and touching my left elbow, gently propelling me inside. "Come on, let's eat, but you're going to have to do the ordering. I don't know a thing about Japanese food."

We sat in a gloomy corner and ordered gluey tempura and colourless raw tuna from a binder of greasy plastic pictures. The food was bad, but I was too busy revising my image of Allan Thackray to care. I caught him peering at me and wondered, was he looking for similarities between father and son? Were there that many to find?

"You know, I often wished I'd been a doctor. Are you surprised?"

"Nothing surprises me anymore," I said.

"I almost was, too, but I had a terrible education. My father ran a men's clothing store in Moose Jaw, and when the new government came to power — I was sixteen — my dad refused to live under what he called a communist regime. He took me out of high school, and we moved to Victoria. I worked in the store."

"So . . . what happened?"

Mr. Thackray grinned, something he did easily and often. He didn't look stern, or watchful, or respectful, or even ironic, any of the things I'd imagined. He looked twinkly.

"I got a girlfriend. She thought a man should be professional."

"So, you got married?"

"Nope. She married a doctor. I went back to school and became a lawyer. But I ended up defending a lot of doctors, some of them multiple times."

"All malpractice suits?"

"Oh, yes. There was one neurosurgeon we dreaded, the guy was so combative in court you had to be really careful."

"Like my father might have been?"

But Thackray wasn't ready to go there yet. "Maybe," he said. "One thing I learned in all those trials: maybe we lawyers weren't sensitive enough to the effects of these lawsuits on some of the doctors. There was one surgeon, we brought him to Vancouver for the trial, put him up in the Four Seasons."

"Like my parents."

Thackray ignored that one too. I realized that he was doing most of the talking. That was okay, but there had to be a reason. Maybe he was working up to something.

"I waited for this surgeon in court, and he never showed up. Finally, we called his family. They got to him just before he went out the window."

Thackray looked down at his sushi. He wasn't twinkling now.

"Well, my father never got over it, you know. I think he kept preparing for the trial, in his mind. Until he died."

Thackray looked as though he had just bitten into something unpleasant. He spoke slowly and carefully, as though he had gone over the words already in his mind. Judging from the memo in my back pocket, I knew he had.

"In the two years I knew your father, he aged a lot. I think now that we should have pushed harder. Your father did very well in the examination. Perhaps we . . . should not have settled."

I thought about the memo in my pocket. The pressure-relieving procedure done on Billy, properly called a lumbar puncture but better known as a spinal tap, had proved indefensible. But my father hadn't *done* the lumbar puncture; Billy's pediatrician, Dr. Beamish, had. Whether my father had authorized it, nobody would ever know, but in his discussions with Thackray he'd had "great difficulty defending the puncture." So, if he had taken the stand, he might have cleared his own name, but the suit would probably still have been lost, and a colleague fingered. This case was full of rocks and hard places. Whatever my grasp of this exquisite dilemma, Thackray's was probably better.

"I just wanted to tell you that," he said.

I didn't push it. We went quickly over the main points. The judge trying the case was known to frequently find for the plaintiff, including in cases involving children. The settlement was big — "huge, even today." But the real question, the one that had got me started on that rotting cardboard box in the first place, clearly still eluded both of us: "Why couldn't my father get over it?"

Mr. Thackray paid for the meal, although it would have been fairer if we had shared. As we got up, he said, "One thing has always puzzled me about your father."

"Only one?"

He laughed. "I've always wondered, why did he stay in Victoria? With the kind of training he had? I just don't get it."

It was a fair question. His training in Chicago was second to none, so why confine himself to a minor Canadian city? It was as puzzling as his inability to get over the trial. If I solved one problem, I'd probably have the answer to the other; for now, they were both unanswerable.

"I'm working on that one," I said. We stood up, and Thackray winced. "Knee replacement," he said. Back in the bright sunlight of Hornby Street, he told me one final story. "I did some lecturing, you know. To doctors about lawsuits — how to avoid them, how to prepare for them. One time I came over to Victoria to talk to a group of doctors but, you know, it was the oddest thing.

They couldn't seem to pay attention. I finally concluded it was something to do with Victoria."

He had the twinkle back. I sensed a punch line.

"They kept looking at a bunch of snapshots, really getting their heads together over them."

"Girlfriends," I asked, playing along. "Houses?"

"Sailboats," said Thackray. "I couldn't believe it. But then, I'm from Moose Jaw." He grabbed my hand, touched my elbow again, and was gone, limping back toward the courthouse.

The Second Law
of Thermodynamics

Disorder is the natural state of the universe, and it's expressed in the concept of entropy. The second law of thermodynamics is simple: entropy increases. Mechanisms that attempt to reduce entropy (a wristwatch, a water pump, the cerebrospinal fluid system of the human brain) require constant care and feeding in the form of external energy (a battery, food, the attentions of a surgeon). It's the energy that keeps entropy at bay. But everything, eventually, breaks down.

A boat is a pretty good entropy machine, a floating collection of improbable mechanical and electrical contraptions that nature is ceaselessly doing her best to disassemble. But the best one, the most audacious anti-entropy device of all, is the human body.

"I'm falling apart," my father told me disgustedly, a few months before the end. He rose from his chair in the care home, pushing once, twice, three times before he came out in a wavering crouch. He was right, there wasn't much left of him. The hands searching for the walker handles looked as though they belonged to a much bigger man. So much of him had already wasted away. For him, entropy was increasing with a vengeance. We could see it.

On a boat, you can practically hear it. After we'd owned *Vera* for a few months, I began to imagine a peevish, feeble chorus of nautical senior citizens silently thumping the table, trying to get attention.

"I'm going," wheezes a hose clamp fastened around a sea-water inlet. "What do you expect, I'm only nickel-plated. I'm supposed to be stainless steel! When I let go, this hose will slip off and down she'll go. Cheapskate owner!"

"Don't look at me," croaks the automatic bilge pump switch. "I stopped working years ago. My contacts dissolved, and I've got algae in my joints. If this boat floods, I'm going down with it. They installed me before they even put the floorboards in, for God's sake, how do you expect someone to fix me?"

Leaking pumps, fading-out radar screens, fraying steering cables, weeping autopilot rams, corroding metal pins about to detach the boom from the mast without warning and turn it into a flailing twenty-foot metal club. All of these happened to us on *Vera*, and many more, so getting to know her had been a matter of singling out a voice, any voice, and doing your best to silence it. I felt like an attendant in my father's care home, grabbing my pager with one hand while I poked applesauce at a grizzled face with the other. At least my marine seniors *could* be fixed, unlike the old people who were literally on their last legs, who might better have been allowed to let nature's ineluctable prescription take effect rather than be subjected to the medical profession's determination to keep them going with more spare parts, more medicines, more duct tape.

When I began the real process of getting to know *Vera*, I surprised myself. I folded myself into tendon-snapping positions to get at deeply buried batteries. I hung upside down, batlike, under the cockpit floor, working by feel to unscrew the faulty electronic compass that fed the autopilot, remove it from its obscure hiding place (why would anyone put it *there*?), and replace it with a half-price used one in a more sensible location. I took a saw to the three cantaloupe-sized aluminum pods that housed the obsolete depth sounder, knot meter, and wind direction indicator. I cut them off flush, carrying them away by their electrical wires, three severed heads dangling from a handful of arteries.

Little by little, I learned *Vera*'s smells and sounds and secrets, as one would a lover's. I washed the previous owner's blue coveralls and even wore them a few times, poring over his logbook. At every step, I pestered anyone who would listen, uncovering a community of like-minded sailors who believed that doing it the hard way was a form of insurance. The worst was when I lay on my back under the foredeck with my head in the chain locker, hands behind my head, working mostly by feel to disconnect the massive electric motor that ran the anchor windlass. When it finally loosened, the smooth shaft came down through the deck and the housing barely cleared my head to crash into a pile of rusted chain. It was like delivering an infant. I staggered out cradling my forty-pound baby, trailing a greasy umbilicus of electrical wiring.

From the moment they take delivery of their boat, middle-aged sailors find themselves in a never-ending game of catch-up. It's unfair because the players are too old for it. Not the physical part — today's sixty- and seventy-year-olds are as fit as their parents were at fifty. Mentally, though, the facility for learning is tapering off. Sailors begin to dream about Tahiti at about the time they catch themselves stock-still in the middle of a room, wondering how they got there. If you can't even cross a room without getting lost, how are you going to cross an ocean?

One answer seems to be by going back to school. Week after week, through fall and winter, greying would-be voyagers get up from an early dinner, clutch their backs, and set out for whichever rented church basement or community hall is on their list. Converging slowly on the darkened doorways, they look like the undead.

Most of the boating courses available to me and Hatsumi were volunteer efforts, by more or less knowledgeable people who'd been there, done that, and wanted badly to talk about it. But there were so many courses to choose from! Heavy weather. Medical emergencies at sea. Radio communication. The psychology of cruising. There was even one for women only, to discuss the problem of overbearing skipper-husbands and how to deal with hot flashes in the tropics.

I was excused from that one, but I still managed to attend a few semesters' worth of classes, beginning with the best known and most general, the Power and Sail Squadron basic level course. This three-month program covers all the basics any boater needs to know, short of actually getting out on the water. Hatsumi and I enrolled even before we took delivery of *Vera*, and my reasoning was faultlessly self-serving: Hatsumi, a complete novice, desperately needed some basic knowledge, and I, a seasoned sailor, would magnanimously sit alongside her, encouraging, translating where necessary, maintaining solidarity. There wasn't much these squadron people could teach *me*, but my wife needed them.

We all sat at long tables in a church hall, like a collection of couples awaiting counselling. A succession of volunteer lecturers ranging from the highly competent (a Brit engineer who covered sailing theory with dry humour and diagrams) to the very annoying (a bubbly lady who did buoys by showing endless slides of her own boat: "There I am, next to a port-hand day beacon!"). A husband-and-wife team seemed fixated on death by explosion and noxious gases. Their presentations featured grainy Coast Guard footage from the 1970s of flaming hulks and masts receding beneath oil-slicked waters. One gloomy video was a re-enactment of the death of an entire family from CO_2 inhalation: the actors rolled their eyes and went down like tenpins. I still check reflexively for this couple's boat each time we drop anchor, in case one of them rows over and demands a description of the main classes of distress flares.

For the first two weeks, Hatsumi had to be dragged into class. Then *ganbatte*, the Japanese version of "never say die" kicked in, and she agreed to continue. But she refused to write the final exam. In the end, she stuck that out too, emerging last from the examination room but with a 92% score. A week later, we all attended a graduation ceremony in a rented golf clubhouse, where we ate tiny triangular sandwiches and marched up to receive diplomas from the commodore, a determined, grey-haired lady wearing a meter maid's hat.

The Power and Sail Squadron course convinced me to eat my words. Thirty years of so-called experience might have made me comfortable around boats and even pretty good at boat handling and seamanship, but it had left me with no more than a sketchy knowledge of things that really mattered: weather forecasting, navigation, safety. I'm not sure how our family cruises ever got from point A to point B because I never saw my father laying out a course with protractor and compass. No weather forecasts either — no wonder we ran aground on Sidney Spit. It was an odd sort of lapse because in all other things he was meticulous and left nothing to chance.

⌇

The Squadron course was just the beginning. There were plenty of other courses that homed in on a single facet of long-distance sailing, which was what we planned ultimately to do. Medical Emergencies was presented by a doctor who'd been cruising for decades. From her, we learned about water-mixable fibreglass splints, how to re-set a dislocated finger, and the care and treatment of butt boils, which you develop from lazing around naked on sunny, salt-soaked decks.

The Sail Repair course was practical too, and we got to go to a real sail loft. Its owner, Rick McBride, wore a ball cap and faded jeans and spoke slowly, as though thirty years of punching a needle through heavy sailcloth had turned his thoughts into a thread that was collected on one side of the sail, pushed through with a gloved fist, then pulled clear on the other side. His words seemed hand-stitched.

"My number one piece of advice?" said Rick, settling himself on one of the sailmakers' benches that occupied strategic positions around the sail loft's hardwood floor. There were four such stations, each with a sewing machine pit in which the sailmaker sat, half-submerged before the tide of sailcloth that would flow through his machine.

"Use your imagination. You can repair most sail disasters without any of the equipment we have here, and anyway, you're not going to have it with you. Look around."

He gestured. We pivoted obediently on our stools. There was a gallery above us where the patterns for new sails were created. Down here on the main floor was where assembly took place, and the walls were hung with spools of rope, prewaxed thread, seam tape called "insignia cloth." Staplers, drills, and tape measures in orange-handled spools dangled from the ceiling, along with wire cutters and an assortment of thrashed knee pads. Long slabs of batten material — the flexible plastic stiffeners that help the sail hold its shape — drooped over racks above our heads.

"You don't need any of this stuff. Well, some of it — thread, needle, a bit of seam tape. But look."

He grabbed a sail, pulled out a pair of nightmarish scissors, and ripped a three-foot gash. Several of us groaned.

"Not to worry, this one's already toast. But you can fix it, on board, good enough to get you to Hawaii and back." And he proceeded to patch the rend, duct-taping the edges together, double-taping the patch around the cut, fencing the whole thing off with insignia tape, and hand-sewing around it, twice. We all came up to try out the stitch; I could barely get the needle through the sandwich of sailcloth that Rick had been methodically perforating.

The difficulty of sail repair didn't worry me because I knew in my bones that if anything went wrong with *Vera*, it would be something mechanical and would probably involve the engine. And I was right.

Herringectomy and Rising Sun

We spent a quiet night at Westview. I'd fallen asleep to the muffled rumble of cars driving off the ferry from Comox, and I awoke at 5 a.m. to the reassuring sound and stink of large marine diesel engines. The fishing fleet was heading out. We ate breakfast with the VHF radio on; the weather looked good all the way to Refuge Cove, well into Desolation Sound. Another long day after that and we'd be halfway through the rapids, almost as far as we'd made it last year before chickening out and turning back.

"We'll probably have to motor," I told Hatsumi as I dried the breakfast dishes. "But the engine's been fine so far. And anyway, if something goes wrong, we're a sailboat, right?" Nothing was going to go wrong.

We cleared the breakwater and turned north. The ferry from Vancouver Island, across the glassy strait, was well off in the distance. "We'll be long gone by the time it gets to this side," I said. "Don't worry about it." I put *Vera* on autopilot. "Is there any of that coffee left?"

Then the engine died. To be strictly accurate, it didn't die, it began a death rattle. Normally, the sound made by the exhaust is a rhythmic throat-clearing, like an old man ambling down the sidewalk, hawking and spitting. What comes out is seawater, after it's been circulated through the engine to keep everything cool. That gentle *hawk-splash-hawk-splash* is the most reassuring sound a boater can hear, and it goes with you everywhere, always in the back of your mind, whenever you're shuffling along under power.

But now it had stopped. The old man wasn't spitting anymore, he was just coughing, a tubercular rumble that Hatsumi and I caught at the same moment.

"Shut it down — *now!*" She reached the kill switch first, and suddenly it was very quiet. We were right in front of the ferry dock.

"I just *rebuilt* the water pump," I said.

"There's no wind," Hatsumi said.

"And there's a ferry coming."

"What should we *do?*"

Ferries seem slow and stately when you're on them, but when you're in their path, their advance is inexorable and, frankly, frightening. This one would be on top of us in ten minutes. On board, passengers were probably already listening to the docking announcement and looking for their car keys. I could radio the vessel, state the obvious ("We're the idiot in your path and we can't move"), or I could fix the engine. I clambered down below, found my cellphone.

"What are you *doing?*"

My friend Chris answered after two rings.

"*Ho!*" he said when I'd described our predicament. "It's not the pump, right?"

"Can't be."

"Then it's perfectly logical. Close the seacock and start taking the cooling system apart. Something's stuck inside. What fun! I wish I was there."

"Me too," I said. After that, Hatsumi may have said, "What are you *doing*?" several more times, but I ignored her. "Just keep your eye on that ferry," I said. "Dear."

The seacock lets the ocean enter a fat rubber hose that leads to the water pump. In a minute, I had the clamp off. There was a brief, savage struggle while I yanked on the hose, then off it came too, depositing me on my backside with the thing clutched in both hands, like a teenager caught masturbating. Protruding from the end of the hose was the tail — just the last inch or so — of a fish. It came out reluctantly, with a noise like a kiss.

What kind of malign fate had sent a juvenile herring up our cooling hose? I knew it was a herring; despite having been squeezed cylindrical in cross-section, it still had the characteristic bulldog lower jaw. But what were the odds? They had to be astronomical.

I flicked the herring over the stern and screwed the hose back on.

"*Clupea harengus!*" I shouted up to Hatsumi. "*Nishin*, you know, a small one. Let's get out of here." She started the engine, which cleared its throat mightily and spat a herring-free jet out the stern. The ferry was close enough to see passengers on the deck. They stared at us as we splashed away.

That made two engine problems for sailboats at Westview. First Valma's boat, and now ours. Did a herring committing suicide in your water intake qualify as an engine problem? But I'd fixed it, and the solution had nothing to do with all those boating courses. I switched the autopilot back on, *Vera* performed the usual drunken lurches while the machine's obsolete Australian circuits came to an arrangement with the rudder, and we gradually settled into a northwesterly course along the mainland shore.

The day was brilliantly clear, the barometer skyrocketing, and the view west reminded me how much of Vancouver Island was serious mountain. With the binoculars, I could clearly pick out Mount Albert Edward, high above the city of Comox, where Hatsumi and I had backpacked before *Vera* came along. To the east, I knew, were more mountains, many more; we were on roughly the same latitude as the ski mecca of Whistler. As soon as we rounded Sarah Point into Desolation Sound, the views of the Coast Range would open up, and for the rest of the trip north, we'd be in a corridor of snowy peaks. There were places in Desolation Sound where, anchored in your boat, you felt as though you were in an alpine lake.

But we wouldn't go to those places this time. We squeezed past the reefs that pepper the water around croissant-shaped Savary Island, making yet another mental note to visit its famed white sand beaches "maybe next year." Off to the right, Dinner Rock was a forlorn hump a half mile off the shore, its peak marked by the cross commemorating the four people who lost their lives when the MV *Gulf Stream*, a ferry on its way from Powell River to the town of Lund, hit the rock at night in 1947. The wreck is still down there, a popular dive site.

How many wrecks would we pass near, even *over*, on this trip? Especially on the west coast. The Graveyard of the Pacific, people called the southwest corner of Vancouver Island. Many of the maritime disasters of the last century involved ships coming from California and across the Pacific as the colony of British Columbia began exporting lumber, coal, fish. Again and again, especially in winter, vessels lost their way trying to enter the Strait of Juan de Fuca. The accounts were so similar: the weather closed in, the captain thought they were some-where else, the sudden, horrifying glimpse of breakers before hull met rocks. The chances of getting off a holed ship were slim, especially when an SOS described the wrong location. Those who actually made it ashore often died of exposure. Finally, a life-saving trail, complete with a telegraph line, was constructed from Bamfield to Victoria in the early twentieth century. If everything went well, we would be in Bamfield in a month.

Dinner Rock is only a few miles from Lund, the town founded in the late nineteenth century by the Swedes Frederick and Charles Thulin and is literally the end of the road. The Pacific Coastal Highway is a network of roads that starts in Chile and ends in Lund. As we chugged past, water taxis streaked back and forth from the beaches at Savary Island, and the boat traffic increased as we squeezed through Thulin Passage a few miles further north. Thulin Passage separates the mainland from the Copeland Islands, a chain of jewels that was already jammed with cruisers at anchor. The Copelands are popular with kayakers, many of whom start out in Lund or are dropped off by water taxis, and I picked out the emerald greens and cherry reds of their long noses pulled into the trees. Now that we were in kayak country, we had to be extra careful. Even though they tended to travel in groups, their cigar shapes all but disappeared whenever the surface was disturbed by even the slightest chop.

"Not now," I said to Charley, who had been up and sniffing hard from the moment we entered the passage, as though trying to pull everything, islands and kayakers included, into his nose. "You can do your thing in Refuge Cove. Hold it for another hour."

Twenty minutes later, we were around Sarah Point and officially in Desolation Sound — itself a relatively small open area bounded by West Redonda and Cortes islands and the B.C. mainland, although the name is loosely used to mean the region "north of Campbell River and south of the Broughton Archipelago." Suddenly we found ourselves looking down the long corridor of Homfray Channel, and there, twenty miles away, was the snow-slathered exclamation point of Mount Denman. From this point on, there would be lots of mountains.

Who was this Denman? He seemed to be all over the place: both Victoria and Vancouver have a Denman Street, Denman Island was a day behind us, and now this mountain. To answer this question, and hundreds of others like it that niggle at me every time I look at a chart, I had invited John Walbran along with us.

Captain Walbran was a character. He was born in Yorkshire in 1848, served as a ship's officer all over the world, and went to work for the Canadian Pacific Navigation Company in 1888. Then, as master of the government steamship *Quadra*, he spent what looked to me like a fantastically eventful five years charting the British Columbia coast, filling in the gaps left by earlier British and Spanish navigators and, more importantly, getting involved with the locals by servicing lighthouses, inspecting boats, transporting police, and rescuing whoever needed rescuing. Those five years furnished him with the material for his next big project, the writing of *British Columbia Coast Names: Their Origin and History*, published in 1909. The book is addictive, despite being more than a century old.

So, what about Denman? There he was in my copy of Walbran: Rear Admiral Joseph Denman, commander in chief of the Pacific Station. In 1864, the year he'd bagged his own mountain, Admiral Denman had taken the ship *Devastation* around to the west coast to "punish" the Ahousaht people for murdering the crew of the trading vessel *Kingfisher*. If we made it around the Nahwitti Bar, we'd be in Ahousaht in a month.

Refuge Cove, the place Charley was so looking forward to peeing in, is soaked in history too. A perfect harbour tucked into the lower lobe of West Redonda Island, Refuge Cove has been the social centre of Desolation Sound since its settlement in 1866, gradually accumulating a collection of float homes, boats, and cottages, the population rising and falling with the vagaries of logging and fishing. Most of the land was bought in the early 1970s by a group of Vancouver academics who formed a co-operative and who still own the place. The weathered wood store that sits on dubious-looking stilts is a madhouse from mid-July to the last week in August, providing the flood of cruising boats with groceries, popsicles, charts, and fishing lures.

When we got there, the store's owner, Colin Robertson, still had the wary look of someone waiting for something to happen. It was July 11, a Sunday. "They're coming," Colin told me as he handed me the diesel hose to top up our fuel tank. "By midweek, give them time to get here from Seattle if they left today."

By the last week in August, Refuge Cove would be thinning out, and the store shuts down again in October. Not much of a season. We weren't much help with Colin's bottom line; we only needed twenty-five litres of fuel.

"You need some big powerboats in here, fast," I said. Colin just smiled.

"Oh, they'll come," he said. "Maybe they'll bring us a break from this weather."

It was so hot, the creosote on the exposed pilings was dripping, like enormous black candles. Charley developed sunstroke and began to squirt diarrhea onto the dock. I hosed it off and then turned the tap on him while he stood, shaking. We did laundry, and I bought a copy of *Anna Karenina* from the tiny used bookstore run by the acerbic Reinhold Hoge, one of the founding members of the co-op. It cost me $3. I took it below, where Hatsumi and I flopped, boneless as starfish, waiting for the sun to go away.

And then, in one of those little wrinkles in the order of things that, at least for me, seem to happen more often in boats than anywhere else, Charley began to emit a low gargling sound from the cockpit.

"For God's sake." I dragged myself up the ladder. The setting sun lit Refuge Cove like a stage. On the concrete fuel dock, the hoses lay like a nest of torpid serpents. The weathered sides of the Refuge Cove Store glowed, and their reflected image rippled out over the calm water below. A retired couple in the *Lucky Louie* sipped drinks in lawn chairs arranged on the dock, attended by the strains of oldies. Was that what Charley was objecting to?

Then I saw the white sailboat. She went past us, quite close, turned slowly and headed for the opposite finger. Charley muttered some more.

"I think you should see this," I called back to Hatsumi. The boat was flying the Rising Sun.

"Let's go," I said, untying the dinghy.

"But we don't *know* them!" Sometimes, my wife could be quite Japanese. For her, hurling yourself, Western style, at someone you didn't know was simply uncouth. And maybe she's right, but this time, I insisted. How often do you see the Japanese flag flown from a sailboat in Desolation Sound?

Yoshio Asanuma and his wife, Fumie, were on their way back from Alaska and Haida Gwaii. They'd sailed *Foxglove* from Yokohama the year before, a violent ride that cost Fumie two broken ribs, and they planned to leave the boat in Vancouver for the winter. Next year, when they returned to Canada, they'd take her south, the beginning of a planned six-year voyage through the Panama Canal, up the eastern seaboard, and over to Europe.

Yoshi was barefoot, wiry, and burned brown. It didn't matter that he was getting started on his sixties; the face beneath the salt-and-pepper hair was still a boy's. Yoshi's rudimentary English was about as good as my Japanese, but he was obviously banking on a combination of his own considerable charm and the exoticism of a Japanese flag to get them into places we'd never manage to penetrate. Within minutes we were aboard, Hatsumi and Fumie were off and running, and Yoshi and I set about getting to know each other without sharing anything more than a love of boats and a determination to get the most out of life.

Descending into *Foxglove*'s cabin was like climbing into a hermit crab's shell. Yoshi and Fumie's boat was as crammed as a bachelor apartment in Tokyo. Every surface, including the cabin ceiling, was stuck, stapled, hung, or simply jammed with the necessities of life for a cruising Japanese couple: post-it notes in English and kanji, eagle feathers driven between books on Panama and the West Marine catalogue, a spinning rod and reel, cans of engine oil and juice, a propane-fired rice cooker. He rummaged under his berth to produce a six-foot-long tuna gaff, the lethal hook made of stainless steel and frighteningly sharp. When Yoshi caught a tuna, he meant to keep it.

Yoshi and I soon became adept at conversing by scribbled diagram — an engine coupling, more fishing gear — and these got added to the piles. We drank beer from the stainless steel freezer that protruded through the chart table next to a weatherfax receiver. A half-completed weather map of the North Pacific hung out of the machine like a tongue.

"Low pressure," Yoshi intoned, stabbing at the riot of whorls. "I don't like." Yoshi, I would learn, would do anything to avoid heading out into a low. We learned that he'd taught himself to sail in the tricky conditions of Japan's coastal waters, and his first offshore experience was sailing *Foxglove*, single-handed, from New Zealand to Yokohama. I have a copy of the book he published about this voyage; I don't understand a word of it, but that's definitely a younger Yoshi on the cover flap.

To get where he was now, Yoshi had put in long years as master of a Yokohama Port fireboat. "Very slow. All day, sit in office. Many reportings." In all his time with the fire department, there wasn't a single emergency. Then he spent a couple of years operating a monstrous power cruiser for some rich businessmen needing a place to entertain their cronies ("Very old!"), and finally retired at sixty. Now he could throw away his monogrammed coveralls and go around in a faded T-shirt and shorts. His life was just starting.

Yoshi had opinions about everything nautical. Before long, we were on our knees in front of his engine. He drew my attention to the tension of the alternator belt.

"Loose," he said, tugging the floppy rubber belt to and fro.

Conventional wisdom has it that belts should be tight. But Yoshi was a mechanic too, among other things. He had his engineer's ticket, which included diesel repair.

"Loose! Good!" I made a mental note to back off on *Vera's* alternator belt.

Regarding the constant problem of the weedy tendrils that grow on your waterline, where sunlight is strongest, Yoshi dove once again into a storage locker, like a squirrel scrabbling in its nest. I watched his butt for a moment, then he resurfaced with several small green cans.

"Mix with paint! Then, smooth, smooth." He mimed a careful sanding of the entire waterline. "Then paint, paint . . . *good!*" He held up a triumphant thumb and pressed the cans of wasabi on me, his face alight. Maybe it really does work; wasabi is, after all, antibacterial and was traditionally added to raw fish for just that reason. It's likely it kills algae too.

And so it went. There were Yoshi's charts (ancient paper charts covered in scribblings, and a pirated, out-of-date disc of dubious electronic versions on Windows 98); there was the way he navigated by feel; there was his deathless celery plant growing in a bucket in the cockpit ("Fresh! Always!"). Yoshi was addictive.

We cobbled together a meal from our combined supplies and exchanged plans. We might see Yoshi and Fumie again at the end of the summer, when (if) we made it back down the west coast to Victoria. The tangle of wires erupting from their ham radio meant they could send and receive emails; they'd let us know when they arrived. Fumie left that sort of thing up to Yoshi.

"I don't know anything," she told Hatsumi, although that was patently untrue. "Then I can't be frightened. Just I *encourage!*"

When we told them we were going around Vancouver Island, Yoshi became solemn. He held up his hands, palms out, as though fending off an *oni*, a devil.

"I look at chart, don't go," he told me. "Very bad, many many rocks. And all . . ." He asked Hatsumi for the English word. "Ah. Lee shore, yes. Very bad." This from someone who had single-handedly sailed to Japan from New Zealand, crossed from Japan to Alaska, and explored Haida Gwaii.

"Lots of people do it," I said defensively. But I wondered if he was right. Yoshi navigated like a Japanese fisherman, many of whom don't bother with charts. He looked around, sniffed the air, and fed the data into some kind of genetic seafaring computer that told him where to anchor, how close to go to shore, when to chance the rapids, and whether to venture out at all or spend a week smearing wasabi on his waterline and fiddling with his alternator belt until conditions improved. The west coast of Vancouver Island gave Yoshi a bad feeling, and that worried both of us.

We exchanged Japanese goodies (dried squid, sour plums) and said our goodbyes. Refuge Cove had finally cooled off, and a quiet game of horseshoes was going on further down the dock, where several people lived in houseboats. We rowed back to the muffled *thunk* of iron shoes in sand. The *Lucky Louie* couple were already in bed, dreaming of the '60s. I decided to put in a few hours in the following decade, with Billy.

Billy

We'd been gone almost two weeks, but I hadn't gotten very far with the trial. The fact was, ever since we'd left Victoria, I had a conflict that I hadn't anticipated. How could I buckle down to the assignment I'd given myself when what I really wanted to do was fret about the next stage of our journey? Which was more important, the thousand and one uncertainties of the trip or the single mystery of my father's trial?

Lots of other people had sailed around Vancouver Island, so maybe the trip wasn't that big a deal. On the other hand, nobody knew or cared about the struggles of a feverish infant surrounded by doctors and nurses in the wee hours of a Labour Day weekend thirty-five years ago, so maybe that wasn't such a big deal either — except that I knew there was a story there that was every bit as compelling as pushing yourself around an island. But I had to care enough about it to put the hours in when I'd rather be clearing my mind for the next leg of our trip.

What I wanted out of it was pretty clear. It was the thing most people spend their lives trying to figure out, namely what made their parents tick. It amounts to a responsibility: you've got their genes, so you'd better find out, because those genes are coming to get you. And there's no better way to do that than to look hard at what happened when they were put to the test. Most of us don't have the documentation describing life-altering crises that might have befallen our parents, but I did. I couldn't back away from the chance I'd engineered for myself by doing all that background work on cerebrospinal fluid and children with big heads.

I decided that, like the sailors who fritter away decades getting ready to go offshore, I was suffering from "over-preparation syndrome." All I really had to do was extract the day-to-day story of Billy and his doctors and *tell* it. Beginning at the beginning. So I started reading again, in Refuge Cove, to find the bare bones upon which so many layers of meat would be hung. For starters, who was this kid?

Billy was born of an unwed teenage mother who immediately relinquished him to a childless couple keen to adopt. How much of Billy's subsequent travail was written in his genes, how much was caused by events right after he was born, and how much by events in the O.R. eleven months later? This was what my father's trial boiled down to.

Billy already had two strikes against him. The first was prematurity; he weighed just three pounds when he was born. The second was lack of oxygen because Billy didn't begin to breathe for three minutes — an eternity. Within hours, he was in a respirator in intensive care, a tracheostomy tube poking from his tiny neck. I thumbed through the charts and imagined the premie ward, the row of struggling babies in their plastic boxes, the swish of starched white dresses, the squeak of rubber-soled shoes.

His lungs gradually cleared, but his head circumference began to be a worry. When Billy was finally discharged to his new parents six weeks later, the family doctor told them of the possibility of hydrocephalus. "I advised [the adoptive mother] not to sign adoption papers right away," it says in one pediatrician's notes. But she was adamant.

Six weeks later, Billy was re-admitted. His head was getting too big, too fast. My father's first appearance in the file is a brief consultation record; he ran his tape around Billy's head and got forty-six centimetres. I put down the file and grabbed my own tape measure from the tool kit.

"Charles!" A click of toenails on the deck, and a pair of eyebrows emerged around the corner of the cockpit.

"Hold still." Charley's head was thirty centimetres, deducting a couple for the squashed ears. He pirouetted, trying to snatch the tape. I wound it around my own head: fifty-nine. So, somewhere in between. I looked around the boat: the fire extinguisher on the engine bulkhead was about right. Pretty big for a six-week-old child.

My father did a ventriculogram and diagnosed "communicating hydrocephalus." Five days later, he inserted the standard hardware of the time, a shunt that diverted the excess fluid from Billy's brain to his heart. The report of operation is a terse three paragraphs: burr hole in the side of the head, expose the jugular vein, catheters into the ventricle of the brain and the atrium of the heart. A run of tubing in between, and a Holter valve, all sutured with silk. It was June 1976.

I read this laconic narrative over and over. This was what my father did for a living. Inserting a shunt, don't forget, was somewhere on the low end of complexity for a neurosurgeon. But for a baby? I thumbed my way back to the admitting record: Billy weighed in at 4.5 kilograms, almost ten pounds. No longer the size of a newborn but still a small target for the doctors and nurses bending over him. Charley weighed twice as much.

Now that Billy's first operation is over, let's let the nurses tend to him. We need to take a closer look at the shunt itself

— because it's about to become a victim of the second law of thermodynamics.

～⌒

The great thing about my father's little library of scientific papers, some of which I had brought along, was that it was roughly contemporary with Billy's case. I learned that the chances of surviving hydrocephalus were pretty good back then, but definitely not plain sailing. I found some interesting statistics from 1983 (nine years after Billy's operation): mortality in treated — that is, shunted — patients was still 7 percent. And only half of the survivors had normal mental function.

This pile also shed some light on the difficulty of a standard shunting operation. To me, just placing the burr hole looked like a nightmare. Then you had to make it through the various layers wrapping the brain, cauterizing as you went so as not to provoke a bleedout later. And *then*, after advancing your catheter halfway into the brain, you had to penetrate the lateral ventricle just so. It looked to me like trying to drill a hole through one side of a chair leg and have it come out exactly where you wanted it on the other side. It never does, but chair legs don't hemorrhage to death in front of you.

Then there was the other end of the shunt to worry about, the drain into the heart. This seemed to me like going from the frying pan into the fire, surgically speaking: enter the jugular vein by sneaking in through the facial vein and pass the slender tube down into the right chamber of the heart. In 1974, you could only tell where the end of the tube was waving around by connecting it to a pressure-measuring device and gingerly advancing it until the pressure readings balanced out.

Yet shunts could turn out very well.

"There is no reason," wrote one surgeon, "that the child with hydrocephalus who is treated early cannot lead a normal life and have a normal-sized head." But then I read the caveat: "Unless there is an underlying brain impairment, congenital or acquired." And I thought of Billy and his small army of experts and lawyers, and the glorious grey area those few words opened up.

When shunts did go wrong, the biggest reason was infection. Around the time of Billy's operation, your chances of a surgical redo were 50 percent. Very few writers had much advice on what to do if pressure shot up when an infected shunt was removed — yet this was the crux of the case against my father.

I felt comfortable with these old scientific papers, probably because they talked the language of experimentation and statistics that I was familiar with. I knew not to put too much faith in any single report, but my father had compiled a pretty comprehensive snapshot of hydrocephalus and its complications from a few years before the time he operated on Billy to a half-decade later. It was like a scientific time capsule. All the papers were heavily marked up, with highlighter (again in his favoured orange) and his own handwriting. My father really was preparing for battle.

Bit by bit, I began to discern his strategy: from the moment Billy was born almost two months premature, his risks just kept multiplying. John Harvey's argument would be that a high-risk infant had received a high-risk operation for a condition that was extremely common in low-weight babies. The outcome was *bound* to be iffy, and it was impossible to tell whether the subsequent problems had anything to do with the surgery at all. One 1983 study he'd photocopied looked at nineteen such children; two died, and only two were neurologically normal at one year.

Asleep on the cockpit seat next to me, Charley was half-buried in paper. I felt buried too. Charley whimpered, looked up, then went back to sleep. I knew what was coming.

"You're making it much too complicated."

It was getting dark in Refuge Cove; I hadn't noticed him in the gloom. He looked especially ghostly.

"Nobody wants to read all that stuff about survival rates."

"Who said I was writing anything?" I didn't mention the book he had kept trying to write.

"You have to keep it simple, or you'll lose your readers. Get back to Billy's story."

"Simple, as in . . . ?"

"As in, hydrocephalus in premature infants caused many problems, even without the complications of shunts and infections. That he was anoxic for the first three minutes of his life. That the deck was already stacked against that little boy."

"That's exactly what I plan to say! I *do* know how to write."

"I was a good writer too, you know."

"Yeah, but this book — assuming I'm writing a book — isn't about you. I mean, it might be, but . . ."

"That was uncalled for. A person in my position, I couldn't be waving my own flag. If you're going to do it, you have to do it *right*."

"Maybe you should have waved your own flag a bit more. Truth and justice don't always prevail, you know."

"Well, I thought they should."

"*Again?*" called Hatsumi from below. "Aren't you ever coming to bed?"

"I'm coming, I'm coming," I said. "And don't worry, he's gone. I think I hurt his feelings."

Turbulence

By the time we got away from Refuge Cove the next morning, it was already hot, and when we turned the corner into Lewis Channel, the long conduit that would take us northwest between West Redonda and Cortes islands, the wind was in our faces. The narrower the channel got, the harder it blew, and I knew this would be the pattern for the next week or so, until we made it past Johnstone Strait and into the Broughton Archipelago.

Narrow channels funnel wind as much as they do water, and in fact the two substances behave the same way in a constriction, speeding up to squeeze through. The more I cruised in these waters, the more I began to recognize the landforms that determined conditions: the humps and headlands, the constrictions, the forested valleys down which the evening wind began to whistle just around the time you were brushing your teeth and getting ready to turn in. The weather forecasts, updated four times a day and listened to religiously by even the most careless of boaters, only provided the big picture — all the way up the east coast, for example, we would receive forecasts for only five geographic regions. That left a lot of brushstrokes to fill in because each region was a maze of humps, channels, headlands, and the rest of it. You had to start thinking like Yoshi in order to realize that a forecast like "winds northwest, twenty to twenty-five knots" described what you might be expected to encounter out in the open. Throw in a dozen mountainous islands and a fjord or two, and you could just as easily get the wind from the opposite direction. Local knowledge was everything.

We popped out of Lewis Channel into a space like a busy intersection in a great city — Piccadilly, perhaps, or Tokyo's Shibuya. The waters (and winds) from eight channels meet around Raza Island, seemingly uninhabited and featureless except for the single symmetrical mound in the middle. Our speed rose and fell as the currents found and released us, and we broke for lunch in the open space, setting the storm staysail and the steering so that *Vera* would try to go forward, stall, fall back, and try again (it's called *heaving to*). I ate a sandwich and pondered the logging on the humped northern end of Redonda Island. We would begin to see serious timber harvest now; on Redonda, the trees had been raked off in strips. We made coffee and killed another hour, waiting for the right moment to enter the rapids that began just a few miles north. This was where we would turn away from the winds in Johnstone Strait — but there was a price to pay.

We had to make the first three rapids — Yuculta, Gillard, and Dent — in the same day. Yuculta and Gillard are close together and can be run as one, but Dent is another two miles up Cordero Channel, twenty minutes in *Vera* going full out under power. And Dent is the worst of the three, getting up to eleven knots of current in the Devil's Hole — a mass of water moving faster than I can run. My well-thumbed copy of *Proven Cruising Routes* has a sequence of photographs of a forty-foot fishing boat being spun end for end in the Devil's Hole, one rail submerged. You *must* take Dent Rapids at slack current, which means sneaking through Yuculta and Gillard a half hour early.

The rapids were dangerous, I had no doubt of that. Strange things happened in rapids — I once met someone whose throttle coupling had simply let go in the middle of one. If Charley chose a rapid as a good place to go overboard, he'd simply disappear astern, a tiny orange speck turning circles until it caught in a whirlpool and capsized. And now, because of my recent medical reading, rapids had become metaphoric. Every time I entered one of these constrictions, I thought about the calamity that happened on a microscopic scale when a passage in the cerebrospinal circulation got a little too tight.

"Let's move," I said. I clipped Charley onto his retaining line. "We've got an hour to get to the Yucultas."

Halfway there, Hatsumi let out a shriek, and I realized we weren't the only sentient beings out here. A school of white-sided dolphins suddenly surrounded *Vera*, hundreds of them, arrowing out of the water just off our bows, or diving beneath us so that I could follow the grey, bubble-trailing torpedoes right under our keel. Hatsumi whooped and filmed, Charley barked and I wondered if I was the only boater to know that dolphins could get hydrocephalus too. We followed our escort toward the opening, now visible as a notch in the trees a mile or so ahead. Soon, we started noticing other boats, until by the time we had reached the turnoff to Hole in the Wall, another nasty shortcut, there were six of us, all steaming hell for leather for the Yucultas. Everybody was afraid to arrive too late.

And then, of course, everybody stopped. We were all too early. The dolphins lost interest and headed toward Hole in the Wall to look for more entertaining playmates. We puttered in a circle, trying to avoid all the other boats puttering in circles. Through binoculars, the opening to the Yuculta Rapids looked innocuous, but it was as though an invisible force field was keeping us all out. Finally, I advanced the throttle and swung *Vera* around to face it. Hatsumi grinned.

"You never did *that* before," she said.

"Somebody has to. This is getting ridiculous." We swept past the other boats, who fell dutifully into line. Was that all there was to leadership? Once past the light on Harbott Point (forty-five minutes early, I realized with the delicious sense of having just thrown caution to the winds), the washing-machine and pursed-lip graphics on the chart began to come to life as whorls and rips that nibbled and nudged at our keel. The wheel jumped uneasily in my hands as the water, unable to make up its mind about which direction to take, tumbled through the gap. It got noisier, the churning water like a river now, punctuated by alarming random knocks from directly beneath my feet, as though someone was tossing rocks at the propeller. We reached nine and a half knots as we yawed down past Big Bay and into Gillard, the next set of rapids. At that speed, I could still steer but only just. Any more current and we'd just be another piece of flotsam going through. A 13,000-pound piece.

We passed Big Bay in a long, skidding turn, past the shiny new Sonora Fishing Lodge on the left and the rapidly emptying Big Bay Marina on the right. When we squirted through Gillard Passage, *Vera* slewed hard as we caught the edge of a whirl-pool playing with some ragged chunks of Styrofoam. Then we were out onto a creased plain of uneasy water that was rapidly becoming choppy as the freshening northwest wind collided with the current. For the two-mile connecting flight to Dent Rapids, we throttled back and let the dying ebb take us into the wind, which by now was taking the tops off the waves and snapping the flag on the backstay behind me. Charley put his head between his paws.

"Look," said Hatsumi, delighted. The other boats were still behind us. We led them through Dent Rapids, hitting the open-ing exactly at slack, although *slack* isn't really the right word to use for such a turbulent place. "Not totally terrifying" would be better. But we'd done half the rapids, and we'd knock off the other three tomorrow or the next day. Unless, of course, the wind got worse. It was still right on the nose. Halfway up the inside of Vancouver Island and we'd had the sails up, what, five times? At this rate, we might as well be a powerboat.

We settled in for another pounding run, this time to an anchorage called Shoal Bay. The wind rose some more. In the confined space of Cordero Channel, the whitecaps were vertical, the low sun on the chaotic water forcing me to squint. On the mainland side, the mountains seemed close enough for me to lace on my hiking boots and step onto the trail. Suddenly we were in a sea of peaks and icefields. Mount Waddington, the highest in the Coast Range at 13,000 feet and one of the world's most challenging climbs, was in there, beyond the head of Bute Inlet, the opening to which we'd passed as we went through the rapids. A horsefly the size of a raisin arrived in the cockpit and Charley made a few half-hearted lunges before settling down again.

We crashed along. I found myself wondering about salmon, whose route from the Fraser River to the Pacific we were more or less tracing. Did the migrating fish, especially the young ones heading out to the North Pacific for the first time, go through the rapids? Or did they all use Johnstone Strait? This would never had occurred to me if I hadn't just done the rapids myself, but the answer might even be important, especially when people worried about the locations of salmon farms and whether they might spread diseases to young salmon wandering past. Could young salmon make it through Dent Rapids against the tide? Did they wait for slack, like boaters? How would you even study such a question, short of radio-tagging thousands of fish? I made a note, for when I returned to reality in the fall.

Shoal Bay's come-as-you-are kind of dock is run by an affable American called Mark. You can anchor in Shoal Bay, if you don't mind wind, or you can tie up, if you don't mind shoe-horning into whatever space is left and can figure out what Mark's vigorous semaphoring means. Like any other haven within a few hours of a tidal rapid, Shoal Bay gets its customers at highly predictable times. I imagine Mark sitting on the verandah of his cottage in the meadow behind the bay, the mountains with their abandoned gold mine above him, looking at the current tables for Dent Rapids and then at his watch. Another twenty minutes, he says to himself, adjusting his hat over his eyes, cowboy style, and going back to sleep.

Shoal Bay gets just enough protection from the northwest wind: the seas disappear, but gusts still get in around the corner to remind you that, eight miles away as the crow flies, Johnstone Strait is howling. We dropped anchor off the end of the already-jammed dock, tucking in between a kelp bed and another sailboat. Kelp meant a rocky bottom and iffy holding, but I was too tired to look for a better spot. The anchor bounced a few times, then grabbed.

At the end of the nineteenth century, there were over four hundred gold claims around Shoal Bay and the magnificent mountainous backdrop of Phillips Arm. In its heyday, Shoal Bay had everything: a school, a trading store, a hotel, shacks for the Indigenous prostitutes who serviced the loggers and miners. There was even a police officer, whose job must have been interesting: his beat ran from the Thurlow Islands south to Campbell River and across Georgia Strait to Lund. Now there was only Mark and his neat vegetable garden with kale and carrots and herbs. He served the yachties beer on his deck, where they sat next to a spray of red geraniums in a toilet bowl and looked up Phillips Arm to the ghost mines of the last century.

We had a terrible night, the swirling gusts relentless into the wee hours. Anchoring over a rocky bottom is never sleep-inducing, especially when the gusts are strong enough that you drag your anchor chain back and forth across the bottom, like the fetters of a monster. *Vera* snatched at her tether and the gusts moaned in the rigging. I kept telling myself that, yes, the anchor had caught solidly and, yes, we'd given it a good pull to set it before shutting down the engine. And, yes, we were far enough away from that other boat.

When I woke and dragged myself out to the cockpit, we had completely turned around. The kelp patch I'd been careful to avoid now caressed *Vera*'s flank, and the other sailboat was nowhere near us. *Sanctum*, I read on its transom, a comforting name. The man in her cockpit raised a hand in greeting, as though to say, "That was nothing special."

I tried to do the same. Because he was right, it wasn't so bad. Last year, Shoal Bay was where our trip had fallen apart. I'd returned from watching Charley dig for clams near the remains of an old logging skid to find Hatsumi down below, surrounded by charts and tide tables and books.

"This isn't fun," she said. "It was better when I didn't know anything." Her face was closed; she wouldn't look up; these weren't good signs.

"These rapids, the wind, they're driving me crazy."

We'd lost our nerve the next day, ducking into Loughborough, the next major inlet, then slipping away early the next morning to head back downstream to calmer waters. Everything seemed to be against us: the endless gale warnings for Johnstone Strait; the careless timing that had landed us at the rapids at full moon, when tides and currents were at their peak; our own inexperience.

But Hatsumi was tougher now. We both were. Failure that's no more than a breakdown of resolve is just an invitation to get it right the next time; we both felt that if there had to be a bailout on this trip, it would be in Bull Harbour, the last shelter before going over the Nahwitti Bar and around Cape Scott. Not here. We got the anchor up, festooned in slippery brown kelp blades and letting go without resistance; probably the only thing keeping us in place all night had been the weight of the chain strewn around the seabed.

❧

Now our appointment was with Greene Point Rapids, which split the two Thurlow Islands. Then, still following the sheltered back-door route behind Johnstone Strait, we had to make Whirlpool Rapids in time to find a place to anchor before we finished off the last stretch of Johnstone Strait. We were like a fugitive darting through back alleys, parallel to the thoroughfare where we didn't dare show our faces. I looked up Thurlow later in Captain Walbran's book (he was another person with streets in Victoria and Vancouver named after him) and found that Captain Vancouver had named the Thurlows in 1762, after being turned back by rapids. "The tide made so powerfully against us as obliged us to become stationary," Vancouver wrote. That made me feel better. Thurlow was lord chancellor at the time of Vancouver's voyages, and a very unusual one: he was a commoner, not born to the peerage at all. He actually made it to the top through hard work. Maybe that's why Vancouver gave him two islands, not one.

The current picked us up as soon as we left Shoal Bay and forced me to steer at a thirty-degree angle to our intended course. The walls of this channel were precipitous and green, with trees to the water, and the place felt empty. The crowds of boaters in Desolation Sound had evaporated, held back by the force field of the rapids, and the only signs of human life were clear-cuts and the occasional salmon farm.

The farms radiated corporate correctness. Each one had the same neat outbuildings painted dark green and mothering a network of metal catwalks picked out with bright yellow buoys. It all looked very anal-retentive, as though to say, "Look, we're harmless! See how small our footprint is, how well we blend in. Let us stay!"

Every time I passed one of these farms, I grabbed the binoculars. I never saw *anything* happening there. The young Pacific salmon from the Fraser River would be swimming past these farms along with *Vera* while, inside the cages, their distant

Atlantic cousins circled silently through the oxygen-rich currents, eating, shitting, growing, occasionally being rudely snatched through the mesh by a prowling seal. In a month or so, when my contract came through, I would have to buckle down and try to decide if the local fish were catching anything nasty from the imports. I didn't look forward to it.

The clear-cuts, though, seemed to be everywhere you looked, and to me those vandalistic swipes at the hillsides said something different: "Look, we've been here for two hundred years, so you can just go and *fuck* yourself." Some of them, above the remains of long-abandoned log skids, were old and nearly grown-in again, like a cancer survivor's hair. Others were more recent, with purple fireweed just starting to come up through the slash. I saw one that could have come out of a textbook on the environmental effects of logging: above, the scalped hillside, immediately below, the caved-in cliff that had let go when heavy rains rolled straight off the treeless patch.

But many clear-cuts were still active. Across from the salmon farm in Bickley Bay, I watched the goings-on at a booming ground dominated by a barged-in bunkhouse whose side was spray-painted in letters ten feet tall. "AQUATRAZ," it said. On the shore, two yellow machines the size of buses sorted logs into bundles and laid them behind a metal gate that overlooked the bay. They worried at the trees with crab-like pincers. In behind, fully loaded trucks inched down the switchback that wound into the clear-cut. Without warning, the gate fell open and the piled-up trees rumbled down the skid, sending up a geyser of water.

Greene Point Rapids is at one end of Chancellor Channel (that's *Lord* Thurlow to you); at the other end, an hour and a half further on, is Whirlpool. The plan was to shoot both in the same day, hole up for the night, then scoot down into Johnstone Strait early the next morning before the wind could get up. Even near slack, the water flowing past Greene Point was roiled and tangled-looking, the kind of place that can whip your boat around in the time it takes to let go of the wheel and take a swig from your water bottle. But it's a short rapid, and we shuddered through it ahead of *Sanctum*, which seemed to have the same idea about where and when to go. And we'd picked up another sailboat somewhere, a dark green wooden vessel with a determined-looking, toqued individual at the tiller.

Our little train bucked along, and the lord chancellor funnelled the wind into our faces, and after five miles or so of this, we realized we'd seen this movie before. Too late, I watched *Vera*'s dinghy, which I had stupidly left on a long tether, begin to climb up and launch itself off the tops of the swells; in the gusts, which seemed to have come from nowhere, the dinghy darted sideways like an unruly dog. If one of those gusts flipped the dinghy over, there was no way we could get it back. We'd have to cut it loose.

"Forget this," I yelled to Hatsumi. She was in the shelter of the dodger with Charley, a miserable bundle curled up next to her beneath a blanket. *Vera* reared, caught the next oncoming wave solidly, and I ducked a bucketful of water.

"I'm bailing out at Loughborough. Again. We can't keep going into this mess." Loughborough Inlet is one of the many blind alleys that extend up toward the Coast Mountains; Lord Loughborough was — well, he would have to wait. Once around the corner, we would escape the gale that was blowing down Johnstone Strait and spilling into Chancellor Channel.

But the corner before Loughborough Inlet wouldn't be easy. It took forty-five minutes to make a turn that would have been simple in calm seas but had become a nail-biter in winds that would send us sideways once we let them onto *Vera*'s flank. Finally, we veered hard to starboard, and the dinghy took a heart-stopping run until it was right beside me, threatening to somersault. We wallowed around the foaming shore of the island guarding the entrance, and then we were in the lee of the mountains. The dinghy retreated.

"I hated that," I said.

"No, we should celebrate," said Hatsumi. "This is as far as we got last year, remember? From now on, everything is new."

Had I been pushing too hard? Had we been in danger? If I wasn't sure, what was my Tokyo-born wife to think? I shut the engine down and rolled out the jib, and we coasted silently up the inlet between vertical walls of green. That was the problem: no matter how much you thought you knew, there was always another situation to demonstrate that, really, you knew next to nothing. For the hundredth time, I wished I could have learned it all much earlier, that I had been raised in a truly seagoing family, not as a sometime crewmember on board an infrequently used family sailboat. I looked back at *Sanctum*, also sailing now behind us, and at the other boat. Were they feeling the same fears? Or was I the only person who would admit to such failings?

There aren't many anchorages in Loughborough Inlet, the bottom falling away within metres of the shore. We tied up at the same place we'd ended our trip the year before, at Dane Campbell's cobbled-together collection of docks across from his house in Sidney Bay. If I were asked to imagine the kind of person who could survive for twenty years in such isolation, pulling trees from his woodlot, tending a shellfish lease, running this little haven for freaked-out summer boaters, I'd probably come up with someone bearded, lumberjack-shirted, booted, and rough-edged.

That wasn't Dane, who showed up later in the evening in his aluminum workboat, connecting up a few more overflow docks and accepting the absurdly low moorage we owed him as though it was the farthest thing from his mind. Not this slight, soft-spoken man in socks and sandals, straw hat and a neat beard; he looked as though he'd wandered out of a poetry reading. At least his jeans were dirty.

There were only the three sailboats this night. Last year, the place had been jammed with boaters waiting out an endless series of gales in Johnstone Strait, and we'd tied up to a dock that had been discarded by a salmon farm. It was littered with cables, bent-over nails, loose shackles, and worn hawsers that led somewhere far away, presumably tethering the whole thing in water that was over a hundred feet deep but still just a stone's throw from the trees. You had to watch where you walked, stepping over gaps and clumps of Indian paintbrush sprouting from the weathered planks. Now, Charley and I sat on the corner of the same dock, listening to the wind in the trees and staring into the water. Charley seemed close to testing his theory that the dinner-plate-sized purple jellyfish pulsing slowly at the surface was in fact a stepping-stone.

"Don't even think about it," I told him. "You can't swim."

I needed someone to talk to, someone who had been there, someone who wasn't my wife or my dog. Suddenly Charley whirled and catapulted down the dock toward the other boats. A man had just stepped out of *Sanctum*, and in seconds Charley was literally bouncing in front of him, all four feet lifting off simultaneously, like a sputtering rocket with four jets.

"Quite the talker, isn't he?" The man wore a floppy white hat and sandals, and he seemed to be smiling.

"Just ignore him, if that's possible. Charley, Jesus, shut *up!*"

"That was getting a little ugly out there. Thirty-five, gusting forty."

"No wonder I nearly lost the dinghy."

"We were worried about that. There, that's better. I seem to have been accepted." Charley had his paws up on the man's legs.

"Were you planning to come in here?"

"Nope, we wanted to get through Whirlpool. But we figured you had the right idea. So did he, I guess." He pointed to the third sailboat. The owner of that one was ambling toward us. He still had his toque on. It seemed never to have been washed.

"Wind against a flooding tide, always seems to happen," said the man. "So here we are."

Laconic seemed to be Dave Young's default mode. It took me half an hour to get out of him that he was the retired master of the *Uchuck III*, the coastal cargo ship that's serviced the west coast of Vancouver Island, in several incarnations, for forty years. The guy scratching my dog behind the ears had been into every hole on the west coast, in every kind of weather, collecting people and dropping off cargo along a stretch from Kyuquot south to Barkley Sound. The *Uchuck* was an icon; there was nothing in the way of wind and wave and human behaviour he wouldn't have seen.

"So," I said, "you guys are heading north tomorrow?"

Dave contemplated the waving tree-tips. "That's the general plan," he said.

I threw myself at his feet and screamed, "Take me with you!" Actually, I didn't, but my inner voice was rolling around, pounding its forehead on Dave's sandals.

"Yeah, we were sort of tending that way too," I said. I squinted appraisingly at the sky. "Depends. Maybe we'll run into each other. In the morning."

"Round about seven, I may take a look." I think he was onto me.

Later, Dave shared a ling cod he'd caught, and we took over a loaf of freshly baked bread. Dane Campbell reappeared late in the evening, with crabs for us to split. We shared them with the third sailor, the Ancient Mariner. He must have been seventy-five, with a big corrugated nose beneath mirrored shades.

Hatsumi and I passed the rest of the evening on the windy foredeck, trying to hoist the dinghy aboard. The dinghy was a charming thing, the same emerald green as *Vera*, but it weighed a ton. We wound it painfully aloft using the spinnaker halyard and an improvised harness, and our audience winced and maintained a diplomatic silence as it scraped and swung. At one point, it got loose and swept across the deck, pinning Hatsumi to the lifelines like a boxer on the ropes.

"We can do this," I said. "Honey."

Hatsumi crawled free and gave me a dirty look. "It's impossible."

"Well, I don't know about . . ." I finished the job myself.

Tiptoeing North

We escaped Sidney Bay the next morning. The weather forecast was the same as it had been for a week: twenty knots in the morning, rising to a gale in the afternoon. Last year, we would probably have stayed put; this year, with Dave's example to follow (I still couldn't admit we were following *him*), getting up at 5:30 a.m. seemed the obvious solution.

Loughborough Inlet was calm. We turned right at Chancellor Channel and right again at the much narrower Wellbore Channel, closing in on Whirlpool Rapids. I wolfed down the fried eggs and toast passed up from the galley, warming myself against the cold wind.

"I had the dream again," Hatsumi said, refilling my coffee cup from the comfort in the galley.

"The dead guy?"

"It's like, the boat isn't really moving. We're just floating. The three of us."

Now she had me worried. "You do realize," I said, "dreams don't *have* to mean something. They can just be dreams."

"Not mine," she said.

Two salmon farms slid by, one of them directly beneath an even more chaotic than usual clear-cut, and I couldn't help wondering, which was the lesser of two evils? Salmon farms were under sustained assault from environmental groups, something I was familiar with as a fisheries biologist, and I kept trying to push away the unfashionable suspicion that the critics had simply changed horses. Funding was easy to get if you wanted to oppose salmon farms, while logging protest seemed to be on hiatus.

The sun came out as we turned right into Wellbore Channel. As though following a hackneyed script, the clouds parted, four mountains revealed themselves alarmingly close on the north side of the channel, and a dolphin cut across our bows. The ebb tide emptying the channel picked us up and hurried us through Whirlpool Rapids. Just as Dave had assured us the night before, Whirlpool's flow wasn't especially turbulent, and going through felt like stepping onto the conveyor belt in an airport, with the billboards replaced by hills on vertiginous hills. We sprinted through at eleven knots, an all-time record, nearly twice Vera's cruising speed. Then another hard right into Forward Harbour, following Dave's lead to an overnight anchorage in Douglas Bay, a delicious scoop out of the peninsula connecting Forward Harbour with Bessborough Bay (named after the "noble house of Bessborough," rather a disappointment after all those lord chancellors). It was only ten in the morning. One more early start and we'd be through Johnstone Strait and into the Broughtons. We anchored while three wolves patrolled the pebbled crescent of beach, long-legged and in no hurry.

We spent the rest of the day exploring while the wind built to a gale around the corner in Johnstone Strait. The wisdom of waiting for a weather window was beginning to sink in, although it ran contrary to my nature, and there wasn't any evidence of high winds where we were (which was, of course, the whole point). After lunch, when the wolves seemed to have moved on, we manhandled the dinghy into the water, persuaded Dave and his wife, Nancy, away from the books they were reading in *Sanctum*'s cockpit (they seemed to have no problem with the waiting thing), and went ashore.

The incoming tide was filling the beach like a bowl. A notch in the trees opened into a trail flagged with marine detritus: faded net floats, unravelling lengths of hawser, lengths of PVC tube jammed in tree forks. We clambered over roots and under fallen trees. Charley stopped every few feet, riveted by the smells of strange animals. When the trail opened out onto the other side of the peninsula, the wind barrelling down Sunderland Channel hit me in the face. This was the weather from Johnstone Strait; this was what we weren't seeing in our little bomb-proof haven in Douglas Bay.

Back on the Douglas Bay side, only the tops of trees gave any sign of the gale a mile away. The bowl was now brimming, the beach obliterated, and *Vera*'s dinghy floating serenely at the end of its long yellow tether. We had to scuttle under cedar branches to get in.

That evening, Hatsumi and I gorged ourselves on Dane Campbell's crabs, sitting in the cockpit and tossing the remains overboard. We went through three of them, creating a slow-motion fountain of crab shards. Eating crab was one of those activities that always reminded me, "You're not Japanese, and she is." I dismantled my crustaceans using bone shears from the first aid kit and dug the sweet meat out with a knife; Hatsumi cracked the claws with her teeth and inhaled, making a whistling sound. We wiped our chins and agreed that tomorrow we would listen to the early forecast and decide whether to leave. I might even pop over to *Sanctum* for a word.

Next morning: another gale forecast. If we left, we had to make it through the last, unavoidable ten miles of Johnstone

Strait. We dithered. I rowed over to *Sanctum*, feeling weak-willed, and rapped on the cold hull. Dave emerged, sniffed, looked around.

"We'll likely just poke our noses around the corner, see how it goes." I rowed quickly back.

"We're out of here," I told Hatsumi. It was warm in the cabin but cold outside. Charley peered up beseechingly.

"He's going to have to hold it."

Sunderland Channel was gusty and cold, a working corridor of salmon farms and clear-cuts. Once, I did a double-take: a B.C. ferry, one of the big ones, sat tethered to the shore beneath a clear-cut. So that's where the old ferries went — housing for loggers. It looked preferable to Aquatraz. The northwest wind was already peering around corners, looking for boats to harass. But Dave had been right, an early morning run would get us to safety, and we left Johnstone Strait for good to turn up Havannah Channel. Behind us, on the Vancouver Island side, Mount Palmerston looked as though it had risen straight out of the ocean. Which, geologically speaking, it had.

We stopped for lunch in Port Harvey, a place that, despite its name, I took a dislike to. The bay itself was clotted with logging equipment, barges, a collection of salvaged salmon cages. The ridge above it all was an old-man stubble of stumps — yet another clear-cut. Someone was trying to make a go of a new marina at the head of the bay, with a floating store, a small restaurant, and invitingly empty docks. If you wanted a corn popper or a fish bonker, maybe some Kraft Dinner or a watermelon, Port Harvey was the place.

Most such places on Vancouver Island, once away from the cities, are laid-back and casual, and the really small ones, like Port Harvey, usually have an owner whose story alone is worth the moorage fee. But this one's docking instructions seemed strangely anal-retentive for a person with two hundred feet of unused space. Maybe he didn't like Charley, who leapt ashore to bark at anything that moved, including the horseflies. Whatever the reason, I didn't want to hear this guy's story. Ex-fisherman, failed stockbroker, axe murderer, I didn't care. We followed Dave and Nancy out.

"Let's try Boogie Bay, around the corner," Dave said, and that was fine with me. It also told me how to pronounce "Boughey," the name on the chart. Speaking of names, I couldn't resist looking up the Harvey who'd had this place named after him. At first, it seemed too good to be true: Captain John Harvey, Walbran informed me, was master of HMS *Brunswick* in the battle of the "Glorious First of June," 1794, in which Harvey's ship grappled with the French frigate *Vengeur* and sent her to the bottom. Captain Harvey received his death wound during hand-to-hand fighting, dying after being relieved by another ship captained by his brother. What a glorious career — and the same name as my father! Unfortunately, Walbran's book had several historic Harveys, and this was the wrong one. John Harvey *did* have a mountain named after him, but Port Harvey, it turned out, commemorated the less remarkable commodore of the British South Pacific Fleet.

We rolled out the big genoa jib and followed *Sanctum* up Havannah Channel, the rising northeaster catching *Vera* perfectly on the beam so that she gambolled past all the other landmarks named for the survey ship's officers: Mist Bluff, Malone Point, Bockett Islets. Boughey was the *Havannah*'s first lieutenant, but his bay was taking the wind dead-on, so we turned north and found shelter in Burial Cove, from where we would have access to the Broughton Archipelago by any number of passages.

Burial Cove was pleasant enough, but the name cast a pall over the place for me, and the trees sighed all night. *Vera* dragged her chain to and fro across the bottom, and I came awake repeatedly to the grumble of metal on rock and the moan of wind in the rigging. I wondered when the dead man would step out of Hatsumi's sleep and silently take his place on the cabin floor.

Sanctum motored past us early the next morning, heading for Malcolm Island, where a daughter worked in the Co-op store in Sointula. The night before, saying goodbye, I realized that, in four days, Dave had told me nothing specific about how to comport myself on this coast — about wind direction and weather forecasts and waiting. But, in his own self-deprecating way, Dave was such a potent mixture of confidence and humility that some of it, if only the faintest smear, had already worn off on me. And that was a good feeling. This coast was so pockmarked, so hazard-riddled, I desperately needed to kick-start my own competence.

"By the way," I said, as the dinghy drifted away from *Sanctum*, "yesterday, when we were coming up Chancellor Channel, you stopped for a while. What was all that about?"

"One of those clumps of floating kelp," Dave laughed. "I ran straight into it. Couldn't have done it better if I'd actually been aiming for it. Nearly seized the engine."

I was paranoid about floating kelp myself. And now this paragon of seamanship had hit some. That meant I had the right idea, but sooner or later, I was still going to screw up. Somehow, that made me feel better.

With *Sanctum* gone, Burial Cove seemed even colder and emptier. It was still early, and neither of us felt like going anywhere. Hatsumi was still in bed; Charley's ears poked out from under the covers beside her. Sometimes I wondered if I was being displaced.

"I'll just do a little reading," I said.

Spinal Tap

I was now into my second day of the scientific papers I'd gotten waylaid by in Refuge Cove, trying to make sense of the shunting hardware my father had installed in Billy. I had to finish them, here in Burial Cove, because they furnished the technical argument he was counting on to clear his name. Then I could pick up the second act of Billy's story, where everything went wrong.

Unfortunately, what I had expected to be an easy breeze-through of the science had turned into a time-trip that visited every one of the medical issues in Billy's case. There was no excitement here, just the dry language of clinical science stuttering slowly forward. Important, yes, but maybe a tiny bit boring.

I turned to the Perinatal Anoxia folder. In English, this means "lack of oxygen around the time of birth." Billy was very slow to take his first breath, and after he did, he remained in "acute respiratory distress," tubed and incubated, for weeks. A 1976 chapter on pediatric neurology told me anoxia was the single most important neurological problem for a newborn, causing "mental retardation" (now termed intellectual disability), seizures, and cerebral palsy. Premature infants seemed to be most at risk, and the consequences were often insidious. Intellectual disability was one, along with various dyslexic syndromes and "perceptual disturbances" that surfaced at school age. I already knew that lack of oxygen fries your brain. But it was still a shock to see so many of Billy's problems (especially his cerebral palsy) explainable by lack of oxygen immediately after birth. Anyway, that was enough on anoxia; I got the point.

On to meningitis, always bad news for any infant, and especially so for a hydrocephalic baby that had been shunted. I found several articles. Mortality from bacterial meningitis in infants was in the 30 to 40 percent range. If you had a feverish, vomiting, shunted infant on your hands, you *had* to check for meningitis, and there was only one way to do that in 1976: withdraw and examine some cerebrospinal fluid. How did you do this?

With a lumbar puncture.

When I saw those words, I knew the 1970s-era science was critical to my father's case. It would be another week at least before I could start to piece together the blow-by-blow drama of what happened to Billy after the shunt had first been put in, but I already knew "lumbar puncture" was the reason the case was settled before my father could take the stand.

What did I know about lumbar punctures? I knew that doctors abbreviated the name to LP (I will too), that most people knew their more gruesome and descriptive name *spinal tap*, and that they hurt. How you did one, and especially the dos and don'ts that seemed such a big issue with Billy's case, were mysteries to me. But there was a folder here, labelled "Lumbar Puncture," so I opened it up.

In the mid-'70s, the use of an LP in diagnosing neurological disorders — especially meningitis — was still high, even given the knowledge that an LP itself could actually *cause* meningitis! But the big problem occurs when pressure inside the brain is already high — major causes are injuries to the brain, tumours, and untreated hydrocephalus — because a lumbar puncture can make things worse. Elevated pressure does some gruesome things to the brain, especially where it joins the spinal cord; it's called herniation or "coning." I learned that, yes, an LP can reduce pressure on the brain, but if it was performed when pressure was *too* high you risked eliminating the back-pressure normally provided by the presence of spinal fluid. Top-down pressure from the brain would win out, and down would bulge the base of the brain.

My head was spinning. Lumbar puncture, on which the lawyers had caved in and settled the lawsuit, looked to me like the Devil's Pool in Dent Rapids: you can get close to it, but stay away when the current is really running. I needed more up-to-date information, and that meant the Internet. In Burial Cove? I did a quick check on my phone. There was a weak telephone signal, enough to patch my phone to my computer and use it as a router. I would have to be fast because the data charge would be astronomical. But I really needed to know what doctors were thinking *today* about the risk of doing an LP when intracranial pressure was already high. Did the LP cause herniation (the dangerous bulging of the brain) or didn't it? Could we even say? If the LP that was eventually done on Billy was so crucial, I had to understand why.

But the Internet, usually so eager to throw information at me, was stingy on this one (and spectacularly slow). There didn't seem to be much solid evidence that an LP could actually *cause* herniation, but what if you had elevated pressure to begin with? It began to look as though I wouldn't get a clear answer about lumbar punctures and herniation. Back and forth the opinions went. Don't do an LP. Go ahead, but do a CT scan first. Depends on the kind of hydrocephalus the patient has. Finally, I gave up. It was like asking three boaters about the best paint to use on your hull, or how to fix a leaking hose, or what to do if your engine started smoking. Three different answers, guaranteed.

But I did turn up something interesting: the Lumbar Puncture Simulator Mark II, made by the Australian company Limbs & Things. For around $3,600, novice puncturers got the ultimate pin-the-tail-on-the-donkey game: a "lifelike lower torso" with a removable skin flap that hid the "puncture block," a plastic chunk of lower spine plumbed with fluid from an external reservoir. You filled the reservoir and poked away through the skin flap, trying to get in between the vertebrae and puncture the cerebrospinal space.

"That's the stupidest thing I've ever seen," my father said.

"Yeah, but look." I angled the laptop and pointed. "You can even buy different kinds of puncture block. See, they've got 'normal,' but you can order 'obese,' and 'elderly,' even 'elderly obese.'"

"I hated doing back operations on obese people," he said. "Like cutting into a whale."

"Well, then, can I ask you about lumbar punctures in general? Risks and all that?"

"I'm not in the mood," said my father

"Are you finished with the computer?" called Hatsumi. "And Charley wants to go ashore."

I said good night to the lumbar simulator and handed Hatsumi the computer; she handed me a small dog with a bursting bladder. It seemed like a good exchange.

Murderers and Marijuana

Even after I'd spent two hours confusing myself about intra-cranial pressure and lumbar punctures, Burial Cove was still as cold as the grave. I rowed Charley to the single, gritty beach. At low tide, it was littered with old logging cables and a rusted-out fuel tank. Getting ashore was messy, and clams launched silver spurts in protest as I picked my way across the mud. I could hear the persistent whine of a large saw in the woods, some-where in behind a weathered cedar house. Maybe there was a mill in behind. Small-scale logging; perhaps a second job with a salmon farm; subsistence.

Chatham Channel, just around the corner and the quick-est route to the Broughtons, woke us up. It separates the two Cracroft Islands (East and West) but not by much, as though someone started to scratch a pathway and gave up when it was half-done. Chatham Channel really wants to be deeper. It's a mile long, only a quarter-mile wide and twenty-odd feet deep, and a couple of rocks a metre under the surface pretty much eliminate any margin for error. The chart shows you how to get through the old-fashioned way: a single straight line connects two range markers, red-painted posts about a hundred feet apart on the shore at either end. All you have to do is line up your boat with the first set of markers, keep it that way until you can see the second set, line yourself up with those, and keep on trucking. I found that a mile is a long way to walk an imaginary line and that when you drift off course, which way do you turn to get back on track?

We poked our noses into Cutter Cove, but it seemed a desolate place, shallow for most of its length and topped with a vast estuary overlooked by forbidding cliffs. Plus it was too windy, no place to spend a night alone at anchor.

"What about this place?" I said to Hatsumi as we turned back and began to buck our way out again. "Minstrel Island. Look, there's even a public dock. And a resort. You'd like that."

She studied the guidebook carefully, something she had never done in our first few years of cruising. Perhaps she had learned not to accept my recommendations so quickly.

"It says the resort is closed."

"Give me that." I looked. "Okay, it's closed. But you can still tie up there, apparently. And it's free!"

"I don't know." She frowned. A wave caught *Vera* on the quarter and sent a splatter of water across the windscreen.

"See? Too late to dick around. And look, Charley really has to go." Charley drove his nose even further under his blanket. "It'll be great!"

And that was how we met the axe murderer.

There wasn't much choice, really. It was either the free dock at Minstrel Island or squeeze through a little constriction called the Blow Hole to get into the marina at Lagoon Cove. *Everybody* went to Lagoon Cove; according to the glowing write-ups in the guidebooks, Lagoon Cove had showers and a store, charming hosts and daily happy-hour potlucks with marshmallow roasts. Marshmallow roasts? *Singalongs?* Versus a free, and probably empty, dock? I knew which one John Harvey would have chosen.

The old public dock at Minstrel Island definitely wasn't crowded. Its three fingers extended beneath the obviously defunct hotel, two robin's egg blue wooden buildings with a boardwalk connecting them. The boardwalk had given up, collapsing into a shallow V and bringing down the hotel's verandah with it. The only boat at the dock was a twenty-five-foot converted fishing boat with a ramshackle African Queen–style roof held up by lengths of galvanized pipe. A fat smokestack protruded through this makeshift canopy, to which was screwed a hand-lettered sign offering "Marine Services."

Wonderful, I thought, the local mechanic. I can tell him about the herring in our cooling system, share some guy time. We tied up across from him, and I followed Charley past upturned office chairs, abandoned crab pots, and a houseboat with a long-overgrown vegetable garden. When we got up onto the upper dock and I looked back, I saw a dark figure unfold itself from the wheelhouse of the boat across from us, step carefully onto the dock, and look around, as though coming out of hibernation.

"Finish up," I said to Charley. This was our chance to meet the local expert. When we reached the man, he was still in the same position. Charley ran up to him, stopped, growled, and hopped back onto *Vera*. I'd never seen that behaviour before.

"A dog in a fucking life jacket," said the man. "Hah."

"He can't swim," I said.

"Whatever. What's it *like* out there?"

The man wore black socks and a week's growth of beard. Stringy hair stood in all directions, as though he'd been the wrong way down in a sleeping bag. He sucked at a piece of orange and the juice ran down his chin.

"I've been waiting here five days."

It looked more like five years. His eyes were red. The African Queen was piled with old VHF radios and tape decks, dismantled outboard motors, fuel cans. A portable Honda generator putted away from somewhere in the pile of junk.

"Waiting for what?"

"You can't see those fucking boats?" He waved angrily. "Five of them, I gotta tow them all down to Egmont. Has to be a straight shot."

I could only count one, a small runabout I'd missed before. Maybe he saw five. One, five, the real problem was that Egmont was way back down the Sunshine Coast: through Johnstone Strait, five rapids, the Strait of Georgia. In one go? In a boat that — I looked over his shoulder — didn't even have a towing post?

"That's tough," I said. Man to man, trying not to make it sound like "that's insane." "Well, gotta go."

"Enjoy your day," he said, staring hard at the invisible boats.

Down below, Hatsumi pulled me hard into a corner. "What's *wrong* with him?" she hissed.

"Who?"

"Is he okay?"

"Well, maybe you should meet him." I could see his feet through the porthole.

"We can't stay here. What if he's an axe murderer?"

"Oh, Jesus. He's just . . . look, I'll go back and find out a little more. Would that make you more comfortable?"

Of course, Hatsumi was right; her sixth sense about people was rarely far off. He looked like an axe murderer to me too. Back I went.

"To answer your question," I said, "it's windy. On the nose. Not so bad at night, though. Can you go at night?"

"I can go any time I want!"

"Then . . ."

"I've got everything on that boat, radar, GPS, the iron compass."

Iron compass?

"Look, I can navigate to *Japan* if I want. I've done it! I'm a fucking tugboat captain!"

Hatsumi would be hearing all this. So far, he hadn't actually admitted he was an axe murderer.

"I just have to feel good first."

How do you deal with irrational people? Especially when you're tied up next to one at an abandoned dock? Listen to their concerns? Call the cops? There weren't any cops on Minstrel Island. But there was someone else, or there would be soon. Over the maniac's shoulder, I watched a handsome converted tug, grey, maybe fifty feet long, nose toward the empty finger across from our little tableau. Reinforcements.

"You don't feel good?" I said.

"No! I had a stroke! Three days ago! Look at my hand, I can't feel nothing." He made a claw. "I can't go anywhere, see? And nobody tells me what to do. You smoke?"

"Do I smoke?"

"Don't. If you do, quit. This is what it did to me." The claw again. "Marijuana too, thirty years of it. Doctor told me that was even worse. I was in hospital three days ago."

That I could believe. He needed to go back. He was getting worked up. If I thought he was crazy, what was he thinking about me?

"Well," I began.

"Dog in a life jacket. Hah!" He limped back to the runabout behind us and began fussing with the motor. In a moment, he was gone, rounding the end of the dock and heading at high speed toward the Blow Hole. It was going to be some singalong tonight.

Hatsumi crept out, following the small boat with her eyes until it vanished into the narrow channel.

"Maybe he is a little eccentric," I said. "But look! We've got company."

"The batteries stopped working," she said.

"You're kidding. Well, maybe they can help. Not the weird guy, those two." A breezy attitude seemed important.

A man and a woman were coming down the main dock. Hatsumi was in no condition to talk to anyone, so I strolled down to head them off.

"I'm Brent." The man stuck out his hand. There was a lot of dirt under his fingernails. Brent had a huge head, tangled grey hair, and yellowish horse teeth that I would see a lot over the next few hours. His high forehead was creased in parallel chevrons, as though he was constantly struggling with some weighty conundrum. We shook hands while I read his T-shirt: Garden Naked. I could see checkered boxer shorts through a tear in his sweat pants. He looked slept-in.

"Far *out*! This is Kim."

Kim's hand wasn't horny and grease-stained, like Brent's. It was slender, like the rest of her, and quite young. I thought, twenty? Twenty-four, tops?

"Here's the thing," I said. "You know this guy?" I pointed to the African Queen.

"Never saw the boat," said Brent.

"But you're from here, right?"

"Alert Bay. Kim's from Amsterdam."

"I just landed in Vancouver," Kim said. "I'm a little tired."

This was more like it. An axe murderer and a fifty-year-old hippie satyr; finally Vancouver Island was producing the characters I'd come to expect.

"Welcome to . . . where should I welcome her too, Brent?"

"The real world, man." Brent threw his arms wide. "Don't worry about the weirdo, we'll sort him out. Where is he?"

"Out . . . there. But he'll be back. In the meantime, what do you know about electrical systems?"

The willowy Kim drifted off to explore the ruined buildings on shore; Brent lumbered aboard *Vera*; Hatsumi watched warily from a corner as he peered at what little you could see of *Vera*'s network of electrical veins without ripping the boat apart.

"I think it's the main battery switch," I said.

Brent fiddled with the main electrical panel. His fingers were twice the size of mine.

"I dare say it is," he said finally. "I've got a box full of switches at home." He brightened. "But hey, this'll all look better after a bottle of wine, right? Come on over, later." He climbed out and lumbered off after Kim.

"See?" I said. "I told you everything would work out."

We didn't see anyone for the next two hours. The axe murderer's generator droned on. I wandered up to the ruined resort with Charley and saw no sign of Brent or Kim. Back in the bushes, behind the sagging main buildings, a shack with its step rotted away might have been a school; peering over the ledge, I thought I could see a blackboard and a faded picture askew on a peeling wall. Out back, a tangle of rusted fuel tanks had tumbled to the ground beneath a gnarled and barren-looking apple tree, a porcelain cream jug in the dirt, hummingbirds. I dug out the jug while Charley rooted half-heartedly in a musty corner. Even the rats had abandoned the place.

When we emerged from the bush, I saw Brent heading back down the dock, trailing a length of rusty exhaust hose.

"Let's take them up on their offer," I said to Hatsumi. "Anyway, we can't cook with the house batteries kaput."

"Take it back," she said, pointing at the cream jug. "It's bad luck. And I'm freezing."

We both needed to mellow out. I pulled my wife up the companionway and led her across to Brent's boat. "It'll be cozy in there," I said, rapping on the varnished mahogany door.

But Brent's boat was freezing too. He and Kim didn't seem to notice; they sat at the wooden galley table next to an inviting-looking but unlit diesel stove, with a bottle of wine and an ashtray between them. Only Brent had a glass.

"Far *out!*" he said, deftly picking up the thread of our earlier conversation. He got up and fetched two more glasses. "Lots of good times, right here." He patted the table, and I could believe it. The galley was a generous space, with plenty of windows and a view forward to the wheelhouse. I could easily keep an eye on the axe murderer's boat. Brent, it turned out, was a contractor for the Department of Fisheries, taking biologists out for weeks at a time to sample for young salmon. It would have been a nice place to unwind after a long day with the plankton nets — as long as Brent turned the stove on. I drained my glass in an effort to warm up and reminded myself it was mid-July.

"Now *you*" — Brent jabbed an oily finger in my direction — "you need to loosen up. I can see the boy inside you — let him out, man!" He turned to Hatsumi, who was now chugging steadily. "Don't you think so, Hattie? You don't mind if I call you Hattie?"

Kim wasn't drinking. If I was going to be taken to task for not loosening up, it was going to be a long night. Axe murderers and battery switches wouldn't be on the agenda. A doobie appeared in Brent's fingers. He began to orate.

"This whole area is dead now, but when I was a young guy, it was rocking. I had a bachelor's in psychology, but I couldn't wait to get on the fishboats. Guys were making a hundred thousand a season, all kinds of boats working all day and all night, you could get fuel everywhere, not just a couple places like it is now. Stayed at that hotel up there. I was nineteen. They had to sneak me drinks. That's how I got this rum-soaked voice."

He dragged on the joint and waved it at us.

"I don't," said Kim.

"Me neither," I said.

"You need a good spanking," said Brent. "Come on Hattie, there's a good girl." Polite to a fault, my long-suffering wife pulled some marijuana into her lungs. Charley coughed from his place on the floor.

"That dog gets between you guys," said Brent. "I know. I'm a good judge of feelings."

Outside in the dark, a blue heron let out its warning *craak*, and Brent grinned. "Hear that, man? That's what it's all about!" He pinched the joint out and went back to the wine. My wife was turning green. We sat back and listened, and I let my mind wander. Was Kim his girlfriend, or just a visitor he was showing around? Did Brent's fisheries clients smoke pot in the evenings? Was marijuana bad for dogs?

Finally I said, "Brent! Early start."

"Roger that." He jumped to his feet and shook my hand and we filed out. I drew the heavy door open and inhaled cold night air.

"I dare say it's the battery switch," said Brent.

Across the way, *Vera* was dark and cold. We ate some dried squid to soak up the alcohol and Hatsumi crawled into the V-berth. I gave her a goodnight kiss. Her hair reeked of pot. She mumbled something into her pillow. It sounded like, "I want to go home."

Kill All the Lawyers

After Hatsumi went to sleep, I cleaned up a day's clutter in the galley, retracing the steps of the dishwashing ballet that I would perform twice a day: wet the dishes with a little water from the foot pump, squirt soap onto a cloth, scrub and rinse with another few foot-strokes of precious water. Then drain, dry, and refile everything in rack and drawer. The battery problem Hatsumi had discovered didn't seem to extend to our dedicated engine-starting battery, so I poached enough electricity from that one to light the sink. Outside, the moon was pallid behind a veil of cloud. The axe murderer's generator droned on.

Already our boat was changed, the tangle of tools and wire and grease guns that filled *Vera* in the weeks before departure had miraculously transformed itself into books, dog toys, basil plants, and laundry dangling from the clever Japanese drying racks Hatsumi hung from the cabin ceiling. But I couldn't relax; tomorrow would take us through an unavoidable section of Johnstone Strait and then to the town of Port McNeil, the second last settlement of any size before we took the irrevocable step of crossing the Nahwitti Bar. I needed something to take my mind off it all, so I dug out my father's file on malpractice suits. An hour of legal nuts and bolts, *that* would put me to sleep.

The first thing I found was this quotation, from the Nicene Creed of the Anglican church: "We have left undone those things which we ought to have done, and we have done those things which we ought not to have done, and there is no health in us." The words introduced the chapter on "Malpractice and Negligence," which my father had photocopied from a book called *The Doctor and the Law: A Practical Guide for the Canadian Physician.* The adversarial system, its author felt, should not be the only way of dealing with problems in medical practice because there will be times in a surgeon's life — many times — when the right thing to do and the wrong thing to do are equally risky. Medicine was full of Catch-22s.

The author of *The Doctor and the Law* also wasn't much in favour of contingency fees, which removed the objectivity of lawyers by giving them a financial interest in the outcome. Contingency fees incensed my father, as might be expected of someone who had just watched more than $400,000 go to the lawyers who had bargained a settlement against him. Doctors and lawyers are never likely to see eye to eye on this subject. Doctors say, "We have to treat everyone who comes through the door. We can't cherry-pick and take only the ones we're most likely to get a good result with. So why should a lawyer be allowed to?"

At the time of my father's malpractice case, anguished commentary abounded: on the rapid increase in awards, on the cost of insurance literally driving doctors away from their practices, on the unseemly profits made by lawyers. Even back in the 1980s, most malpractice suits didn't go to trial; if they did, the courts would have been hopelessly tied up. For a case to go to trial, either the issues were highly contentious, or one side would rather fight than flee. That was my father. I shouldn't have been surprised; as a boy, he'd taken on all comers. "You helped your friends," he wrote in his memoir. "Fighting was as natural as breathing."

And so, after spending a few hours trying to understand the legal process, I found myself back at my Big Question: When the result of his obstinacy came crashing down on his head, why couldn't he get over it? Why couldn't he say, as my wife and 167 million other Japanese say every day, *shikata ga nai*? ("It can't be helped").

Before we left, I'd called up his last family doctor, a man about my age who I'd come to know and like. We'd met for lunch at a Polish delicatessen, taking our glistening mounds of artery-clogging food to an out-of-the-way table.

"I don't eat like this that often," he said, forking a sausage. If he did, he must burn it off somehow; he was lanky and fit-looking. I asked my question before he'd even stopped chewing; I couldn't wait. He swallowed and said, "His ego, of course," as though I'd asked him one of those skill-testing questions to which nobody could fail to know the answer. "Just couldn't take it."

"Yeah, but don't other doctors have egos? Don't lots of them get sued?"

"Sure we do," he said. "I did, along with a couple of other doctors, just like your dad."

"And?"

"We lost."

"And?"

"I got over it. Part of being in practice. I acted to the best of my ability with the information I had."

I couldn't imagine my father leaving it at that.

"We get these newsletters from the Medical Protective Association. You know what they keep reminding us? The ones who get sued the most are the ones that don't communicate well with patients. The godly ones."

"Like my dad?"

"I never saw him in practice. You know what else they tell us? Don't be defensive. Don't ignore people. If something goes wrong, apologize. It reduces the number of suits."

"Never happen," I said. A big ego could get you a long way, I was beginning to realize, but once it was conclusively deflated, especially late in life, there was no recovery. I'd heard the same message from another physician, Charley Brown.

Charley Brown was a little younger than my father. He appeared often in family photo albums, sailing, playing Ping-Pong, mugging in a lawn chair. In my father's last months, Charley came faithfully to the care home, cajoling him outside, mediating in disputes about the best way to care for a crotchety and still-imperious retired neurosurgeon.

I went to Charley's townhouse shortly after my lunch in the Polish deli. Outside, sunglassed retirees crept past pastel house fronts. Inside, Charley's place was tidy and dark. His wife had died a year earlier, from cancer; like all doctors, he was able to provide a dispassionate description of her condition while clearly still reeling from the loss. A large grey cat wandered through the empty house, tinkling.

"He was crushed," Charley told me. "Those headlines, terrible, his reputation. Some of the other doctors . . . they backed off."

"I thought you were supposed to close ranks," I said.

"They didn't. He didn't make it easy on himself."

"No kidding. What was he like, professionally?"

Charley considered. "Crusty," he finally said. "Fantastic training, but there was always something. I had him and two of the neurologists at my kitchen table once, trying to get them to get along. It didn't work out."

Charley had arrived in Victoria in 1952, the year after we did. He'd been mediating ever since.

"The funny thing was, he didn't like operating. He told me once he wished he'd become an internist like me, where you could do the detective work, and others could do the surgery. That he'd gotten to the point where he just didn't want to cut anyone anymore. He was dedicated, though. In the early days, he flew up north in a private plane to see a young woman who'd gone over her horse's head. He brought her back to Victoria; we both worked on her. She never came out of the coma."

I remembered that case; it was one of the ones he'd talked to us about. The woman's family tried a faith healer brought in from England. When that failed, they took her off life support. It never stopped nagging at him. Very Harvey Cushing.

"But he was definitely different. You know about the concerts, in the pediatric ward?"

"Concerts?"

"He used to play his violin for the sick kids at the old General Hospital. I never forgot that he did that."

"You're kidding," I said. "When was that?"

"Back in the mid-seventies, I guess." Exactly the time he operated on Billy.

⤳

I shoved the stowaway's legal file back under the seat, tried a few pages of that incomprehensible book on Buddhism that my father had been trying to get through when he died, and finally crawled into bed with my wife and dog. Charley was on my side of the pizza slice–shaped berth, so maybe Brent was right: he *was* coming between us. The wind moaned in the rigging, *Vera* snatched nervously at her mooring lines, and I thought about the axe murderer next door. Or wherever he was. What if he really did have to deliver five boats a hundred miles to Egmont, alone and at night, piloting a daisy chain of derelicts through the rapids? What if he was just a loner trying to make a living, instead of the ogre my wife was probably having nightmares about already?

Finally, I fell into an unsatisfying sleep. I dreamed I was eight years old again, trapped in the middle of Haro Strait. This time, though, I was sitting on Zero Rock with the seals, watching my father struggle past.

My Friend Phil

When I woke up, the droning noise next door had stopped, but there was still no sign of our troubling neighbour. His generator had probably just run out of gas. Brent's boat was shuttered and looked even colder than it had the night before. Should I walk over and say goodbye? I tried on a couple of scenarios: Brent in his sweatpants, spread-eagled and snoring? Kim cupping a steaming mug in Brent's fatherly embrace? Neither appealed. We'd sort out the battery problem ourselves.

I started the engine with the remaining battery, untied the boat while Hatsumi jumped into her clothes, and headed for the closest town with a chandlery, Port McNeill. We squeezed through the Blow Hole, a tricky tidal constriction, past the celebrated Lagoon Cove, and then started a long swim up the arteries of Clio Channel and Baronet Passage. As usual, the northwest wind funnelled down the narrow passage, but we were getting used to it: the serious wind wouldn't arrive until mid-afternoon, by which time we'd be through the last section of Johnstone Strait and tied up in Port McNeill.

I wolfed down the breakfast Hatsumi passed up to me, remarkably chipper once we had severed ties with Minstrel Island. Besides eating, my responsibilities were limited to keeping *Vera* midway between the clear-cuts on either side. Only two weeks in, and the trip was becoming a grind. When Baronet Passage finally opened into Johnstone Strait, the sea became lumpy and confused, and that was exactly the way I felt. If we turned right, literally thousands of small islands would lie before us. We could slow down, kick back, and get lost in Broughton Archipelago Marine Park. To the left lay another two days following the smooth curve of Vancouver Island, with a stop in Port McNeill for groceries and minor electrical surgery. And after that, the Nahwitti Bar.

We turned left.

For its last fifteen miles, Johnstone Strait behaved itself. From now until the Nahwitti Bar, we'd be in the much wider Queen Charlotte Strait. Vancouver Island was beginning to narrow toward its northern tip, drawing away from the mainland. The last sizeable island was Malcolm, where we'd first gotten the crazy idea of buying a sailboat four years before. Tucked in its lee, the small crescent of Cormorant Island was home to the 'Namgis First Nation. Brent, who I imagined still sleeping it off back on Minstrel Island, lived in its main town, Alert Bay.

Suddenly the wheel jumped in my hand, as though seized from below. *Vera* lurched and a wave slapped the hull. Where was *this* coming from? Another one batted us from the other side. Charley got to his feet.

"What's happening?" said Hatsumi.

We were surrounded by standing waves, a clearly delimited field of them extending a half mile or so in all directions. Currents snatched at *Vera*'s keel.

"Aha!" I pointed to the chart. "The Nimpkish River, look, it empties right over there. We're on Nimpkish Bank." The Nimpkish was short but significant, a major salmon producer draining the elongated Nimpkish Lake. The darker blue of shallow water bloomed halfway across to Cormorant Island. We were where the chart said we should be, well outside the shallow area, but the sea was still chaotic.

"Same idea as the Nahwitti Bar," I said, as we passed into normal water again.

"It'll be like this? I mean, that's all?" Compared to some of the tidal passes we'd been through, the Nimpkish Bar had been a blip. But Hatsumi sounded worried.

"Nothing to it," I said.

If you look at a small-scale chart of Vancouver Island, the contrast between the two coasts is striking, like two brothers who have gone down different roads. The east side is smooth-shaven and respectable. Yes, all those narrows and constrictions lend character, but it doesn't actually *look* menacing. But the west side — the bad brother — is another story: grizzled, unkempt, taking the wind in gapped teeth.

Port McNeill was still on the respectable side, well sheltered at the end of a long east-facing bay almost directly across the island from the forbidding stub of the Brooks Peninsula. I liked it immediately. How could you not like a place where a sign at the marina entrance says, "No welding permitted in the harbour"? Where commercial fishing boats unloaded great arrowhead-shaped halibut onto idling trucks at night, and the morning low tide laid out a feast of carcasses for eagles to tear apart? You could hear the twist and snap of beak on bone, as the big birds worked their way along the vertebrae.

Port McNeill has around four thousand residents, and in the days we spent there I felt as though I had met most of them. People smiled at us in the street, they squatted to make friends with Charley, a knot of teenage boys on bikes actually moved aside to let us pass on the sidewalk. Almost everyone in Port McNeill, it seemed, was friendly.

Except for Phil.

Phil ran the chandlery. If you were a boater, you needed Phil. And Phil needed you — or at least, basic business logic suggested he should. I did everything I could to make Phil like me, beginning by buying the simple battery switch I foolishly believed would end my electrical problems, and spiralling to levels of expenditure on things I didn't even know had gone wrong. But he resisted my advances to the end. By the time we left Port McNeill, I was in love with the town but I wanted to kill Phil.

The battery switch couldn't have been the problem: a new one only cost fifty dollars, a number that, in a chandlery, is more like statistical noise than actual money. Replacing it was, of course, hell, since all the "hidden" electrical wiring on a boat is crammed into inaccessible, knuckle-shredding spaces. But the batteries still refused to work. I retightened every connection between batteries and the electrical panel. Still no go.

"I dare say," I could hear Brent intone through a marijuana haze, "it's the batteries themselves."

Vera takes her everyday electrical juice from a bank of four "golf cart" batteries stacked, two on two, in a cockpit locker beneath the water line. I can barely lift even one of them. Replacing all four meant rigging up a pulley system suspended from the boom. I pulled, Hatsumi guided, and one by one the heavy batteries swung over the side and into a dock cart. Then we dragged the contraption, its tires flattened by all that weight, all the way up the sloping gangplank and across town to Phil's shop. Charley nipped at our heels.

"How do you know he has the right batteries?" panted Hatsumi, as usual speaking the thoughts I had decided to keep to myself.

"Of course he does," I said. "He runs a chandlery, doesn't he?"

But Phil didn't have four golf cart batteries, he had one.

"It's bent," I said. "Look, the terminals are wrecked."

Phil fingered a leaning lump of lead. He managed to look surprised. "Somebody must've dropped it off the pallet. Now, when do you need these for?"

"Well, we can't actually go anywhere without . . ."

"Just a moment, my friend." He punched the offending battery lightly, as though it had let him down, and dug a phone out from under a sea of junk on the parts counter: a dead oil pressure gauge, a stack of unpriced boxes, a pile of unsent invoices.

"Jesus Christ," he said to a beaten-looking employee cradling a phone to one shoulder. "Go lock yourself in a room and type up all these work orders." Then, into his own phone, "Who've I got? Okay. Phil here, Port McNeill. Look, I've got a customer, wants some six-volts so he can get on his way. What about tomorrow?"

That sounded better. Because was anybody going to say no to this guy? Phil was big, a head taller than me, with an aggressive gut and a greasy white pompadour. He'd run a boat-building business once, he told me. Now, the added cares of operating a chandlery in a seasonal town seemed to have pulled his features into a lugubrious slide so that the face below the shock of white hair was an avalanche zone of pouches and jowls. The voice travelling down the line to whatever hapless distributor Phil was bullying was a sepulchral, carton-a-day rasp. He put down the phone.

"Tomorrow," he said. "Eight thirty. You can pay me now."

I paid him $850 while a lineup of yachties and sport fishermen fumed behind me. We spent the rest of the day buying groceries and doing laundry. While the sheets levitated and collapsed in the dryer, we crossed the street to the Port McNeill Museum. The place was crammed with lethal-looking logging gear, including a two-man chainsaw the size of a surfboard.

"What happened when it bucked?" I asked the elderly guide.

"What?"

I yelled my question again, and he shouted back the answer.

Maybe he'd made himself deaf by talking too much? I tried to find out.

"So, were you a logger too?"

"No! Driller-blaster! Come from Alberta originally, moved up to Campbell River to meet girls! And I did, not the kind you'd want to marry, if you get my meaning!"

He was a nice guy, and we were his only customers. I bought a "Hug a Logger Today" sticker, and we went back to collect our sheets. Outside, a man walked past carrying a carved and varnished salmon under one arm. Apart from Phil, Port McNeill was turning out fine, and we still had the rest of the day to kill before our shiny new batteries showed up. We walked back to the boat trailing the smell of clean laundry. Hatsumi pulled out a book in Japanese and left me to my stack of elderly papers.

❦

Enough scientific background. Now, I wanted to pick up Billy's story after my father had done the first operation, inserting the shunt that would relieve the pressure on Billy's brain.

When we last saw Billy in Refuge Cove, he'd just been operated on; I guess you could say Act One was almost over. Fever spikes kept Billy in the hospital another three weeks, while his family doctor and two different pediatricians did two lumbar punctures to check the cerebrospinal fluid for signs of meningitis (there weren't any). The pediatrician noted that the baby cried during the spinal tap. I would have too. Three different antibiotics, plus phenobarbital and Tylenol, were dripped into Billy. In the file, vital rates charts took up an inch of paper. Finally, he went home.

Two months later, it was time for Act Two. Billy was back in the hospital. The fever wouldn't go away. Blood cultures grew *Staphylococcus epidermidis*, convincing his doctors that the shunt had gotten infected. And so my father removed it. Billy was getting standard treatment for the time.

But even the standard treatment, as I'd learned in my research over the last week, could go off the rails. With the shunt removed, Billy's little train took a shunt of its own. The source of the infection was gone, but so was the pressure relief, and Billy still had hydrocephalus. It was now wait and see: Billy had entered the no man's land where his doctors were banking on infection subsiding before the lack of a drain caused danger-ous pressure on their patient's brain. I reminded myself this was standard procedure and, not for the first time, was profoundly glad that I had never had to make such a decision. The doctors' order sheets tick off the days with blood tests and adjustments in antibiotic dose. Do this, do that, continue this, add that. At twenty-five minutes past midnight on an uneventful day, there was my father's unmistakable handwriting: "Please give 2 a.m. and 8 a.m. cloxacillin." He may have been a martinet, but he was a polite one, even in the middle of the night.

But the race against time and infection was lost. Billy became lethargic. He started to vomit. Something was going really wrong. For the next thirty-six hours, the records are in minutes, not days. Time began to elongate. At 4:20 a.m. on Labour Day, Billy had a seizure. The most likely cause was increased pressure on the brain. An hour later, his pediatrician, Dr. Beamish, did the thing that led eventually to $1.5 million changing hands and my father's name in the newspapers: he put a needle into Billy's spine to relieve that pressure.

This was the lumbar puncture that would become the stick-ing point in the case against my father, the reason I had tried so hard to understand lumbar punctures and their risks. Because half an hour after the LP, Billy stopped breathing. He turned blue. Working fast, Beamish "bagged" him with oxygen and tubed him through the trachea. Billy started to breathe again.

There was no gloss of hindsight or accusation here but, despite my idyllic surroundings, I found myself transported to a scene as vivid as any movie. The child struggling beneath the O.R. lights in the wee hours, the pediatrician and the nurses fighting along with him; I could almost hear the pounding soundtrack.

What happened next? At 7:30 a.m., my father installed a new shunt on the other side of Billy's head. How long he had been present — what time in the early morning he had gotten up, pulled on his clothes, driven through empty streets to the hospital in the ritual I had slept through all my childhood — was maddeningly unclear. But once the new shunt was in, Billy settled down. The records went back to daily; normal time resumed. Billy stayed in hospital another month. Was he visually impaired? It was impossible to tell. I leafed through the many reports — hematology, urinalysis, bacteriology, CSF analysis, infusion therapy, neurological vital signs. Billy kept the lab busy. His mother was so traumatized by the experience that she demanded, and got, a completely new team of specialists.

With that, my father's role in Billy's life was over. A hydrocephalic infant had been shunted; infections predictably ensued; the shunt was removed; there were some dicey hours when cerebrospinal pressure built; a new shunt was put in. The child recovered. Life went on.

In preparing for his trial, my father had obviously gone over these records meticulously. Even after fifteen years, the splodges of his highlighter were still bold, and some sections of notes had been bordered in heavy black lines. I added my own markings, struggling to piece together what the nurses were contending with.

Most of the record was legible, but it was impossible to know how complete it was. In particular, what should one make of blanks in the "doctor visited" box? Were they real? Or did a nurse simply forget to tick the box? I totted up the number of times *any* of Billy's several doctors came to see him and found ten days for which there were no recorded visits. Real or not? Which was more likely, that none of the doctors bothered to look in on a shunted, feverish hydrocephalic infant with a swelling head, or that their visits didn't get recorded?

I was still left with the impossible-to-answer question, the one any son had to ask: when the critical decision to do the third LP on Billy was made, was Dr. Harvey there? Was he at least consulted? Ten years after the incident, by which time he was in his mid-seventies, he remembered nothing about Billy. But for someone whose father used to appear at the breakfast table with blood spatters on his horn-rimmed glasses, who was so seldom "off call" that I gave up wondering who was more important, me or some patient with his head wrapped in gauze, the answer to that crucial question was easy: of *course* he was there, and the nurses forgot to write it down. But I knew that answer really only had meaning for me. What other people said — the nurses, the doctors, the child's family — was just as important, at least to a court. Because, after the crisis had passed and Billy went home, his road got rockier, not smoother. Labour Day was just the end of Act Two.

～

For the next year or so, Billy got physical therapy at an institution for children with disabilities. A brief stay in hospital for croup provided the last of the hospital records, a thin coda to the operatic fistful of Labour Day. The E.R. doctor who cleared up Billy's croup described him as "grossly normal" neurologically.

But Billy wasn't "grossly normal." He was myopic, with cerebral palsy, and he had trouble walking, so he was more than the usual two-year-old handful. At first, there was some question about visual loss after the shunt replacement — an observation that would become a key part of the lawsuit years down the road. Although six months later, the children's clinic reported that, "according to [the mother], Billy seems to have recovered some if not all of his vision."

I leafed through the clinic's typewritten records, a file that covered his life from just after the shunt replacement to age six. When he was two, the clinic's doctors found him doing better but still mentally impaired. Billy was obsessed with TV game shows. He had trouble walking. In other words, a handful of worry. At three, Billy was small, social, a chatterer with cerebral palsy and one leg shorter than the other. He wore a helmet because he sometimes fell. His verbal ability had shot ahead of his age group and was described as "adult-like." He had an enormous rote memory. At four, he was way ahead verbally, a year or so behind socially, with lousy eyesight.

Closing in on five years of age, myopia was a handicap, and Billy's eyes darted around involuntarily. He couldn't deal with pressure or failure. But he could catch, throw, kick a ball, even though his fine motor skills and balance were below age level.

After I had read this far, it seemed to me that, for a premature, oxygen-starved baby with hydrocephalus, Billy was doing all right. I knew this wasn't an entirely fair judgment. I had never had to raise a child with a disability. If I had, maybe I wouldn't be so quick to judge. But I had read enough of medical history to know that, so far, doctors had salvaged a life for Billy.

The clinic records chugged on until he was nearly six. Billy continued with his therapy. He was a friendly, talkative child with a leg brace, one divergent eye, and a perfectly functioning shunt. The last entry described him as sociable but distractible with iffy eyesight and a tendency to walk into things.

I was sorry when I came to the end of the file; of all of Billy's medical history, this bundle of reports was the only evidence, outside of his family, of commitment, of being there for the long haul. That clinic was Billy's interface with the world, the place where he learned to function. But once the clinic was out of the picture, the reporting on Billy got a little shoddy.

Thus I would find things like a pediatrician's official hospital record, written when Billy was six, that says the infected shunt was out for two weeks (it was actually 2.5 days), followed by "severe loss of vision with optic nerve atrophy" (not at all what Billy's ophthalmologist wrote in *his* report). The harder I looked, the mushier the evidence became. Reading *everything* (which my father and I may have been the only people to do) was like launching yourself down a ski run on a cold, clear morning after a fresh snowfall: the first few runs are pristine and exhilarating, but by afternoon, the fresh snow has turned to slush that grabs at your skis and threatens to snap your legs off at the knees.

Some doctors actually wavered. Billy's family doctor reversed herself. When first asked about Billy's problems, she wrote in a long letter that it was "difficult to know" whether they had arisen at birth or later, as a result of the Labour Day crisis. Three years later, after reading the "expert opinions" the plaintiff's lawyers had obtained, she agreed completely with them. In other words, "Okay, forgot the ten-pager I wrote three years ago, I'll go along with what the experts say."

A bony hand scrabbled through the folder open on the table in front of me.

"*Forget* it? They did better than that. They even tried to make it disappear! Did you see this?" The hand emerged, brandishing another stapled-together letter from the family doctor. "This one!" my father said.

I looked it over, then consulted the one I'd been taking notes from. "It's a copy," I said. "Same letter. Your files are full of duplicates."

"It's not," he said. "Look at your page seven."

I thumbed back. "So?"

"Look at *my* page seven." He tapped it dramatically. There was one paragraph, then the rest was blank. Gone were the paragraphs about pre-existing conditions, and doubt, and (I had hoped) fairness.

"Look at the top of the version you've been reading. Don't you read my notes?" Another tap. There it was, in his hand-writing, "Obtained by A.T. with difficulty. I got it near the termination of the trial."

"The doctor backed down. She tried to cover it up."

"Great," I said. "Trust nobody?"

"I didn't say that."

"Then who do I trust?"

My father didn't laugh a lot in life, but he produced a sem-blance of one now.

"You should know the answer to that. Help me out of this awful seat. I'm going."

"Going where?"

"Back to where it's warm," he said, clutching his checked jacket and shuffling along the deck. "And you can interpret that any way you like."

So Billy limped along, a little pied piper dragging his bag-gage of self-referencing reports, trailing his team of specialists and handlers and his exhausted family from home to hospital to therapy to school, until, at age nine, he found his way back to my father's door in the writ of summons. I tossed the papers aside in disgust. I'd found so many omissions and mistakes and so much sloppiness that I began to doubt whether anything approaching the truth my father claimed to revere was there at all. But if I couldn't rely on the record, how could I stay objective?

Port McNeill was quiet now. For the last hour or so, I'd been reading by headlamp; I turned it off, and the twilit marina slowly revealed itself. The boat nearest to *Vera* emitted a muffled clink of crockery; a heron let out an annoyed croak from the darken-ing shore; down below, Charley mumbled in response. Cabin lights came on, and the North Star materialized above the sil-houettes of trees, a pinprick through the canopy of the heavens.

Utopia

The next morning, the batteries arrived as promised, and we did the trundling and hoisting thing in reverse. By ten o'clock, we were ready to leave. There was one last stop to make before we headed up the final leg to the Nahwitti Bar and Cape Scott. Sointula, the funky, failed Finnish settlement where we'd first gotten the idea of buying a boat, was just across Broughton Strait, a half-hour hop. We'd spend a day there, then head north to Port Hardy. The electrical system was reborn; I'd never have to deal with Phil again; life was good.

Sointula is in love with a memory. To an outsider like me, the community has a wistful feel, permeated by a sense of failure and decay. And perhaps that's all it is, a sense and nothing more, but for me, the bright cottages dotting the crescent of beach near the harbour, the well-maintained houses farther inland, even the new construction near the Co-op store that anchors the village can't dispel the impact of the bleached ribs of ruined storehouses and abandoned boatsheds along the shore. Fishing boats dissolve, infinitely slowly, into the mudflats, reduced to a backbone and rusted engine mounts.

There are plenty of failed settlements along the Vancouver Island coast — Cape Scott, where we were headed, had its doomed Danes, determined to farm in a place blanketed by fog and scoured by year-long winds — but Sointula is the best known. Even if you don't know the history, the names of places and people remind you that something unusual happened here, and the fact that a functioning community replaced the utopian experiment somehow sets Sointula apart from a town like Port McNeill, where Europeans came to log and fish and get on with their lives, not to remake society.

Sointula's utopia was Finnish and it failed not because the resource base wasn't there but for lack of sustained leadership (always a conundrum when your community is founded on harmony and equality). Fisheries, the mainstay of any coastal community, didn't show serious signs of faltering until the 1990s, although the industry has been in free fall since then, with commercial salmon boats being "retired" by the thousands amid an orgy of finger-pointing. The list of culprits is long, and interaction between them makes things far worse: depending on your affiliation and knowledge, you can take your pick from over-fishing, government mismanagement, habitat loss from logging and industrial expansion, pollution, and the effects of climate change on ocean conditions. And, of course, salmon farms.

When a few local entrepreneurs began farming Pacific salmon in net cages along the coast in the 1980s, nobody took much notice, but consolidation of ownership, a switch to Atlantic (that is, non-native) salmon, and massive expansion of net-pen farming in the 1990s gave people another salmon threat to worry about. By around 2005, large-scale farming of Atlantic salmon by a handful of Norwegian companies had, in the public mind, risen high on the list of suspects in the decline of the wild fishery. And when researchers found irrefutable evidence that the salmon in net cages were amplifying the numbers of sea lice, a naturally occurring (and loathsome-looking) parasite on salmon, to the point where baby salmon migrating past the cages were starting to die, people mourning the decline of wild salmon had an enemy to take shots at.

The heavy artillery was deployed in the Broughton Archipelago, just north and west of Sointula. There were lots of salmon farms there (and we'd already passed plenty further south). Alexandra Morton, a biologist living in the archipelago, raised the alarm about louse-infected pink salmon, and the interactions between salmon farms and wild salmon became a feeding trough for scientists and activists looking for funding and for media looking for a story. Sorting the science from the rhetoric became thankless and near-impossible. Few were interested in the buts or the details; salmon farming was a canvas with only two possible colours, black or white.

Alexandra Morton lived in Sointula now. As we neared the harbour, I wondered how an ex-utopian, ex-fishing community would take to having such a famous face in their midst. Now, when I had more or less agreed to go to work analyzing the impact of salmon farms on sockeye from the Fraser River, a six-month job that would have me poring over piles of data and interviewing people on both sides of the controversy, I realized I didn't really want to know. Salmon farms and disappearing sockeye would come soon enough. First, I had to get around Cape Scott and down the west coast; now, I just wanted to walk around Sointula with my wife and dog, enjoying the beaches and the cottages and the bleached bones of fishboats like any other tourist.

"Rough Bay Harbour, this is *Vera*."

Or was it Rough Bay Marina? I throttled back just outside the breakwater and waited for the harbour master to come back on the VHF. Announcing yourself on Channel 66 before landing is the normal drill; someone will respond, take down the name and length of your boat, and assign a spot. I tried again.

"Rough Bay, this is *Vera*." I began to feel silly. Charley jumped up on the cockpit coaming and sniffed hard.

"Maybe we just tie up anywhere. There's lots of space," said Hatsumi.

"You talking to me?" said a voice on Channel 66.

"Screw it," I said, pointing to an open spot across from a derelict tug. "Let's go over there."

We made fast, and while Charley rocketed up the dock, I had a closer look at the old tug. The hull paint was long gone, and the iron cladding was curling off the wormy-looking wood in rusty leaves, like scales on a dried-out fish. Someone had rigged up a steering station on top, a thick metal column to which were bolted a rusty wheel, a throttle and shift lever, and two incongruously shiny searchlights. The captain's seat, lashed to the top of the metal ladder, was a rusted-out metal chair that looked as though it came out of a high school auditorium.

There were few pleasure boats in Rough Bay. Most of the vessels were work boats: fishing vessels with blunt, business-like bows and foot-high licence numbers painted on their cabin sides, or battering rams with rusted teeth for butting logs into position. Behind us, a gillnetter called *Ocean Buster* steamed around the breakwater, dug into a long turn, and disappeared into the maze of wharves on the opposite side of the bay. Charley was already challenging a fisherman walking along the dock.

"Does he like cookies?" the guy asked, grinning. Without breaking stride, he dug a dog biscuit out of his pocket and tossed it to Charley.

"Does the pope wear a funny hat?" he said over his shoulder.

I knew I would like Sointula.

Captain Walbran was no help for the name of Rough Bay, a shallow but dramatic indentation in the elongated south shore of Malcolm Island, like a bite out of the middle of a croissant. By mid-afternoon, the answer was self-evident: any kind of wind from the south swept straight into Rough Bay, whipping the shallows into nasty whitecaps. Rough Bay was . . . rough. Even with the breakwater around the harbour, the outermost boats rolled wickedly and snatched at their lines. Land was the place to be. We hiked up the brand new gangplank being finished off by a couple of cheerful contractors ("You're the first to use it. Put that in your logbook!") and set off for the village a few kilometres away. The town's Finnish past announced itself immediately with the Tarkanen Boat Yard, where a fifty-foot fibreglass seiner was hauled out. I caught the tang of epoxy resin.

The next stretch of road was scattered with beachfront houses, some of them new and expensive-looking, others no more than cedar-shake cottages facing the southwesters. A spanking new tennis court looked out over the strait. Did Finns play tennis? Probably not, but retirees did. Charley lunged and strained at a couple of deer grazing at the edge of the court.

I began to see bumper stickers on fences or gates: "Salmon Are Sacred." This was the first time I'd heard of salmon worship. Japanese Shinto held that all things possess a spirit and might thus be considered sacred — was this the evidence of some obscure Shinto sect, come to Sointula to spread the word? If so, they had spray cans, because I started to see *Salmon Are Sacred* on walls too. Then I saw a T-shirt displayed on a tree trunk next to a sheaf of leaflets, and a painting lashed to a pair of nearby hemlocks. It was a knock-off of Munch's *The Scream*, with the yawning, bug-eyed creature standing not on a bridge but in front of a salmon cage and brandishing a fish. I thought it was pretty good.

It wasn't hard to figure out who lived here. Beside the little maroon-coloured cottage on the beach was a vegetable patch, and Alexandra Morton was bent over in it. The nemesis of fish farmers and bureaucrats was hoeing her garden. Was this the time to drop in and introduce myself? This was Sointula on a sunny summer day, not a Vancouver meeting room full of media. Half an hour in the lettuce beds and I might have a unique perspective on one of the better-known activists in the country. Turn right, let Charley off the leash to make the introduction for me, that's all I had to do.

But I kept walking. This was my holiday, and her backyard. Discussions about farmed salmon and sea lice could wait for the fall. We made a loop at the village, a little farther down the road, past the ferry dock and the Co-op store that's the hub of the community. The restaurant on the pier, which I remembered as loud and lively five years ago, now had an emptied-out, downsized look. We doubled back to the harbour, found the very spot where, five years before, we'd gotten the idea of buying a boat, and took each other's picture. I felt slightly silly, standing next to an unremarkable piece of wharf, but a turning point is a turning point.

The past attended to, we explored the other side of Rough Bay, where the ghosts of Finns and fishermen are everywhere. The tide was out, and a dozen collapsing float homes and boat sheds seemed beached on the muddy shore. Most were falling apart, the roofs lumpy and green with moss and the peeling window frames like gaping sockets in a bleached cedar skull. A fence enclosing the back of one of the old homes had sagged open into a snaggle-toothed fan. One shack was reduced to a skeleton, the remaining gable framing a view of the other side of the bay. Ghosts would have no trouble passing through these walls.

We passed more derelict boats along the curving shore of Rough Bay, as though this was the place they had come to die. The *New Joy*, a pocket troller, still sat upright against a rock wall, as though waiting for owners who would never return. Just down the beach, another fishing boat was no more than a few ribs and a driveshaft. I bent down and sniffed the wood; you could still smell the diesel soaked into it. But there were metal boats in this graveyard too, flat-bottomed aluminum skiffs with outboard motors still attached, pulled high and left to oxidize behind the grass.

Back at the harbour, I stopped in at the wharfinger's office to pay for our moorage while Hatsumi fed coins into the shower across the parking lot. The office was papered with curling snapshots of fishermen and their boats, and within minutes the tsunami of sentiment I thought I'd ducked by walking on past Alexandra Morton's house had caught up with me.

"I'm a third-generation fisherman," the woman told me, her pen poised over the receipt book. "And I can tell you, it's dying here. The department is just figuring out new ways to make it impossible to fish." She looked out the window over the docks. An eagle swept by close overhead with a fish wriggling in its beak.

"But there are still boats going out," I said, remembering the *Ocean Buster* that had followed us in around the breakwater. "What are they catching?"

"Chinook. But now the sockeye are coming." She looked up at the sky and her voice broke. "They're coming, I can *feel* it."

"Yeah, but last year was a disaster, wasn't it?"

"Not this year. This year'll be good. I can feel it," she said again. (She was right. The return of Fraser River sockeye that year was huge, catching everyone off guard after the disaster of the year before.) This was my cue, the moment for me to identify myself as a biologist, someone who'd be back in Sointula in six months with a contract and a tape recorder. But she beat me to it.

"Thank God there's someone to speak for us," she said.

"Yes."

Another woman in the office looked up and nodded. "She's got that, you know, charisma? That's what we need in this fight."

What could I say? If I introduced myself now, I'd never get away. Hatsumi would run out of quarters before I was finished.

"It's dying here," the harbour master said again. "Every year, more boats on the beach. We just want it to be the way it used to be."

Don't we all, I thought. I stuffed my biological baggage firmly out of sight and shook her hand. Better now than later, because reviewing fish farm effects was a thankless job. Neither side liked grey areas, and either one could come down hard on you if you identified one that wasn't to their liking.

"Get some of those sockeye," I said and went out to find my wife, whose own country was far more fished-out than this one. In Japan, it was rare to find a protected bay without a small aquatic city of nets and cages. I found her reading an enormous bronze plaque erected at the entrance to the parking lot. There were three such, each with three columns: boat, crewman killed, and date. The dates ran from 1937 to 2001, and I counted thirty-one names. Half of them were Finns, two had the same last name. Brothers? Or father and son? One boat, the *Ocean Star*, lost five men in 1966.

Beached boats, decaying boathouses, and the bones of all these men somewhere at the bottom of the sea. Theirs was the past that the woman in the wharfinger's office refused to let go of, and if it took a high-profile activist to somehow stop time and get it back, who was I to question their motives? I was right to have stayed out of it, to go back to my waiting piles of data. Facts are emotionless, and that's what I would be paid to analyze. The story told by the ruins and the memorials to missing fishermen were the same up and down the coast: people died for the fishing, and now we'd somehow managed to kill off the fish themselves.

Back down at *Vera*, someone had tied up behind us. Our new neighbour was taking his black and white tabby for a strange, stop-and-start walk along the dock. I asked him about his boat.

"Used to be a gillnetter," he told me. "I found it in the bushes, rebuilt it myself. Kind of a retirement project."

"Retirement from what?"

"Commercial fishing. I spent thirty years in the Charlottes.

All that time, I told myself all I wanted was a hidey-hole away from the wind." He gestured at the whitecaps in Rough Bay. "And there's still too much of it!" His cat leapt onto the derelict tug and disappeared into the chaos of the wheelhouse. "Jeez. I gotta go rescue him. Last time he fell in, we had to net him like a salmon."

I lay on my stomach and watched a school of coon-stripe shrimp on one of the pilings that secured the dock. Do shrimp form schools? Probably not, but this group was definitely interacting. It seemed to me they were having a kind of meeting, as though the piling was a wrap-around boardroom table. The longer I peered into their world, the more of them I counted, and once my eyes adapted, I saw that the creosote-black pole was studded with their greenish bodies. Now and then, one of them would do the shrimp equivalent of getting up from the table and stretching its legs. They swam horizontally, front legs extended as though readying for an embrace, propelled by the flutter of paired swimmerets that allowed them to go backward and forward with equal speed and ease. Sometimes they took a brief yoga break, flinging all of their appendages straight out and sinking, perfectly motionless, until I lost sight of them.

I suppose that a competent crustacean biologist could have told me what all these behaviours meant, but I was happy just to feel the sun on my back and watch. As always, when confronted with one of nature's marvels, I found myself guiltily unable to summon up much interest in how it worked, or what it meant. Wonder was enough.

Guts

The next morning, the wind was smacking Rough Bay by nine o'clock. Breakfasting inside *Vera*, we could feel her snatching at her mooring lines, like a dog on a chain. It would only get worse. We wouldn't be leaving Sointula today unless we went by ferry.

"Hey," I said to Hatsumi, "let's go and see that processing plant in Port Hardy."

"That what?"

"Processing plant. For the farmed salmon. I met this guy back in Port McNeill who tried to help out with our electrical problem. Ron? Remember him?"

"No."

"Doesn't matter. He turned out to be the manager of the plant. I told him I was a biologist. He said we could get a tour, all I had to do was call." I reached for my phone. Hatsumi looked at the dog curled up between us on the settee.

"What about Charley?"

"Maybe someone can take care of him there. Let's ask."

In five minutes, it was arranged. Ron's wife would pick us up in Port McNeill and look after Charley while we toured the plant. The next ferry left Sointula in forty-five minutes. We'd be back in time for dinner.

We hurried past *The Scream* and got to the ferry just as it was loading. On board, the wind whistled through the open car deck, gathering speed in the constricted space so that I had to pull my hat low over my eyes.

"Too cold," said Hatsumi, handing me Charley's leash. "You take him."

She and all the rest of the foot passengers vanished into the passenger lounge. Charley and I tucked in behind a bulkhead at the stern and watched Sointula recede behind an expanding plain of whitecaps. I sat on a sack of stove fuel and cradled Charley's head in one hand. An eyeball fluttered under my fingers. The deckhands looked frozen, and by the time we walked off to look for Ron's wife, I was frozen too.

The road north to Port Hardy was intermittently bounded by new growth, where a logged-off area was beginning to regenerate. "We call it the salad bar," said Gwen, a solid, cheerful woman who also seemed to work for Marine Harvest, the company operating the processing plant. "See the bears?" I spotted a couple of blacks, nose down, the first large mammals we'd seen since the wolves back in Douglas Bay. On a ridge behind them, what looked like a giant waterslide curved down and away toward the sea.

"What the heck is *that*?"

"Orca Gravel," said Gwen. "Like a treadmill, a kilometre long, from the pit to the port. Look for it when you go past in your boat. You'll see the big bulk loaders. High-quality stuff, they ship a lot to Hawaii."

That was British Columbia all right, ship out the timber, ship out the gravel, and, now that the wild salmon were petering out, truck out the farmed fish. I hadn't told Gwen's husband

I was about to write a report on salmon farms, just that I was a biologist. Had he Googled me? Was the tour a subtle way of getting me onside? How easy was it going to be to stay neutral?

"This really is awfully kind of you," I said.

The plant occupied an attractive piece of waterfront a half mile or so north of the town of Port Hardy. The building, cream-coloured with blue trim, might have been anything — a warehouse, a shoe factory — except for the dock, where a sixty-foot commercial salmon boat was tethered by lines and hoses like a patient in a hospital bed. The reefer trucks, invisible from the sea, were around the back — seven semis a day, packed tight with creaking Styrofoam boxes of farmed Atlantic salmon. Ninety percent went to the United States. I learned all this, and much more, from the production manager, Tanya, an athletic-looking woman in her mid-thirties who escorted me and Hatsumi through the plant.

"I used to be a commercial fisherman," Tanya said. Her office looked out across Hardy Bay to the fishing harbour where a dozen seiners and gillnetters were tied up. "So was my dad. He lives in Sointula." She laughed. "It's okay, everybody gets along. But I don't wear my Marine Harvest jacket when I go over to visit."

"So how does that work, the fishboat down at your dock?"

"We pay them to go around to the farms, wherever we're harvesting. There are three boats on contract."

I didn't bother pointing out the ironies; by now, everybody in this story was long past irony. But I was curious about what happened to the fish. The big selling point of farmed salmon, besides its lower price, was freshness.

"You corner the fish in the pen and suck them into the boat," Tanya told me.

"And then?"

"Electric stunner, then bled through the gills. After that, they're refrigerated in seawater till they get here." She gestured to the dock outside her window. The fish boat was listing to one side, like a glass tilted to get the last of the milkshake.

"And after that?"

"What size are your feet?" said Tanya.

We followed her down two flights of polished concrete stairs to a kind of receiving room where we exchanged our shoes for blue Crocs. "Very Japanese," I said to Hatsumi.

Tanya laughed and splashed through a shallow disinfectant tray, across a plastic grid, and over a yellow-painted curb into a second room where a thickset, hairnetted woman was kicking off a pair of white rubber boots. We shucked our Crocs, selected rubber boots, wrapped ourselves in green smocks, and surrendered our jewellery to Tanya in exchange for blue nitrile gloves and hairnets. Then we stumbled after her through an automatic boot sprayer. Tanya paused at the door.

"Usually we wear earplugs," she said. "But then you won't be able to ask questions. Okay with you?"

"Okay with me," I said. She pulled the door open.

We were on a metal gallery. If our feet rang on the grid, I would never have heard it. The plant howled at us from below, and the noise and motion made it difficult at first to take in what was going on.

"Four gutting machines," Tanya screamed into my ear, ticking them off with a finger. Way across the room, which was the size of a football field, the salmon were arriving on a conveyor that split into four arteries. Each gutting machine was a twenty-foot aluminum box that straddled a conveyor. At one end, a worker fed a whole salmon in, belly up; seconds later, its reamed-out body was grabbed by a worker on the other side.

"I'll show you," mouthed Tanya. We followed her down some steps. Despite the horrendous noise, the two guys servicing the machine seemed to be having a conversation. One of them wore a beard net. Tanya caught my look of surprise.

"Probably talking about the hockey game," she yelled.

But what they were doing here was horrifying. The box that housed the gutting machine sprouted numerous hoses, some of them hardwalled and relatively thin — I figured they would be the supply lines for water and hydraulics — and others, which had to be suction hoses, ribbed, flexible, and much wider. The thickest of these exited straight up, like a kind of chimney, and every time a fish went through the box the hose writhed violently, as though swallowing hard. What was happening in there? I peered through the misted, blood-spattered window.

There were three machines inside, and the first was the scariest: a stainless steel head with spinning blades and a gaping mouth that dropped suddenly down onto the fish's offered belly, punched deep between the pectoral fins and ripped savagely back to the vent, inhaling the shredded viscera and spitting them out through the jerking hose. Then, just as suddenly, the mouth was retracted, jets of water misted the window and two flexible arms rooted in the pink cavity, reaming out the kidney that ran along the underside of the backbone, picking off stray bits of viscera. Up close, I could practically feel the impact of the robots, but the general noise level was so high that what was going on behind that clouded window appeared silent and dreamlike.

The worker on the receiving end ran a practised eye over each fish as it came out, leaning in with a knife from time to time to nick off a dangling fin or an errant length of disconnected esophagus. I thought immediately of my friend Chris, and the awful operation he'd just had. I couldn't help it.

"Do you grade them?" I yelled, and Tanya struggled to explain the computer system that scanned and sorted fish, but I couldn't follow her in the din. All I could see was that, downstream of the gutting, some stayed in the round, while others trundled around a corner into another room.

"Value-added," she shouted. "I'll show you." I looked around for Hatsumi; she looked startled, as though she couldn't take it all in.

"You look cute in that hairnet," I screamed. A salmon landed in a puddle and drenched her with seawater and blood.

"Sorry!" mouthed a jolly-looking middle-aged woman, handing her a towel. Everybody in the plant smiled at us. I made a mental note to ask Tanya what the typical salary was. The workers changed stations regularly, Tanya told me later, and while we were on the floor, I saw a group break away, draw together in the middle of the gutting room, and go through a stretching routine.

"Value-added" meant filleting, and it was quieter than disembowelling. We had to splash through another set of disinfecting baths and jets to get there. As with the gutting, some of the machine's work was touched up by hand; I watched a gowned worker deftly round the corners of a rich red slab before tossing it back on the belt.

"A lot depends on the customer," said Tanya. At least we could talk in here. "Costco is really picky, they want the skin off the fillet."

"Why?"

"Don't ask me, but we do it. I'll show you."

The skinner was a Freon-cooled drum to which the skin was frozen long enough for a blade to flense it off. When I saw it, the machine was being ministered to by two men whose blue suits contrasted with the greens and whites of everybody else.

"Maintenance," said Tanya. "When they move in, everyone else backs off." Ron, the guy I'd met in Port McNeill who'd set this tour up, must have trained this crew, a kind of SWAT team injected onto the floor every time there was a problem. Time down was money lost; no wonder the other workers kept out of the blue-suits' way.

Like the fish that were sold in the round, the fillets were layered in a rectangular Styrofoam coffin, buried under an avalanche of ice from an overhead hose, capped, shrink-wrapped, and palleted for the waiting trucks.

"Some of it even goes to Japan," said Tanya as we shrugged out of our smocks. "For sushi." The product was obviously about as fresh as you could get without catching the fish yourself. But what happened to all that waste I'd seen flying around in there? And where did the water come from?

"It's all local fresh water," said Tanya. "And we built a three-million-dollar wastewater plant to deal with what comes out the other end. We're pretty proud of that."

"What about the guts?"

"We donate it all to a local pet food maker. Truck it over to him."

I felt dazed. The noise, the ceaseless storm of deconstruction we'd just passed through, now this comical image of a truckload of guts and gills sloshing across Port Hardy, it was all starting to get to me. I'd cleaned plenty of fish in my life; when I was a graduate student trying to measure liver enzymes in trout, I briefly became a one-man gutting machine in the service of science. This industrial-scale processing was something different, and it seemed to me that the millions of years of evolution that had resulted in such a superb eating and reproducing machine were being tossed aside every time the saw dropped into a salmon's belly. All those exquisite systems for propulsion, fuel supply, long-distance navigation ripped out in seconds and spat into the cat-food truck. It was like jumping up and down on your iPhone.

But there wasn't anything going on here that anyone could rationally object to, and the opponents of salmon farms were usually silent on the topic of high-paying, reasonably secure jobs. But this wasn't the part I was being hired to assess. The real problems caused by farms were outside the controlled spaces patrolled by Ron's blue-suited SWAT team, out where the perturbations that came from growing an alien species at high density in local ecosystems were complex, hard to predict, and even harder to study.

We thanked Tanya and stepped out into the bright, natural light. Charley was waiting in Gwen's truck. He began yipping ecstatically.

"He didn't chew your seats up, did he?" I asked. "I'm not sure where he stands on salmon farms."

"Nah," she said. "Piece of cake."

Gwen drove us back to Port McNeill, where the wind had picked up even more. With that wind behind it, the little ferry would fly back to Sointula. On the way through town, we passed Phil's chandlery.

"At least we never have to see that guy again," I said to Hatsumi. "Two more days, and we're around Cape Scott."

But I was wrong.

When we got back to Rough Bay, we found a message on my cellphone. It was from Chris.

"What?" said Hatsumi, watching my face as I listened. "*What?*"

Two months after the horrendous surgery to remove his esophagus, a scan had shown new shadows in my friend's liver. The surgeons hadn't gotten everything. The chemotherapy that had started just as we left on our trip had been called off. To go around Cape Scott and back down the other side would take another six weeks. All I could think of was the gutting machine and the eviscerated salmon with the wobbling shred of its torn-off esophagus. Esophageal cancer was a bad one. I cried; we both did.

"We have to go back," I said.

"I know."

I dialled, listened to Chris's voice, left a message: we would return to Port McNeill tomorrow, buy provisions, and ride the northerlies back down Johnstone Strait. If we pushed hard, we'd be home in two weeks.

"Dave and Nancy are here, you know," said Hatsumi.

"They are?"

Where had we last seen them? Burial Cove, another portent. But I could do with some calm, something Dave seemed to exude. We walked over to *Sanctum*, leaning into the gale, and it looked cozy in there; the portholes glowed, and I could hear voices. I leaned over to rap on the hull.

"Can we do this?" whispered Hatsumi.

"They're friends," I said. And they proved to be, again, pulling us down into the warmth of the cave of the cabin, where a daughter and son-in-law were helping finish off the remains of dinner. Cookies and tea materialized.

"We thought you'd be long gone," I said.

"Ah," said Dave. "Water pump. Started dribbling just after we left you. It hasn't gotten any worse, but it hasn't gotten any better either. And I don't fancy losing my engine. I ordered a new part."

"Which came today," added the son-in-law.

"But it was the wrong one," finished Dave. "Another one is supposed to be coming tomorrow. I'm going over to Port McNeill to pick it up."

"If it comes," said the son-in-law.

Nobody seemed much perturbed. "We'll be over there too, tomorrow." I explained about Chris. Dave just nodded; outside, the wind whined in *Sanctum*'s, rigging and the boat fretted against her fenders. But I felt better.

Sometime that night, the wind blew itself out. When I slid the hatch open the next morning, the sun was just climbing up behind the comical wheelhouse of the tug beside us. The black and white tabby padded over to the tug and vanished. The groaning, shifting dock of the night before had become solid again. It was going to be a beautiful day, even if we were about to turn back.

"At least *our* water pump isn't leaking," I called down to Hatsumi, who was boiling water in the galley. "I should probably do an engine check, though. Won't be a minute."

Vera is unusual, for a sailboat, in that you can actually get at the engine from the top. I unscrewed the bronze fasteners in the cockpit floor and lifted the heavy inspection hatch.

"Oh, fucking hell."

"What? *What*?"

"Fucking, fucking hell." I lowered the hatch again and screwed it firmly in place. "Now we *really* have to go back to Port McNeill. I hope they have a good mechanic there."

The engine compartment looked as though someone, some gremlin, had soaked a rag in engine oil and whirled it gleefully around its head. There was a splash circle of oil that went up the sides of the boat and down into the bilge. It looked a little like Saturn's rings. The epicentre seemed to be at the driveshaft coupling, which I'd fixed just before we departed from Victoria. Or thought I'd fixed. Only a day before, I'd been imagining my father's feelings when the shunt he'd inserted in Billy had to be removed. The mess in my engine compartment was the maritime equivalent: fluids where they weren't supposed to be.

"Can we move?" said Hatsumi.

"We have to," I said. "It's only thirty minutes to the other side. We can get parts there, everything. We'll be right at home."

Then I remembered Phil.

Leaks

This latest breakdown wasn't the first time I'd been reminded of the weird parallels between boating and brain surgery. A few months before we had set out on the trip, as the weather softened and the lists of provisions and contacts lengthened, *Vera* had developed hydrocephalus. At least, that's how it seemed to me. I was on my knees in front of the engine, doing a routine check for loose connections, suspicious-looking hoses, horrifying black lakes of oil. Instead, I found seawater beneath the engine, not a lot, but there shouldn't have been any. I traced the rivulet up the cold grey metal of the engine block, under the fixed-up water pump, and toward the radiator, feeling for moisture like a doctor palpating a chain of lymph glands. The moisture started at the seawater inlet to the heat exchanger. The cooling system had sprung a leak.

Most modern marine inboard engines have two complete fluid circulation pathways, one seawater and the other fresh. Only the fresh water actually penetrates the engine and cools it, before passing the heat to a separate stream of cold seawater.

The hand-off happens in the heat exchanger, a honeycomb of tubes (full of seawater) surrounded by a bath of antifreeze. It's elegant — just like in the cerebrospinal fluid circulation of the brain, an inner and an outer system fitted together — but, like the cerebrospinal system, it's prone to leaks and blockages. Sometimes, antifreeze or seawater gets loose; sometimes, the cooling tubes get blocked up with salts and the engine over-heats. Based on my examination, my engine might have both problems. I could hear my father.

"This is going to be really expensive."

"Thanks a lot," I said. "I thought you were dead." This was the second time he'd piped up. The first had been in Baynes Channel, as we spun helplessly in the current.

"You're going to have to operate. And you need a second opinion."

He was right. I knew I couldn't do it alone. Even wrestling the heat exchanger off would need two people, and removing such a big chunk of an engine is really only exploratory surgery. You *will* find something frightening inside. Knowing this, I called Chris, for whom "been sailing all my life" is actually true. Chris, it may fairly be said, loves boat engines.

"I can't even get the bolts loose to look inside," I told him. "Stripped, rusted, you name it."

"*Ho!*" he said. "We'll have to take it off!" He sounded delighted.

"It's big," I said. "I think it connects to the exhaust system too."

"All of it! Off! Where are you?"

"On my knees in front of it."

"I'll bring my biggest wrench."

Chris and I blowtorched rusted bolts loose, knifed off mushy rubber hoses, drained lurid green antifreeze that looked like alien blood, and finally had the whole mess out on the dock. It looked like the aftermath of an accident between very old vehicles. The heat exchanger itself was fine, needing nothing more than a new set of rubber seals; the "something frightening" turned out to be the exhaust elbow, a cast-iron cocked arm that twenty-five years of seawater had turned into a pitted, russet lump. It was quite attractive, in an artistic kind of way. When we put it in the vice and leaned hard on the wrench, the quarter-inch-thick cast iron cracked like a dried-out wooden bowl.

"That's a shame," said Chris. "At least it didn't happen while you were in Johnstone Strait. What was the name of that Yanmar dealer?"

"Willi," I said.

Willi's replacement elbow was $379.

"Cast iron is hopeless anyway," said Chris. "We'll make one out of stainless steel."

To get this far — parts strewn around my basement and Chris's shop, the engine stripped, rags stuffed in its exhaust ports — would already have cost several thousand dollars if I'd taken the problem to a shop. Now we were contemplating a custom-built stainless steel exhaust. Chris began to doodle a design on a piece of paper, like the upraised arm of a Balinese dancer. He handed me a list of parts.

"These two" — he pointed to a connection at the top, a small stovepipe where the water would be injected — "have to be TIG welded. Take them down to Leach Machine Works." He tossed the old elbow into the garbage.

"It was bound to fail, you know."

Over the next week, I cleaned, buffed, and painted the heat exchanger and drove around town looking for stainless steel elbows, sleeves, and nipples, pacing myself so as not to get ahead of the daily design refinements that Chris was coming up with. He kept changing his mind.

"Better make that an eight-inch hose nipple," he would say. A nipple is a piece of pipe with male threads on each end. They didn't resemble any nipples I'd ever seen.

"And some nice anti-rust paint." Only Chris says things like *nice anti-rust paint.* "Your engine is disgusting."

"You want me to paint my engine?"

"Scrub it with solvent first. Use a toothbrush. I'll lend you my compressor to blow it dry before you paint. Just think, all that grease and rust gone. It'll be lovely!"

I couldn't paint my engine until it stopped raining. Instead, I drove out to see Willi and collect as many gaskets and hoses as he could provide. The rows of yachts tied up outside his shop looked miserable, their decks stained green with winter's inevitable algae.

"How was Patagonia?" I asked when I stepped in out of the rain.

"Like this," Willi said, gesturing at the rain running down the window. "Weather was the shits." He cracked open the thumb-smudged Yanmar parts list and led me into the inner sanctum where his stock was kept. For an ordinary person, it was an ordinary place: racks, boxes, things dangling. For someone whose engine was in pieces and who couldn't afford to pay a repairman, it was dangerously exciting. Hundreds of fan belts hung from hooks in the walls, and the ceiling was festooned with refurbished bronze propellers, their blades whorled from the polishing wheel. Cardboard boxes held gaskets of every conceivable size, like stencils created by a madman. The one I needed was $25. Willi found an old plastic container and threw in the parts as he located them: O-rings, rubber seals, copper washers. Now Willi's voice came from within a cardboard box, where he was rapidly flipping through plastic sleeves of gaskets, like a librarian going through an old-fashioned card catalogue.

"What about that elbow, you gonna buy the new one?"

"Making one out of stainless," I said.

Willi emerged and gave me a long look. "Oh, ya," he said. "Good idea."

The last stop before reassembly was the machine shop where

the parts would be welded together. "What's TIG welding?" I asked.

"Tungsten Inert Gas." The guy was in his twenties, in a green shop suit and lip ring.

"Well, can you tungsten-inert-gas these?" I held up an elbow and a small section of pipe.

He took the pieces behind a curtain of vinyl drapes and reached for his welding helmet. I looked around Leach Machine Works. Another young guy was setting up a chunk of metal in a milling machine, adjusting clamps and taking measurements with calipers. There were three other massive metal-working machines in the shop, one of them the largest lathe I had ever seen, not quite as long as *Vera* but close. The chuck alone — the rotating clamp that holds the piece of metal being spun and shaved — was as big across as a bicycle wheel and eight inches thick. "Made in Czechoslovakia," the smudged nameplate said.

While the first guy welded and the second fiddled with his clamps and calipers, I nosed around. The world is full of machine shops like Leach's, places where you can turn a driveshaft on a monstrous metal lathe or weld a trivial little spigot onto a stainless elbow — and everything in between. I wandered into the cluttered office and was pleased to see an adding machine in the middle of the desk. The man at the desk wore coveralls, like everyone else.

"Do you get many people dropping in with stupid little projects like this?" I waved toward the flickering light at the welding station.

"All the time," he said. "Sometimes it's a pain, yeah, but basically we like people coming in with odd jobs. Keeps us connected, you know? That was the way my dad always did business."

"So this is a family operation?"

"Four brothers," he said, gesturing vaguely toward the shop. I poked my head outside again: the man at the milling machine did look a lot like the person I was talking to.

"Dad sold it to us. We pay for it in instalments, so it funds his retirement."

Four brothers, all sorted out by a father who seemed to have known exactly what he was doing. And my own father couldn't get even one of his three children interested in medicine.

At the milling machine, the job had finally gotten under way, the spinning cutter eating steadily into the solid metal that one of the Leach brothers advanced carefully into the path of the blade, each hand caressing a knurled knob that moved the work left or right, up or down. A continuous jet of cooling water drenched the point of contact and flowed down over the work into a collecting pan beneath. A shiny helix of metal grew out of a tendril of smoke and dropped to the floor, joining thousands of other waste metal coils that gave the place an after-the-ball look. A window slid open above the office and a man in green coveralls and a ball cap grinned and waved at me with an apple. Another brother?

When the vinyl curtains parted again and my exhaust elbow emerged from its trial by fire, it was still warm. A bomb-proof bead of stainless steel cemented the two parts.

"Are you happy?" I asked the guy who had welded it.

"I am. It'll last forever."

"It's for a boat," I said.

"That's different." We both laughed.

Reassembly was anticlimactic. New exhaust system, new hoses, new O-rings, bolts, and clamps, and new antifreeze — everything drew together like those movies of exploding buildings run in reverse.

"Aren't you going to fire it up?" asked Chris. He peeled off his overalls.

"I'm nervous."

"For God's sake."

I turned the key. The engine snuffled, cleared its throat, and hoicked seawater out the stern as though nothing had happened. *Vera* was fixed, for now.

Mechanics

An hour after discovering the oil leak, we were back on the dock in Port McNeill. This looked like a no-brainer. Oil in a circular pattern came from something that was spinning. The only candidate was the driveshaft — except that I'd pulled the coupler apart two months before and cleaned out all the gunk. Mind you, I'd paid a mechanic in Victoria to put it back together because I didn't have the special tool needed. But how difficult was it to tighten four bolts?

I picked up the phone to call the mechanic who'd done the job, and it rang in my hand.

"Don't come back." It was Chris. "Absolutely not."

"But I thought . . ."

"A little rot in the bilge? Ha! We've already got an appointment with another oncologist, in Vancouver. I'm fine, never felt better. Finish your trip."

"Yes, but . . ."

"No buts."

"I mean, we *can't* finish our trip. Not until I get the engine going again."

"Now *that* sounds interesting. Tell me everything, but quickly. We have to leave for Vancouver. I'll think about it on the way."

Next, I called the mechanic in Victoria.

"Impossible," he said. "No way oil can come out of that coupling."

"But it *is*!" I said. "You owe me a little time on this one!" I had paid him four hundred dollars.

"I'll think about it," he said.

Port McNeill was full of fishing boats. They all had diesel engines. I buttonholed a water taxi operator and scribbled down two names he gave me. When I called, both were booked solid.

"A week, maybe more," said one. "Or you could try Phil, over at the chandlery. He's got a mechanic."

Phil.

It was Friday. Phil was terribly busy. He didn't show any sign of remembering me or the thousand dollars I'd spent in his store a few days before. If anything, the place looked even more chaotic. I insisted.

"Come with me," he said. I trotted into a loading bay. Time sheets were fixed to the wall. Phil stabbed one with his finger. "Booked solid. See?"

"I know, but . . ."

"Come here." Phil led me back to the service counter and picked up the phone. He stared into space and narrowed his eyes, as though there might be another diesel mechanic hiding behind a ceiling tile.

"Look," he said suddenly. "I've got a gentleman here, his engine's throwin' oil off the ass end. Gotta be the seal needs replacing. You'll have to drop the transmission."

"It's not the seal! There's a brand new seal in it!" I bleated. Phil put down the phone. He continued to look over my head.

"My guy doesn't work Saturday. But he's making a concession. Eight thirty tomorrow, at the dock-head."

The woman who manned the cash register approached and tugged at Phil's sleeve.

"*What?*" he said.

Dave arrived later in the day on the ferry from Sointula, and I walked with him to the parcel depot, which was in the lobby of a motel at the top of a steep climb. I sat outside on the curb and watched the ferry inch back to Sointula. Dave came out empty-handed.

"I guess it was too much to hope for," he said as we trudged back down the hill. He didn't seem fazed by the prospect of spending half his holiday waiting for an engine part. Clearly this was someone I could learn from, on many levels. When Dave thought something was funny, he let you know, but in a sideways fashion. Loud laughter or lamentation seemed equally foreign to him as though, after a lifetime spent moving people and their things around the coast, *anything can happen* was something he felt in his bones.

"I had a friend once," he said, as though reading my thoughts, "he used the phrase, *eagerly awaiting the next disaster.*"

"What happened to him?" I couldn't help asking.

"Lost him to cancer," Dave said, as though reading my thoughts again. He left on the next ferry.

The wind rose again in late afternoon. A sister ship, identical to *Vera* but much newer, entered the harbour and tied up a few fingers away. The owners found me staring morosely at our greasy engine.

"I admire you," the man said. He was shivering, in a red Port Townsend hoodie. He looked like a miserable goblin.

"We had a terrible time getting here," said his wife. They

were both in their mid-thirties; she had the lean, pinched look of a dedicated runner. But not a sailor, apparently.

"The wind was horrible, on the nose all the way. Are you guys going around the island too?"

"If I can fix the engine," I said.

"That's why I admire you," said the man. "I wouldn't know what to do. I'd probably call 911."

"Would you mind sailing along with my husband?" the woman asked. "He has no mechanical skills."

I didn't know what to say.

"She's flying back home tonight," said the goblin. "I'm continuing on my own." He looked at his feet. "I guess."

We agreed to meet later that night, go over the planning he'd done for getting across the Nahwitti Bar and around Cape Scott. I realized with a shock that I'd been so tied up with axe murderers and hemorrhaging engines I'd given no thought at all to the make-or-break question of *when* we would cross the bar. But if the engine got fixed tomorrow, we'd be sitting in Bull Harbour twenty-four hours from now, listening to the surf and gnawing our nails. A chat with Patrick (the goblin's name was Patrick) might be good for both of us.

His wife hurried off to meet her seaplane and Patrick trudged over to the laundromat to download weather forecasts.

"I still can't decide," he said later when I visited him on his boat after dinner. There was a pair of street shoes aligned neatly on the side deck. Unlike *Vera*, which looked strenuously inhabited by two adults and a dog, there were no towels clothespinned to the lifelines, no sandals jammed beneath the wheel, no dangling underwear. Patrick's boat looked as though it had just come out of the mould.

He handed me a notebook. "This is what I figured out, when to cross the bar," he said. "As far as I can tell, we'd have to go in the middle of the night. To hit slack tide."

"Or not at all," I said. He looked terrible, and his calculations seemed way off.

"I'm totally freaked out." He looked at me imploringly.

"Maybe you should sleep on it," I said. "I'll drop by before breakfast, and we can talk, okay?" I felt sorry for Patrick, but I hated being put in a position of responsibility. I had enough troubles with my own inexperience, my own motley crew.

"Okay," he said.

But by seven o'clock the next morning he was gone — almost. I caught up to him just as he was casting off.

"Couldn't sleep all night," he said, fumbling with the engine. Last night he'd looked miserable. Now he looked desperate. "I'm gonna go out there, then decide whether to go north or south." I didn't think there was much question which direction he'd choose. He gunned the engine, swung helplessly into the boat behind him, then scraped noisily along its entire length, removing teak and fibreglass, until he was free. South for sure, I thought. We never saw him again. When I got back to *Vera*, Hatsumi was up, standing in the galley in her pyjamas. She had a serious look on her face.

"That dream again," I said.

"Mmm."

"Who *is* this dead guy, anyway?"

"I can't see his face. He's lying on his stomach."

"Hey," I said, brightening. "Maybe it's Phil!" But she didn't laugh.

⌇

Phil's mechanic was named Danny. He showed up an hour late, a friendly forty-year-old whose complicated explanation for his tardiness I only half-listened to. In my experience, mechanics blame lateness on (a) their other clients or (b) their families. I waited until he'd finished the story about his daughter's hockey practice and pointed to the perfect circle of oil around my shaft coupler.

"It's engine oil, all right," he said, rubbing some between a finger and thumb. "But no way can it come from that joint."

"So where's it coming from? And how does it end up in that circular pattern?"

"We'll just have a look-see." Danny had an easy, aw-shucks manner that almost had me believing he knew what he was doing. He carefully wiped the engine clean and peered hard at it.

"Lookin' for leaks," he whispered, as though the engine might pucker up at any moment. I peered hard too. Even Hatsumi popped her head up through the companionway and had a look. Danny ran practised fingers over the Yanmar's ridges and bumps, like an eighteenth-century phrenologist. He sat back.

"It's coming from around the air cleaner," he said. I felt the air cleaner; it was bone dry. "You just can't see it," he reassured me. "Believe me, some of these oil leaks, well, you just *never* see 'em. Here's what I want you to do."

He took out a pen and sketched a complicated tube and bottle reservoir I could use to measure the amount of engine oil coming out of the exhaust breather hose. "Do it yourself. It'll save you some money." I liked the sound of that. Danny packed up his rags and spray bottle of engine degreaser and heaved himself out of the cockpit. He hadn't actually used any tools. "Let me know how it goes," he said. I'd had twenty minutes of his time.

It took me two hours to find the supplies and rig up Danny's bypass gizmo. The sun got warmer, boats started to leave. On my way back from the auto supply store, I stopped at the chandlery, where my bill for Danny's services was miraculously typed up and waiting. Two hundred forty dollars. Phil stared at me impassively.

"This had better work," I said.

But it didn't. When I ran the engine, Danny's test device stayed dry, and brown oil still flew off the shaft coupling.

"For God's sake," I said. "We paid two hundred bucks for — what was that anyway? A consultation? I'm going to have another word with Phil."

I muttered to myself all the way back up the hill to Phil's kingdom. What, I asked myself, actually happens to men like him when they finally lose their crown? After a career of staring down the opposition and terrorizing your staff, what happens when you retire? When things start to go wrong? When you're crouching in front of the doctor doing up your pants and trying to get your head around the terrible news he's giving you? Well, I already knew the answer to that one; I'd watched my father boil over in a dreary hospital corridor and seen the hollowed-out look he had when he realized nobody was listening anymore.

But Phil wasn't retired yet. He heard me out, staring as usual at the ceiling. His face worked. Was I finally getting to him, reaching the little kernel of decency that surely even Phil retained? He turned on his heel and began to walk away.

"Come with me," he said.

"No." I got around in front of him. He was a big guy, that was part of his power. I had to look up.

"Phil," I said, "I just paid you two hundred forty bucks for a mechanic's opinion. Which turned out to be wrong. And now I can't even get hold of *him*." It was true, I'd tried his cellphone twice; I'd have done anything to avoid having to deal with Phil again. "So, what am I supposed to do *now*?"

Phil looked down at me. Then he looked away.

"My friend," he said, "here's the way I see it. You've reached a point where . . ." Phil thought for a moment. My heart thumped. Phil was going to apologize. He was going to refund my money. He'd met his match.

". . . a point where, well, you've just got to decide what you're going to do next."

I marched out of the store. The four batteries I'd pushed

uphill to save Phil the trouble of collecting them were still stacked by the door. The phone rang in my pocket.

"I know what's wrong with your engine," said Chris.

"Where are you?"

"Vancouver. New doctor. Now listen. It's not engine oil. It's transmission fluid."

"I know! It has to be! Just, nobody will believe me!"

"They don't know how to think," said Chris. "The transmission fluid wicks past the new seal because there's a screw thread on the shaft. Then it collects inside the coupling."

"Until there's enough that it starts to fly out?"

"Exactly. The same thing happened to me. Here's what you have to do."

Hatsumi and I took the shaft coupling apart, doubled like contortionists and working opposing wrenches. Just for fun, she carefully sniffed a sample of the oil that had escaped and compared it with a known sample of engine oil.

"He's right, they're not the same."

When the coupling came apart, a little lake of foul-smelling transmission fluid poured out. Following Chris's instructions, I cleaned the mating surfaces with acetone and a toothbrush while Hatsumi walked back to Phil's shop to buy a tube of gasket cement.

"No way I'm going back there," I said.

When she got back, I filled the cavity with bright blue gasket goop, plastered the mating surfaces, and bolted everything back together. By the time I'd finished, my knees were dancing from being folded up so long. I didn't even worry about whether it would work; I *knew* it was fixed.

That evening, as I walked Charley, we passed a couple of Kelsey Seafoods reefer trucks being loaded with halibut. He darted off to sniff at the seawater pouring from the tailgate. The last of the light behind the green hills of Malcolm Island turned the Coast Mountains into a wavering purple line, like the tracing of an uncertain heartbeat. Charley raced around behind me, playing keep-away with a plastic Listerine bottle and a dog three times his size. I still liked Port McNeill; even the dogs were friendly.

But we were finally on our way. A pit stop in Port Hardy and then a half-day run to Bull Harbour, where we would undoubtedly encounter a gaggle of nervous yachties obsessing about the best time to cross the Nahwitti Bar. We'd join them, we'd figure it out, we'd do it.

Waiting in the Dark

Port Hardy was where we got the first whiff of what I call the fisheries smell. Not fish smell, which, when it exists, tells you the product has already gone bad. What we smelled at Port Hardy, and at many harbours on the west coast after that, was actually the smell of fresh guts. In Port Hardy, where we tied up at the end of the Quarterdeck Marina, it came from both sides: the sport fishermen at the marina and the processing plant at Keltic Seafoods, across Hardy Bay. Wherever the smell originated, Hatsumi hated it. For a while, she held lemon slices to her nose. Then she tried tying a wet cloth around her head. Then she just pulled the hatch closed. But Charley was in heaven.

Keltic Seafoods was the latest incarnation of a processing facility that had been rolling with the punches of west coast fisheries since 1966. After a large food company closed it down in 1999, laid-off employees and local investors resurrected the place, which was now processing whatever came in the door: turbot, pollock, sardines, dogfish, shellfish, halibut, salmon. The sporties stuck with salmon and halibut, and Port Hardy was the first place where I began to get an inkling of why the sport-fishing lobby was beginning to be listened to.

For years, commercial fishermen had suspected that the salmon fishery had fallen off the regulators' table because, statistically, it simply didn't pay anymore. In economic terms, commercial salmon fishermen weren't worth worrying about. It was a vicious circle; once the resource had dwindled far enough, the incentive to spend money on research and management dwindled too. I doubt if it was a conspiracy, but it looked like good news for sports fishermen, who pumped more dollars into the economy.

Or so they claimed — everybody claimed something. All I knew was that, in Port Hardy, the fish guts came at us from both camps. The thrum of charter seaplane flights bringing fresh sportsmen from Dusseldorf and Duluth went right through *Vera*; my teeth buzzed. When we walked into town, we passed a party of sportsmen embracing for the camera in front of Codfather Charters, their fat salmon laid out on the dock.

"A good day's work!" One of them fist-pumped a beer. There was shoulder-punching. Further on, another charter group clustered around a gutting table, joshing while their guide worked through a queue of salmon corpses with a fillet knife.

⌒

Early the next morning, when I took Charley ashore, the docks were coming alive with coffee-clutching sport fishermen heading out for the first bite, stamping their feet and coughing while their outboard motors rattled in clouds of vapour. Hatsumi and I had argued about the Nahwitti Bar the night before; maybe I envied these sport fishermen, who were just out for a good time in local waters, catching their limit and turning back for drinks and congratulations. Things weren't always so rosy with them though, as we would learn firsthand in Winter Harbour a week later.

The hot fishing grounds were just around the corner from Port Hardy, and we counted twenty-two boats already strung out at Duval Point, before the straight run northwest up the gut of Goletas Channel. As usual, the wind was on the nose, and we powered away from the anglers into fifteen knots of it, past grey gravel beaches under a grey sky. Even the trees looked grey, and the only signs of life were eagles and a couple of dolphins. Four months earlier, when there really *was* nobody out here but the occasional commercial fisherman, a sharp-eyed Canadian forces patrol plane crew caught a pair of smugglers on infrared-radar video. The miscreants ferried thirty-seven hockey bags stuffed with more than a tonne of cocaine from their unlit sailboat to one of the islets *Vera* was crawling slowly past. The sailboat and its crew were nabbed in Port Hardy. They had come all the way from Panama.

For a few minutes, the sun appeared over what the newspaper reports had called a "remote stretch of British Columbia coastline," and every wave that smacked *Vera*'s bow created its own little rainbow. But by the time we found the entrance to Bull Harbour three hours later, it was raining and the headlands loomed in and out of a thin, dispiriting fog. For the first time, we began to feel the Pacific swell, the water rising and settling uneasily beneath *Vera* as we turned and headed into the long notch that almost bisected Hope Island. The end of Bull Harbour, I had already been told, was so close to the northern shore of Hope Island you could hear the Pacific breakers hurling themselves at Roller Bay. We groped our way in.

"At least there'll be other boats there," I said. "We'll hang out, talk to them, see when they're going over the bar."

I was talking to Hatsumi, but really I was reassuring myself. And I needed to, because Bull Harbour wasn't full of yachties. There was only one other boat, a bedraggled forty-foot cement ketch from Ucluelet, its stern festooned with fat, faded fenders. We anchored within easy rowing distance, turned off the engine, and listened to the susurration of invisible surf. Six houses and an enormous satellite dish guarded the spit that separates Bull Harbour from the open Pacific; apart from the public dock on the east shore, there was no sign of habitation. The fog thickened. A loon called. You could hear a pin drop.

"I'm going to talk to that guy." I could see the man in the other sailboat fussing with his main mast. "Coming?"

Hatsumi shook her head. I bundled Charley into the dinghy and rowed over. Except for the beach that fronted the houses, the shoreline was clotted with moss-hung cedars whose lower branches extended over the still water in a kind of shroud. Gerry Schreiber was sanding his mast and touching up paint spots. He was alone. It didn't take long to realize that he knew a lot more about these waters than I did. He had to — he'd arrived the day before from the north, after working his way clockwise around Cape Scott. He planned to spend the next few weeks cruising in the Broughtons, then go back the way he'd come — the way we were going now — all the way to Ucluelet. With an itinerary like that, he had to be knowledgeable. Or crazy.

"It's my holiday," he said. "I do it most years." He was full of stories, and on closer inspection, his boat wasn't shabby at all, just eccentric. The mainsail he was working around looked brand new.

"So, we're heading across the bar tomorrow," I said. "As far as I can tell, it won't be windy." I desperately wanted to come out and ask him, *what should we do?* But pride and the image of poor spooked Patrick high-tailing it out of Port McNeill kept me from disgracing myself.

"We thought we'd take the inside route." I permitted myself this overture, at least. The inside route was becoming the popular alternative to actually crossing the bar itself; if you tucked in close to the rocks, found the right spot, and threaded through the kelp along the shore, you could sneak past the bar on the inside. This meant you could time your departure from Bull

Harbour so that you reached Cape Scott at slack tide. You didn't have to play the zero-sum game of trying to cross both the bar and Cape Scott at slack, which wasn't physically possible given the top speed of most boats. In my pre-voyage preparation, I'd read more and more accounts of people cutting through along the shore.

But not Gerry. "I've never done it," he said. "Just make sure you get to the cape at slack."

That seemed to be all the advice I was going to get. I repackaged it for Hatsumi, who was sitting morosely in the cabin with the tide tables and a bottle of wine in front of her.

"Good news," I said. "We're doing the right thing. He agrees, Cape Scott is the critical one, so all we have to do is make sure we hit it as close as possible to slack tide."

"Where are all the other people?" she said.

"How would I know? Now, what time is slack at Cape Scott?"

"Nine o'clock tomorrow morning," she said. "Look it up yourself."

I must have looked it up a dozen times already. I knew it was nine, and I knew the Nahwitti Bar would be slack even later, at ten or so, but we'd decided that didn't matter because we had just taken the bar out of the equation. Instead of being caught between a rock and a hard place, we'd eliminated the hard place.

"We'll have to get out of here by five," I said. Twelve hours to kill. A gillnetter came through the gap, tied up at the public dock, and blasted its horn. Five minutes later, we watched a pickup truck pull out from one of the houses and reappear at the dock. Unloading ensued, then another blast, and the fish boat took off again into the rain. After dinner, I rowed Charley to the dock to try to get him to pee, but he only patrolled the beach, toying infuriatingly with sticks and rotting crab shells.

"You're going to regret this," I told him. "Tomorrow morning, forget it, we won't be stopping until the end of the day." I even urinated myself, spattering the rocks to give him the idea, but he just sidled away. He wasn't the only nervous mammal around here.

Before going to bed, we wrestled the dinghy onto *Vera*'s foredeck, tied it firmly down, and set the alarm for 4:45.

"Are you nervous?" asked Hatsumi.

"No," I lied. "Anxious to get going, though. It seems like we've been thinking about this damn bar for the last month. I'll just be glad when it's over." Then, still hedging, I said, "We'll listen to the weather forecast tomorrow morning and take it from there, okay?" I crawled into bed with the portable VHF radio and tried not to listen to the faint thunder of the waves in Roller Bay. Charley curled up at our feet, and Hatsumi mumbled something into her pillow.

"What?"

"Maybe I'll have a panic attack," she said.

I lay back and tried everything. Counting sheep. Counting fish. Meditating. A glorious morning, magnificent Cape Scott saluting us. None of it worked. So I got up again, got dressed, lit the oil lamp, and sat down with someone who knew all about rocks and hard places. I'd been through the three acts of Billy's travails. Now it was time to raise the curtain on a different play: my father's trial.

~

Billy's family was officially upset in 1976, when the first shunt was put in. The evidence of just how upset they were arrived at my father's house in an envelope, dated December 5, 1984, an early Christmas present. Billy was now nine; my father was seventy-four.

There were four defendants: three doctors plus the Victoria General Hospital, but my father's name was first, and that's the way all the publicity would go. The writ claimed that most of

Billy's problems at age five resulted from injuries to his brain and nervous system over a four-day period when he was ten months old (the Labour Day episode). It was the classic "bad baby" lawsuit: doctors' negligence causes brain damage that's responsible for the child's later problems.

Next to the copy of the writ was a letter from the Canadian Medical Protective Association, which told my father what to do next: write a narrative account, "from first to last." Just what a retired surgeon would love to do. But he had the narrative ready in a week, plus his old office files. Whatever was in those files, it was all he had to go on, because he didn't remember a thing about Billy. That wasn't surprising; it would be like asking a retired mechanic to give you the details on the brake job he did on your 1976 Volvo.

The next letter in the file was from his new lawyer, Mr. Thackray, directing him to think harder about what, if anything, passed between him and Dr. Beamish on the morning Billy stopped breathing. Right from the start, the LP that Dr. Beamish did that night was critical. My father shot back, "I do have views about lumbar puncture in general, and this one in particular." In other words, "not a great idea." Over the next year or so, documents kept coming in, and the correspondence between doctor and lawyer got fatter. Finally, they had dates: examination for discovery in a year, followed by trial a year after that. In all, three years of waiting and worrying and trying to remember.

Examination for discovery — was there ever a better name? A prospective witness is sat down with his lawyer and peppered with questions from the other side's lawyer. That's the examination part. The *discovery* comes about in the way the witness answers or evades. Weaknesses emerge (are "discovered") and become the basis for a trial strategy. Examinations seemed to me to be the first opportunity for advocates to enter the ring, circle cautiously, and begin to take the measure of their opponents.

Discovery transcripts can make surprisingly entertaining reading, and I had six of them. My father's was the fattest, a spiral-bound inch of paper; Billy's mother's weighed in at about half of his; Dr. Beamish the lumbar puncturer's was slimmer still. Then two nurses (down to about a quarter of an inch now) and finally the slimmest of all, for the third doctor, a perfunctory thirteen pages. I read that one first.

Poor Dr. Parsons. Billy wasn't even his patient. Dr. Parsons had been covering for Dr. Beamish. He would have been in his mid-sixties when he was suddenly asked to look at a vomiting hydrocephalic boy, putting him in his seventies when he found himself in a closed room with two lawyers. His stonewalling was almost comic. Maybe he really didn't recall, maybe he just didn't care.

Plaintiff's lawyer: "I take it you can't recall whether you ever discussed this patient with Dr. Harvey during the day?"

Dr. Parsons: "Mm, mmm."

Dr. Parsons's lawyer: "I think the answer is no."

Dr. Parsons: "No."

Both lawyers: "No."

Nobody was going to shed much light on the "failure to monitor" question from this corner. The last words were, "Thank you, Dr. Parsons. You can go back to Sooke — I mean Sidney." I could almost see the lawyer rolling his eyes.

Billy's mother's examination was done before my father's, so I decided I'd better read hers next. I tried hard to be impartial, to keep my composure. But my own highlighter was out by page 9:

"If anything went wrong with [Billy], he could help me get a so-called normal child and said he would be a vegetable and not to expect very much when he came home."

That didn't sound like anyone I knew, and doctors don't talk about vegetables. Anyway, he would have been pretty wrong if he had, because on the very next page Billy's mom was describing her son as "very verbal and photogenic." He had even appeared on TV. Next came the odd assertion that my father had told her Billy "wasn't hydrocephalus." That sounded like another clanger to me. Her feelings about doctors came out easily:

"I still do feel victimized by doctors. . . . When I adopted Billy, I was told by no doctor that it was a risk to adopt this little boy."

Now that, I knew, wasn't going to stand up. The pediatrician's warnings about hasty adoption were on the record; I'd read them.

None of this interview can have been pleasant. The mother did her best to present some pretty traumatic events while Mr. Thackray painted a picture of marital breakups, a single mother working in what she called "a laundry situation," a boyfriend that came and went, frequent moves. But she stuck to her story that my father "said Billy is not hydrocephalic." Nobody suggested his head size was large, even for a premie? I counted six instances of "not that I can remember" in two pages.

Point by point, Mr. Thackray compared her statements with the written record. Billy's mother stuck to her guns. And she wanted to tell the story of Labour Day. Everything had been fine, fine, fine, up until the Labour Day mess. The fretting, vomiting baby, the long weekend stretching out, the hallway vigil, and the elusive doctors. And finally, the early morning news that "Dr. Harvey wants to put the shunt back in. I told him Dr. Harvey couldn't touch him without I saw my boy."

But by the time the anxious parents reached the hospital, Billy was in the operating room. "The nurse came up to me and said to me that I don't want to upset you but don't expect him to come back." And, "approximately two weeks later this black intern, I don't know his name, he said to me I was here the night everything went wrong with Billy and I just want you to know that your little boy fought for his life and I have never seen anyone fight for his life like that little sick boy did."

It got weird. News travelled. A nurse's grandson's wife spoke to Billy's mother. The grandson's wife was Billy's mother's friend. I was having trouble following.

"Things went wrong," the nurse's grandson's wife said. And the nurse herself (this would be the grandmother, I think), said that "they left him unattended and uncared for." Nurses who had cared for Billy flocked to "say goodbye" to him because they were "all told that night they didn't expect Billy to live." But, unfortunately, no names. Even the nurse who "sat her down," explained everything, and got her started on the idea of a lawsuit didn't seem to have a name.

And so back to my father, who, Billy's mother said, "never called me back." At the hospital, "he would walk right by me. He wouldn't even say hello. The nurses explained to me he has a terrible bedside manner and he is embarrassed."

Embarrassed? The only time I ever saw him embarrassed was when one of our boats hit the dock.

Finally, as the waiting and watching dragged on, there was a telephone conversation, when "things got a little bit verbal. That's when it was brought up that Billy was a vegetable. I made a comment back that if my son died, I would be at his back door with a shotgun and then I hung up."

The reporters had loved that one. The vegetable and the shotgun, I still remembered the headlines. And asking myself, "Why not the front door?"

Now the examination turned to life after Labour Day, entering the minefield of Billy's precocious "verbal ability." For Billy's mother, this meant that he was "quite a chatterer." For Mr. Thackray, Billy's appearances on local radio talk shows, and articles about him in the newspapers, seemed to be evidence of a parent open to the idea of a little publicity for her exceptional child. For him, a little ode that Billy wrote (it was called, "My Mom") and managed to get read over the radio, was unlikely to have been penned by a carrot.

On and on it went . . . and then it just petered out, at 111 pages and four hours. It wasn't flattering to Billy's mother. There were plenty of inconsistencies with the written record. The mutterings of "the black intern" and the nurses were unverifiable. The most charitable thing you could say was that Billy's mother had made up her mind to adopt a struggling, premature infant and that no amount of alarm-raising was going to undo her confidence in him.

But the unflattering portrait and the inconsistencies weren't what would decide this case. Billy had brain damage. His mother loved him fiercely and had shouldered his care for a decade. He'd nearly died on Labour Day, and there were expert witnesses prepared to say that the actions of at least one of his doctors were ill-advised. The fact that so many of Billy's problems were textbook examples of the effects of lack of oxygen at birth wouldn't mean much in the face of all this emotion. My father and his science versus Billy's mom and her shotgun? I seriously wondered if I should bother to read the rest.

So I didn't, not that night. Hatsumi and Charley were both fast asleep, cuddled under the duvet. I could hear them breathing gently. I did a quick check for dead men on the floor and went out on deck. Bull Harbour was still as the grave and completely fogged in. Roller Bay breathed heavily in the night, like a giant biding its time.

A sailboat alone in a strange anchorage in the middle of the night can be a little island in a sea of wonder, but tonight, Bull Harbour was a frightening place. Standing on *Vera's* deck, the anchor light the palest of moons in a halo of mist, I felt intensely alone. Maybe reading the words of my father's accusers hadn't been the smartest thing to do, but it might have helped bring us a little closer. He probably read the same account in his overheated study, surrounded by his books and his music, but I'm willing to bet the experience placed him in a private little Bull Harbour of his own. We both had a tricky passage coming up.

Crossing the Bar

River bars are dangerous. The United States Coast Guard has actually created regulated "navigation areas" for all coastal river bars in Washington and Oregon, with warning signage that can include flashing lights and radio bulletins when conditions are especially unsafe. Both New Zealand and Australia are notorious for river bars, and people of a morbid bent can choose from a long list of YouTube compilations of boats fighting their way through fields of standing waves, shooting into the air or wallowing sickeningly before pitchpoling end over end. Most were filmed by onlookers on land, but the camera still shakes. I never looked at them before we left on our circumnavigation, and when I see them now, I always think, Well, at least you can see where you're going before you turn upside down. Because when we found ourselves on the Nahwitti Bar, it was still dark, and the fog was so thick you couldn't see the next wave.

Bars are created when rivers that carry a lot of sand dump their contents into the ocean. As someone who had written a book called *The End of the River*, I might have been expected to know a lot about river bars, but I didn't. In that book, I was more concerned with the body of the river and the fish in it, and what happened to rivers when you dammed them or dumped waste in them or sucked most of their water out to grow lettuce and grapes. The meeting place between river and ocean was a special case, and the only one I'd ever paid much attention to was the São Francisco River in northern Brazil, where a chain of dams had had the paradoxical effect of actually intercepting a lot of the silt that would normally have made it to the ocean to form a bar.

The unlucky São Francisco was being strangled; the Nahwitti River clearly wasn't, and it had a formidable bar. Even before we'd reached Bull Harbour, back in Goletas Channel, the evidence of the bar had appeared on our depth sounder. Goletas was a freeway, unobstructed and deep — a monotonous three hundred metres. At that depth, *Vera*'s depth sounder gave up trying to read an echo off the bottom; it just blinked "Last" over and over, as though to say, "Why don't you just turn me off? You're not going to run into anything. There's nothing down there but hatchet fish and ooze."

But, just after Bull Harbour, Goletas ends abruptly. The bottom jumps up at you. "*Whoa!*" goes the depth sounder, waking up with a start. You've just stubbed your toe on the Nahwitti Bar.

And that shallowness is the problem with river bars like the Nahwitti. Not because there isn't enough water for the boat to float in — *Vera* needed around five feet, and the Nahwitti Bar never got that shallow. The problem arises because the water over the bar is in nearly constant motion. First, there's current, which is the net movement of water and reflects the state of the tide. Second, there's wind, which pushes the surface water ahead of it. And finally, there's swell, the long rollers that have travelled across the Pacific to end up at the mouth of the Nahwitti River. All three of these water-movers combine to guarantee a net directional flow of water over the shallow bar.

Why does this matter? Because when moving water encounters a shallow spot, it gets stuck, dragging on the bottom and falling over itself. On a beach, the onrushing waves get bigger and bigger as they drag more and more, and then they break and collapse. If they're big enough, you can ride them on a board. Over a bar, the same thing happens, producing what would look, from the air, like a beach without a shore. Breaking waves, surf, the lot. If you go across when wind, current, and swell gang up, you'll be in trouble.

Around the Nahwitti, even a cursory look at the chart told me it would be shallow — thirty to fifty feet — for at least two miles after we first tripped over the leading edge, which would happen shortly after we exited Bull Harbour. But there was another fifteen miles to go, around the top of Vancouver Island, before we would round Cape Scott, and it was relatively shallow there too. The water wouldn't start to get deep again until we were through the turbulence that was marked by the cheerful little wave symbols on the chart. The place was a boater's worst nightmare.

～

And now here we were in the middle of it. Once our illusions about the "inside route" had been rudely snatched away and I'd made the idiotic decision to chance the bar at the worst possible moment in its tidal cycle, it took us thirty minutes to grind over it. By then, I was puking water. Even throttled back, we were making eight knots as the current helped push us up and over each wave. *Vera* was like a cringing dog kicked from behind. Down below, lockers opened and vomited out their own contents: cosmetics, a bottle of chili sauce, lemons. Hatsumi hung onto the chart table, and I hung onto the wheel.

Finally, the oily rollers ahead began to look less threatening. I found I could change course, get us pointed closer to the direction Hatsumi kept calling to me. On one of my trips to the rail, I looked up after vomiting over the side and saw a sea otter on his back not twenty feet away, feet in the air, an incurious look on his whiskered face. "Don't look at me," he seemed to be saying.

Once we were over the bar, the character of the sea changed. The waves behind us had seemed deliberate, focused, implacable, but now we entered what so many writers have described as a "confused" sea. It's a good term. Around Cape Scott, in fact anywhere close to shore along the west coast, the Pacific swell has begun to catch on the bottom, and to twist this way and that in response to local currents. It's not the lazy roller coaster you envision when thinking of an offshore voyage. It's more like a washing machine.

For the next three hours, *Vera* lurched past the invisible shore while we struggled to keep our footing. I vomited some more. When my bladder would hold out no longer, I urinated down the cockpit drain, or at least in its vicinity. There wasn't a breath of wind. I put *Vera* on autopilot and finally sat down, clinging to a lifeline and sipping the coffee Hatsumi had made four hours earlier. From time to time, a tiny seabird would bob in and out of the mist, riding comfortably. "This is *our* place," they seemed to be saying.

We rounded Cape Scott at nine o'clock, exactly at slack tide. "How about that?" I said to Charley. But we never saw land. An hour or so later, holes in the fog revealed islets, kelp beds, a white flash of surf, before closing again. Finally, a rising wind began to chase the clouds and fog away, and we were able to sail listlessly past Sea Otter Cove and south toward Quatsino Sound, the first of the rock-speckled entrances to the long fjords that cut into the west coast. But it was poor sailing, and the boat rolled sickeningly. When we encountered a pack of sport-fishing boats around the entrance to Winter Harbour, around lunchtime, we took the sails down and powered the rest of the way.

Hatsumi collapsed on a cabin berth and went immediately

to sleep, surrounded by a jumble of foul weather gear, boots, trampled charts, and lemons. A packet of my father's documents had broken loose from somewhere, littering the cabin floor with scholarly articles. After sloshing away the remains of vomit and urine with a bucket of sea water, I sat down in the cockpit and looked around. The folly of what I'd just put us through began to settle in. How many foolish decisions had been made by intelligent, well-prepared people who thought they had every base covered? We had been in real trouble back there, and it was my fault.

I was too tired, finally, to care. And as for not actually seeing Cape Scott, to hell with it. Even the name, it turned out, was a disappointment when I looked it up later in Walbran. This Scott was hardly the hero of the Antarctic; instead, he was a Bombay merchant who helped outfit a British sea-trading expedition in 1786. No matter, we were finally "around the corner."

〜

Winter Harbour isn't technically the end of the road on Vancouver Island, but it's probably the most northerly settlement you can drive to fairly easily — it's straight across the island from Port Hardy. That made it perfect for sport fishermen, who could haul their boats across on trailers, tie up at the dock for a few weeks, and sleep in a tent or one of the small fishing lodges. Nothing fancy, but Winter Harbour was where I finally realized how big the sport-fishing business was.

The smell was the giveaway. There it was again, the sickly reek of fresh intestines that emanated this time from a cleaning table and weigh station on the next dock. The public docks were ramshackle, a listing, cobbled-together collection of blind alleys supported by logs and littered with bleached and crumbling plastic furniture. Seagulls fought over offal, and the bloated, pop-eyed carcass of a red snapper circled endlessly between the docks. *Vera* and the only other large boat, a converted fishing vessel full of good old boys from Washington, were tied to an eroding concrete slab anchored by absurdly long pilings: the tides in Winter Harbour were obviously huge. The tops of the pilings were bearded with grass.

By mid-afternoon, the docks began to repopulate as fishermen streaked in from the grounds, often several miles offshore, where they'd spent most of the day. The two main lodges, Outpost and Qualicum Rivers, relied on twenty-foot open aluminum boats with a rudimentary cabin like a telephone booth. Bench seats, two big outboards, no radar — in the hands of a competent guide, a boat like this got the customers out and back quickly, but at the cost of a fearful pounding. If the weather blew up, they would be sitting ducks.

While Hatsumi tried to sleep off the effects of my decision-making, I sat in the cockpit as the fleet filed past *Vera*'s stern to tie up at the lodge's dock. Winter Harbour felt like a grand place. It was the first safe haven we'd seen for ten hours. We spent a second day there, waiting, as usual, for good weather, but also just to avoid making any decisions. Our dock was managed by one of the charter companies; in their rudimentary store, I asked one of the men from the big Seattle boat whether the fishing was good.

"Oh, excellent." He nodded enthusiastically. "We're getting so many, it's all catch and release for us now. But hey, they're all Washington fish anyway, you know?" He pronounced it *Warshington*.

This was a common refrain, sung by both sides: American fishermen were convinced Canadians were catching "their" fish, and vice versa. With five highly migratory salmon species heading for home rivers from Alaska to California, there was a lot of mixing going on. These guys were probably right, but claiming ownership over a fish that spent most of its life offshore seemed kind of small-minded to me.

"Well," I told him, steering clear of the ownership issue, "if you get one that doesn't make it, we'll take it off your hands."

Two hours later, the man appeared at *Vera* holding a bloody bag containing a thick fillet of chinook salmon. We salted half of it and ate the rest raw, thinly sliced, with ponzu sauce and grated onion. Canadian or American, it melted in our mouths. When I went over later to thank the men again, they insisted I join them for drinks. Their boat was called *Miss American Pie*. We sat around a big table, where the four men fed me whiskey and skillfully extracted information. How old was I? How many times had I been married? Marriage seemed to be a favoured topic.

"I been through three old ladies," said one. Another of the men, returning from a walk to the single pay phone that everyone lined up to use, shook his head in wonderment.

"The wife, you know what she actually said? She misses me!" He adjusted his ball cap and started in on a beer. "No, wait. She said, 'I wish you were here.' I guess that's not the same thing, huh?"

Probably the missus didn't really know where Winter Harbour was. When I'd gotten through to family members on the same phone, more than one had said, "Winter Harbour? I'll have to look it up." That wouldn't last; three days from now, everybody with a TV would know where Winter Harbour was.

We drank. Before the alcohol completely dulled my senses, I came to understand that the four men had fished together since elementary school. One of them showed me photographs of grandchildren with buzz cuts; he was the successful one, who'd bought the *Miss American Pie* off the quietest of the three, the one who was tending the barbecue and refilling my glass. *He* had been a commercial fisherman. It sounded like a weird relationship to me, loaded with simmering resentments, but they all seemed happy enough. Tomorrow, the skipper told me, they would head up to Sea Otter Cove, which we'd passed, unseen, on the way down. But they wouldn't go around Cape Scott.

"Not in this boat," he said, flipping a side of salmon.

I made an excuse about tending to my own wife and stumbled out, followed by knowing, manly laughter.

The next day, we wandered along the old boardwalk that ran in front of the few houses in Winter Harbour. The weathered cedar was springy underfoot. All the houses had their own small docks and cleaning stations. One was hung with a collage of rusted implements: a paintbrush, a buoy, some chain. The bulk of the visitors had created a village in a cleared area behind the Qualicum Rivers Lodge; in the evening, the smell of grilling salmon and steaks hung over a collection of tents and trailers. We saw a few wives, but this was mostly a guy thing.

We followed the path to the exquisite cobble beach at Botel Bay, but it was late July, bear-fattening time. After passing too many piles of fresh-looking bear scat, we collared Charley and headed back to *Vera*, where the only other mammal was the sea otter who hung out near the dock, crunching crabs and urchins. The day went by. Water rose and fell, the shelving beach covered and uncovered. I sat in the cockpit and read.

"I guess we have to go tomorrow," I said, putting down my book. "And we have to decide about the Brooks Peninsula." Brooks was the next major challenge. "Do we go around it or not?"

There wasn't any answer. I peeked below. Hatsumi and Charley were asleep again, cuddled like lovers. It was still only late afternoon, and I'd had my rest. Time for another dip in the pool of pain.

⌇

Why not see what the nurses had to remember? The outcome might be a foregone conclusion, but this was still a detective story, and the nurses were important characters. I dug out their examinations for discovery, which were slender. Maybe there was something in there, even a snippet, about the questions that had been nagging me since my marathon slog through the hospital records in Port McNeill: Where was my father on Labour Day, when Billy started to go downhill? What did he know, and when?

Nurse Chambers was first, and Mr. Thackray got little from her beyond establishing that in 1976 it was *not* standard practice for a nurse to record whether a doctor came to see a patient. She remembered little about her regular shift the night before Labour Day, including whether she made any attempt to contact Dr. Harvey (in fact, the record says she did, at 10:30). Was she the nurse who showed Billy's mother her notes? No. She didn't remember any details of Billy's "fight for his life."

This reticence wasn't surprising when you remembered that the hospital itself was also named in the lawsuit. Nurses were part of the hospital, so I didn't expect them to stick their necks out.

And so to Nurse Wong. *Her* recollection of the number of calls to Dr. Harvey was "at least five." Alas, none of them were recorded on the chart. So the only known attempt was Nurse Chambers's call, which she herself didn't actually remember.

That left Dr. Beamish and Dr. Harvey. In the best detective-story tradition, I decided to leave the star witness for last, so I started with the luckless pediatrician who'd been called in to cover for Billy's regular doctor over the Labour Day weekend.

Dr. Beamish certainly had his own voice. To the opening question, "Are you a defendant in this action and sworn to tell the truth?" his answer was, "I guess so, yeah." He didn't remember much of what happened in 1976 (none of the doctors or nurses did; Billy was one of thousands of patients. Dr. Beamish couldn't even remember if Billy was a boy or a girl). But his opinion of Billy's condition before surgery was the same as mine: prematurity, early respiratory problems, a suspiciously large head, and intraventricular hemorrhage.

Then the examining lawyer went straight to the night before Labour Day. What was Dr. Beamish worried about? Infection and increasing pressure. Examining the child's eyes was difficult, but he found papilledema, swelling of the optic disc. This could mean increasing pressure inside the brain. The problem was, Billy's symptoms could have also have been caused by infection, which was the reason the shunt had been removed in the first place. Which was it, pressure or infection? Maybe both?

I could see his reasoning. You take the shunt out because it's infected. That might easily cause pressure to build. But then again, the pressure could be caused by the original infection. So he waited and watched. He doesn't remember whether he called Dr. Harvey.

"From my notes, I would think that, ah, there was still some time, there's still time that I, I can wait."

But things got worse. Dr. Beamish returned at 5 a.m. to confront a seizure, dilated pupils, no response to pain. Dr. Harvey arrived soon after, so "I assume I did call him." That would make sense: Beamish returns, sees things starting to slide, calls my father sometime between 5:00 and 5:30. Dr. Harvey arrived just before six.

But into the tiny gap between those two events, the phone call and my father's arrival at St. Joe's, lumbered the elephant that wrecked everything — as far as the lawyers were concerned. Because Dr. Beamish hadn't just waited and twiddled his thumbs. He'd done a lumbar puncture. Immediately, the plaintiff's lawyer pointed out that an LP is contraindicated when there's evidence of increased pressure. Dr. Beamish's answer, not unexpectedly, was that the benefits outweighed the risks. He'd done the LP to check for meningitis. He couldn't recall whether he discussed it with my father, now pulling on his pants in the bedroom with the phone cradled to his ear.

The cerebrospinal fluid he withdrew through the LP was clear, meaning, "I would say it's not an infection." So the problem *was* pressure. Great — but then Billy stopped breathing. They got him started again, then Dr. Beamish put a needle through the burr hole in Billy's head to reduce the pressure (a procedure called a ventricular tap). A lot was happening, and fast.

Where was my father? I checked the timing in the hospital records. Dr. Beamish arrived at 5:00 a.m. The LP was done at 5:10. Breathing stopped at 5:30. The life-saving ventricular tap was done at 5:45. And my father arrived ten minutes later. If those timings were reasonably accurate, there would have been time for a quick phone call before the LP, and a longer one after it, but there were no records of any. The ventricular tap was probably being done as my father stepped into his car. We didn't live far from the hospital. By the time he arrived ten minutes later, Billy was responsive again.

Of course, Dr. Beamish couldn't remember any of it.

⤳

It had been a horrible day. My little floating family had survived a stupid snap decision I'd made in the fog and dark of the early hours yesterday, so today probably hadn't been the best time to go back to the early hours of Labour Day, 1976, and poke again at the people who'd been forced to make a judgment call of their own. I was exhausted.

But we'd made it, and Billy had too. I didn't know then how our experience going across the Nahwitti Bar would affect me later but, based on what I'd learned so far about Billy's struggle, the decisions made by his doctors and nurses on Labour Day seemed a lot smarter, more reasoned, and definitely more professional than my own.

All Alone with Nowhere to Go

For the sailor, the western side of Vancouver Island has four major navigational challenges: Cape Scott (behind us now, thank God), Brooks Peninsula (coming up), Estevan Point (south of Nootka Sound), and finally the seventy-two-mile stretch between Barkley Sound and Victoria. The first two are the worst, and the fear factor recedes as you go south. Estevan Point is a smaller bump than Brooks, and the long day back to Victoria is a worry only because all of the anchorages on the way are in bays where you wouldn't get a good night's sleep.

The Brooks Peninsula and Estevan Point are classic headlands, and they do the usual unpleasant headland things to sea conditions. Brooks was especially notorious for making mariners miserable, and even the most cursory glance at a chart tells you why. While most of the west coast of Vancouver Island is perforated by long inlets (the one we were sheltering in now, for example, cuts almost all the way across the island), Brooks protrudes *ten miles* into the Pacific, an almost perfectly rectangular shelf defended by cliffs. It's a geological afterthought, accessible only by boat and helicopter. To me, it looked like a particularly ugly mole, the kind of thing you have to watch out for when you're shaving.

The Brooks Peninsula messes everything up, catching and bending the Pacific swell, getting in the way of currents. The air mass following the contour of Vancouver Island has to play catch-up around the Brooks Peninsula, which means that the weather forecasts for the area often end with the caveat, "except Brooks Peninsula." Going around Cape Cook and Solander Island, the outermost corners of the peninsula, the wind speed frequently doubles. The day I'm writing this, in late November, there's a storm warning out, which is bad enough (thirty-four to forty-seven knots) that nobody in their right mind would leave port. But the caveat for Brooks Peninsula is "hurricane force warning" — an unimaginable sixty-five knots.

That day, the forecast was for fifteen knots, rising to twenty-five at Cape Cook. We decided to try it. We left Winter Harbour in mid-morning, hours after the sport fishermen but taking the same route many of them would follow into Brooks Bay. If Vancouver Island was your side, and the peninsula a cocked arm, Brooks Bay was an armpit, and in a northwester, it became a trap. We had such a wind, and we dithered as we got closer, heading far enough offshore to avoid the five o'clock shadow of rocks that guarded the coast but not committing to Cape Cook either. *Vera* seemed to appreciate the chance to sail, and we lurched south under the big genoa jib, struggling to get used to the swell that had begun to lift us as soon as we left Quatsino Sound. It was sunny and clear, and Brooks Peninsula was visible almost immediately, a green panhandle with a mane of brilliant white low cloud.

That cloud rang a bell.

"Take the wheel?"

I clambered below and dug out a weather manual for Vancouver Island. "A 'cap' on the Brooks Peninsula," the book cautioned, "usually means a gale is coming." *Vera* rolled south, settling into the first decent sailing wind we'd had since before the gale that blew us into Loughborough Inlet. For a while longer, I could still see the distinctive cone of Solander Island guarding the tip of the peninsula before the island, then the rest of the whole promontory, began to slip behind the clouds. Now *Vera* was really flying. The sea whitened. We wound the genoa into a half-reef, Hatsumi wrestling with the wheel while I threw my weight into the winch handle and tried not to somersault over it when the boat rolled.

Then the peninsula disappeared.

"Those guys who gave us the salmon the other night," I said. "They said there was a spectacular anchorage this side of the peninsula. Want to have a look? Try Brooks again tomorrow?"

We both wanted to. By the time we made it to Solander Island, it would be a full gale, probably with zero visibility. So we altered course, heading for the armpit of Klaskish Inlet while trying to keep from being driven into the cliffs. By turning east, we were putting ourselves on a lee shore, a situation that always makes me touchy. "Don't you get it?" I would snap to Hatsumi in our first year of sailing. "We're going *sideways*. It's a goddamn lee shore."

I didn't have to snap at her now; we were too busy threading the rocks, and she now knew as much as I did about lee shores. Two orcas cruised past as we closed in on Klaskish Inlet, and a momentary white flash dead ahead looked like a third.

"You're off course," said Hatsumi. That white flash was Hughes Rock, more than two miles off the coast. I began to wonder whether I liked navigating out here. The entrance was clotted with islets, and although our new GPS told us exactly where we were, I clung to an atavistic need to see for myself, using a much-folded paper chart to match up the landmarks with the lurching landscape. The navigation light I was searching for on shore turned out to be a spindly thing on a pole, more like a garden light than the white-painted concrete tower I'd been looking for, but once we'd passed it, the wind was blocked, and we motored cautiously toward what one of the guidebooks called "the best-kept secret on the west coast" — Klaskish Basin.

It was like going up a river. The entrance to the basin was almost invisible until you were practically in it, but the cedar-lined channel was deep. When it opened up, we were alone in what might as well have been a lake. We anchored across from the only conceivable landing for Charley, a trickle of stream with just enough of a clearing that I could run the kayak next to a rock, let him off, and float around until he'd done his thing or gotten eaten by a bear. The broad estuary of the Klaskish River, moss-green and open beneath an old clear-cut, was too far away to reach by rowboat. We were enclosed by forested hills shot with the silvered trunks of fire-killed trees, like a greying beard. And we were very alone.

We sat in the warm sun while Charley snapped at horse flies. A big jet crawled overhead, a sparkling point of silver trailing twin contrails. Where was it headed? Tokyo? Hong Kong? I thumbed through Captain Walbran's book. Klaskish Inlet had been named seventy years before the Brooks Peninsula; back then, the inlet was known as Port Brooks (to the English) and Puerto de Brucks (to the Spaniards Galiano and Valdes). On the matter of what the Indigenous peoples called this lonely spot, or what use they had made of it, Walbran was silent.

I swatted flies and thought about these long-ago explorers and how they stumbled into this place — on August 5, said Walbran, so the weather would have been similar to today's. Had they too been taking shelter? I imagined their ship anchored uneasily outside while her boats felt their way along the riverlike seam, then the hours of careful soundings before the larger vessel cautiously followed. They must have towed her in.

We tried to round Brooks the next morning, despite a gale warning and an ominous report of thirty-five knots at Solander Island by 4 a.m.

"It's *always* thirty-five at Solander Island," I said peevishly. We'd gotten up early, made coffee, secured the lockers. Outflow winds barrelling through the mountains at the head of the inlet had rocked *Vera* all night. "What the hell, let's try it. We can always turn around."

Outside Klaskish Inlet, the wind was already rising at 6 a.m., and by the time we'd sailed an hour, clawing slowly toward the peninsula that was invisible under a grey, depressing sky, *Vera*'s decks were awash, and it would clearly be another two hours before we could even think of making a wide, cautious turn around Cape Cook. It was a simple enough problem: we had to backtrack, almost into the wind, to get enough sea room to avoid being crowded onto the uncaring face of the Brooks Peninsula. With the wind rising as the day went on, the safety margin would just keep shrinking.

"So much for that," I said, turning *Vera* up through the eye of the wind and all the way around onto a broad reach. She galloped back to Puerto de Brucks like a dog racing for home, but our spirits sank as we dropped the anchor and shut down the engine. It was as silent as the grave. And still only eight in the morning.

"Breakfast?" I said brightly. But Hatsumi looked defeated.

"We'll try again tomorrow," I said. I didn't tell her that something else was worrying me. When I'd started the engine, the first push of the button had produced nothing but a faint click. One thing at a time, I decided, although a failing starter circuit was the last thing we needed out here. Sails were nice things to have, but an engine could keep you off the rocks.

"No people," said Hatsumi in a small voice. She handed me a fried egg. "Drives me crazy."

"No kidding. Not exactly Kugayama, is it?" From Kugayama

to Klaskish Basin: there was a dislocation. But I couldn't find any way to make it better for her.

"We just have to learn to wait," I said lamely. It was true, though. Getting around Brooks Peninsula — like getting around Cape Scott or through Johnstone Strait — was a fight, a lopsided one. The only way you could expect to win was to look for your enemy's weakness. In our case, that meant waiting for a break in the weather. So we listened, on and off throughout the day, to the Coast Guard broadcasts on the VHF radio, infuriatingly faint in our closed-in little world.

VHF weather reports follow a script, of which the actual forecast is only a part, and not always the part you're desperate to hear. Often, the real-time report from a lighthouse or a weather buoy is what you base your decision on; in this case, the Solander Island light was what mattered. So we sat glued to the crackling radio as *Vera* swung slowly at anchor and the signal built and faded, waiting out the reports for all the places that didn't matter, grinding slowly through the list of "local and lighthouse reports" until finally — *finally!* — here it was:

"Solander Island. Winds northwest whistle *pop grrr whooshhh . . .*"

The silver jet crawled across the blue dome of our prison. Same time as yesterday, probably the same destination and the same plane.

"Come on, Charley," I said, heaving myself up. I released him on weed-covered rocks and floated in the shallows while he snooped around. It was warm again. Flies buzzed and the cedars released their summer smell. Again, the idea that we were anchored in an alpine lake was hard to shake. But the moment didn't last long. By lunchtime, the fog began to settle into the basin, sifting down over our little bowl until only the lower branches of the trees were visible. *Vera* ceased swinging and the place became unearthly still and silent.

"Ahhhh-*choo!*"

It was more a roar than a sneeze, and there weren't many people who sneezed like that. It was strangely muffled too, and I had to look hard in the direction of the sound until I could spot him. He was standing in the clearing where I'd taken Charley to pee, holding the red-and-white checked jacket around himself like a blanket.

"We could talk to *him*," said Hatsumi.

"You can see him?"

"Of course I can see him."

"It's lonely here," called my father. That's what he'd said, every day, near the end. "What are you doing in this terrible place?"

"I don't want to talk to him," I said.

"Then turn on the shortwave radio," Hatsumi said. "Maybe we can talk to someone that way. It's about time you tried."

She was right about that.

"I'm trying to get us out of here," I called. "You had a shortwave radio, didn't you? When you were a kid? Well, watch this."

❧

Shortwave (or "high frequency" or just "ham") radio wasn't found on a lot of cruising boats, but *Vera* had come equipped with one of these dial-encrusted monsters. I'd spun those dials a few times when we first got the boat, randomly intercepting excited whisperings in Mandarin, Colombian pop music, the plummy tones of the BBC, and a lot of pops, tweets, whistles, and dishwasher noises. But I didn't understand the first thing about how it worked, and listening was pointless if you couldn't transmit. To do that, with our particular radio at least, you needed a ham licence.

But determining, unequivocally, that I needed a licence, and finding out how to get one took months. There just wasn't a simple answer. So-called amateur radio (the proper name for ham) might be capable of life-saving, globe-spanning feats of communication, but its practitioners were thwarted by simple English. Finally, I went for the bargain-basement option: buy a study guide from the Radio Amateurs of Canada and pay $25 for a locally accredited ham to administer the 100-question multiple choice exam.

The study guide was an inch thick, not counting appendices on elementary math. How could an inch be boiled down to 100 questions, of which I had to get 80 percent correct to receive my licence? In desperation I turned to the Internet, where I was delighted to find the entire bank of 973 possible questions. After three days cramming, there were still 500 questions I kept flunking. There was only one way to get through this hell: forget understanding everything, just memorize the answers, all 973 of them.

Which I did. Two infuriating weeks later, I tossed my cheat sheets in the recycle box and went to see my examiner, Barry Mann. He met me at the door to his apartment wearing a red T-shirt over jeans and slippers. I wondered if he was a typical ham — the receding hair, clipped beard, and pallor certainly fit with the image I had of people hunched over knobs and dials in a darkened room. I followed Barry into his tiny kitchen, where the exam was laid out on a breakfast table next to a coffee mug jammed full of pencils with plump, virginal eraser-ends. Maybe he anticipated a lot of indecision on my part, or an unusually heavy hand. A Mozart string quartet murmured from a small stereo on a shelf next to a framed sepia portrait of a naked youth, knees drawn up pensively at the edge of a lake. Barry fiddled with an espresso machine.

"No thanks," I said. More caffeine would send me into Barry's bathroom. "And look, I like Mozart, but it's kind of distracting. Those formulas, you know?" I was itching to spill them. Barry clicked the radio off.

"Take your time." He padded silently into another room. I heard the mouse-scampering of computer keys. Thirty minutes later, Barry ran my completed pages through a scanner while a shortwave radio mumbled from one corner. There were radios everywhere, perched on brackets or winking from windowsills and all connected to a Christmas tree of antennae. A cluster of handhelds was arranged next to the scanner like some kind of electronic *ikebana*. I shamelessly snooped in his bookcase while he fussed with the answer-key software.

Barry whistled. "Ninety-eight percent," he said.

Of that 98 percent, I understood maybe 40. We filled out and faxed some forms, and I became VA7BJH, licensed to transmit. A week or so later, I got a diploma in the mail. I didn't frame it. But I *had* written down the frequency for one of the boaters' networks that operated daily, providing a shortwave meeting place for anybody with the right radio and a licence. Now, marooned in Klaskish Basin, I dug out the information: six o-clock, 3,010 kilohertz.

"Here goes," I said. While Hatsumi fried onions, I perched next to the radio, fiddled with the tuner, and listened. And there they were! A moderator, a roll call of sorts, and then a string of little narratives, each from a different boat. An ethereal gaggle of boaters had just joined us in Klaskish Basin. Their voices came from all around Vancouver Island, and most of them were clear and strong, totally unlike the feeble whisperings of VHF. With this radio, I knew, we could as easily listen to someone in Fiji, but being connected to these local people, whose reports were edifying, or rueful, or exasperated, was just what both of us needed. Several called from the Gulf Islands, so far behind us now they seemed a distant memory; others were closing in on Alaska.

"Listen," I said suddenly. "This guy's in the Bunsby Islands. That's practically next door!" If the weather showed us its belly, even for a day, the Bunsby group was where we would spend the next night.

"Call them," said Hatsumi. She was grinning now. "Go on, do it. Let them know we're here."

"Well, I . . ."

"You took that course, didn't you?"

Everyone on the Boaters' Net sounded ferociously competent, hailing and signing off with their call signs, relaying each other's messages, even leaving the air, some of them, with the phrase "Seventy-threes, everyone." What the hell did seventy-threes mean? Before I could look it up in the long list of coded signals, Hatsumi nudged me again. I clutched the microphone, waited for a break, and said, reading from my scribbled notes, "Ah, Victor Alpha Seven, Bravo Juliet Hotel." Bravo Juliet Hotel was tricky to say, I found.

"I, ah, don't have you on my list." The moderator sounded puzzled. But he was speaking to *me*! To VA7BJH afloat in a fog bowl and surrounded by frying smells. Barry would have been so proud.

"What's your vessel's name?"

I spelled it out for him, and my own.

"And your crew, who are you travelling with?"

"My *crew*? I don't . . . oh, I get you. My wife, Hatsumi."

"Ah, you're going to have to spell that one for me . . ."

And so we became part of the B.C. Boaters' Net. When I finally signed off, we didn't feel so alone. I looked up "seventy-threes"; it meant "best regards."

The whole experience reminded me of the delight my father had taken, as a boy, in constructing his own shortwave radios and listening hungrily for a voice from England or Australia. In the end, he always seemed to end up with CFCN, the "Voice of the Prairie," but he was as satisfied with that as I was with the B.C. Boaters' Net. I was so happy I climbed into the cockpit to tell him.

But he wasn't standing in the clearing anymore. So instead, I spent the evening reading about him.

The Examination of an Elderly Surgeon

It was pretty clear that the case was going to focus on Labour Day; no matter how provocative the circumstances of Billy's first few weeks of life, this suit was about malpractice and blame. You couldn't pin Billy's prematurity and respiratory distress on anybody, so you had to blame his problems on something else. The lawyers needed something concrete. They chose Labour Day.

I'd read Dr. Beamish's grudging explanation of why he did a lumbar puncture. How he made that decision was a mystery that might only be cleared up by my father's examination for discovery, so that's what I turned to next.

He started out professorial. His lawyer jumped in to remind him not to keep saying, "Right," while the opposing lawyer talked.

Mr. Thackray: "Just try and wait until he shuts up."

Dr. Harvey: "Right."

Billy had "communicating hydrocephalus," something that could be dealt with by a shunt, that didn't involve a tricky tumour, that might or might not turn out to be self-limiting. He was pretty clear about the diagnosis and found it "hardly possible" that he would have told Billy's mother the shunt was temporary. "I can't imagine anybody saying, 'He doesn't need it anymore,' and taking it out."

He wasn't defensive, just confident. And he did go on. Where the other doctors were stingy with information, he tended to expound. Only my father would have described the effect of hydrocephalus on the many bones of the skull this way: "They open out like a flower, you know." He went on for a full page about shunt complications; I could imagine his lawyer twisting in his seat. He seemed so innocent on those early pages, carefully explaining why you had to wait a few days between the ventriculogram and the shunt insertion:

"If you were to immediately shove a ventricular catheter into that situation, you might be getting just air out, for example, and as you know it is not a good thing to pump air into a venous system."

As you know — I loved that. I finally felt I was getting to know him. On why he examined the child daily after the first surgery, he said, "I did the plumbing, you might say, and my chief responsibility was to make sure the shunt was functioning properly."

Why was he being so forthcoming? So entertaining? But once the questions turned to meningitis and sorting out the conundrums of cause and effect (shunt can cause meningitis, meningitis can cause hydrocephalus, a deadly circle), his fuse shortened.

Lawyer: "Was there any additional damage to the child's brain because of the meningitis that developed after the shunt, that you are aware of?"

Dr. Harvey: "There isn't anybody who could answer that question."

I was struck by the elasticity of the division of labour, especially for an infant patient with so many problems and specialists. Here the surgeon deferred to the pediatrician; there, the mechanics took over and it was up to the surgeon to decide what to do. When I read, halfway through the examination, "Dr. Beamish is a far better judge on that than I could have been," I wondered if, by the end of the examination, that deference would be under a magnifying glass and starting to smoulder.

And so we arrived inevitably at Labour Day. The plaintiff's lawyer made much of the timing of Billy's shunt removal ("Could it not have been put off 'till after the long weekend?"), and I wished I could have reached through the pages and into the examination room and said to this man's face, "He didn't *take* holidays. He probably had no conception of Labour Day. Growing up, neither did I."

Lawyer: "What was your procedure for holidays?"

Dr. Harvey: "Just to be there. I was home. It was like any other time. If I had a very sick child on my hands, the holiday weekend had nothing to do with it." That was my childhood.

No time for reminiscing, though, because we were into the nasty stuff now. The shunt was out. For how long? My father answered this way: "The longer you can go, the more likely you are to get a clean field." In other words, once the shunt had been removed, it was a race between dwindling infection and increasing pressure. A race, and for Billy and his doctors, a waiting game while the rest of the city headed for the beach. And so the plaintiff's lawyer probed, and my father carried imperturbably on, so obviously telling the truth that I wanted to reach in there, give him a shake, and tell him: "You can fudge it a little, you know, everybody else does."

"What was your normal practice?" they asked. That he would have checked on the child, that he expected the nurses to call him if necessary. That a visit might be recorded or might not. He could so easily have said, "Of course I visited; there's just no record of it," but he didn't. All he would say was, "It's likely I would have."

He explained the options (there was only one, a ventricular tap to relieve pressure) and the drawbacks (repeated entry through an already-infected burr hole). But "in the presence of meningitis and septicemia, your hand is stayed." So, to determine if the pressure buildup might be due to meningitis, you first had to do a lumbar puncture. When the lawyer asked if he would have been considering these questions at midnight, he said, "I don't even know if I was awake at midnight."

Did he think he was somehow immune from what a skilled lawyer could do with a statement like that? That he was Harvey Cushing reincarnated? The plaintiff's lawyer pressed on about increased pressure and whether my father would have been called or attended. Uncertainties swirled like dust devils. "At some point," my father admits, "the pressure is more important than the possibility of spreading infection by anything you do, so I'll stick a needle into that ventricle and release some of the pressure."

Because the allegation was "failure to monitor," much depended on the understanding between surgeon and pediatricians. The plaintiff's lawyer was determined to know what my father expected in the way of communication.

Dr. Harvey: "I wouldn't expect the pediatrician to go and do something to treat it without consulting me if he thought it was increased intracranial pressure."

Lawyer: "Thank you."

Dr. Harvey: "With one qualification."

Lawyer: "Yes?"

Dr. Harvey: "If it is a dire emergency, if he is there and nobody else is there, then he is going to do the best he can."

There were pages and pages of this. Reading them in this lonely anchorage, where night and fog had now fallen upon *Vera* like a shroud, made me wonder, How alone had he felt, closeted in that room with two lawyers and a stenographer? Was he still defiant, sure of himself and his training? Reading his testimony, I sensed something I had heard so many times as a child that it had become second nature — the physician's credo. My father applied it to everything. It was this: "First, do no harm." He had a horror of making things worse through medical intervention. Dinner-table stories featured ghastly medical disasters where the patient would have been better off left alone. He'd seen too many botched surgeries. "Nature will take care of it," and "Stay away from surgeons," were staples of my upbringing. Once, when I was around ten, I broke my arm falling off a metal grid while scraping the hull of one of our boats. It was two days before he reluctantly took me for an X-ray and a cast. He designed the cast himself, though, so I could remove it when I wanted to go swimming off the boat.

The lawyers couldn't know this; all they saw was a doctor who was content to wait until whichever was worst, the meningitis or the building pressure, showed its hand. He told them clearly: "I was extremely anxious not to interfere. I thought it was absolutely paramount to get rid of that infection. If I did something surgical at that time and the infection blew up again, people would be saying why didn't you — you should have known. You have difficult choices, and this was a difficult choice."

The rock and the hard place. Nahwitti Bar and Cape Scott.

The two lawyers sparred, like hockey players fighting in the corner for the puck, while my father skated reluctantly behind them knowing it would squirt loose and he would have to take another swipe at it. When it did, it was the lumbar puncture that slid and hopped over their sticks as the lawyers tried to determine whether this was where the goal would be scored in the only game that mattered to them, in court. Finally, they agreed that, yes, my father would expect to be consulted if another doctor planned to do a lumbar puncture.

He stayed feisty till the end; he wouldn't give in. A lumbar puncture and stopped breathing "doesn't mean that the prognosis is terrible." He just refused to predict, because, "Well, it goes on forever."

His examination for discovery seemed to have gone on forever too, but it finally ended, with a lame attempt to get him to comment on the mother's accusations about Billy being a vegetable, Billy being replaceable by another child, the shotgun. The newspapers would love these stories when the trial was opened to the media months later, but my father brushed them off. I can even imagine a little smile. It looked like he was ready for a fight.

When I'd finished his examination, I noticed, inserted at the end, a collection of loose-leaf pages covered in a handwriting I realized was his lawyer's. Page and line numbers on the left, notes on the right — here was what the lawyer had made of the transcript I'd just finished reading. A few of Mr. Thackray's notes had stars beside them, all drawn the same: five rapid strokes of the pen to produce a happy and oddly human figure, tilted to one side, one arm lifted to the note it was meant to highlight. Only once does he resort to capital letters, rewriting in full the words of my father: "You have difficult choices, and this was a difficult choice."

Pan-Pan

Early the next morning, the hoped-for chink in the enemy's armour revealed itself: the wind at Solander Island was a reasonable thirteen knots and not forecast to rise above twenty-five. Brisk, but not a deal-killer.

"We're out of here," I said, and although it was foggy (fog and low winds often seem to go together), we knew the way out by now, and by seven, we were already farther than we'd got the day before. Once again, the starter had failed to respond on the first try; once again, I reminded myself that sooner or later it would stop working altogether. The fog kept us in our own little universe until we finally rounded Cape Cook a respectful mile offshore. As predicted, the sea humped and roughened near Solander Island, and the wind increased enough to have us hanging on even when seated in the cockpit. It was as though the invisible peninsula was letting us know it was there, waiting for us to make the slightest mistake. Somewhere off to the left, I knew, there were cliffs that soared straight up into the warty forehead of this improbable land mass; on the chart, I counted fourteen peaks higher than a thousand metres. If we could see the Brooks Peninsula, I thought, it would look like Tahiti.

We did see it, finally, the fog grudgingly thinning once we had rounded Solander. The west-facing shore was all black cliffs and log-strewn beaches below the improbably green hills. There was Banks Reef — could that be Sir Joseph Banks, president of the Royal Society? The man who accompanied Lieutenant Commander Cook, as botanist and naturalist, on Cook's voyage around the world in 1768? We were under power, so I could easily consult Walbran. It was. Solander Rock, which we had finally rounded, turned out to be named after Banks's easygoing assistant, the Swedish botanist Daniel Solander.

It was nice to find a few scientific names among the endless list of British and Spanish naval men and royalty that filled so much of Walbran's addictive book. Joseph Banks became scientific royalty himself, politically unassailable in his later career, with a finger in every pie. His reef, well out from shore, was white with breaking waves, and the rocks looked like the stubs of an eighteenth-century sailor's rotten teeth. It terrified me.

The retreating fog was like a curtain lifting. We began to see seabirds: guillemots and, a first for me, a pair of tufted puffins, their sturdy black bodies an afterthought to enormous orange beaks. They reminded me of the false nose and Groucho Marx glasses we used to play with as children.

Once around the peninsula, the wind fell to nothing and the sun began a long game of hide and seek with holes in the fog. The Pacific swell was more or less coming from behind us now, and we surfed an undulating sea of mercury that, when the sun was out, threw back a dazzling reflection of towering white clouds and blue sky. The horizon, at those moments, became a wavering silver ribbon. *Vera* was on autopilot now, and the motion was lulling and seductive — or would have been had we not entered the stretch of coastline where there were exposed rock pinnacles as much as five miles out to sea. The chart looked as though a waiter had leaned over my shoulder and murmured, "Some ground pepper with that?"

Between the corner of the Brooks Peninsula and the Bunsby Islands, where we had decided to spend a few days, we had to find our way through a minefield of reefs. Some of them we saw, poking evilly into a bank of low-lying fog. Some of them we only thought we saw.

"Oh my *God*!" Hatsumi shrieked. Charley and I jumped. There wasn't supposed to be a rock this close, and definitely not to starboard. But this rock was smooth, and it moved, flexing through the oily surface in a glistening grey hump that was long gone before I could grab the binoculars.

"That was *big*," she said. "Same as *Vera*, maybe more." I found my marine mammal book and keyed it out from the profiles of surfacing whales: it was a humpback, long teetering on the endangered list and now making a strong recovery. I realized that the orcas we'd seen yesterday in Brooks Bay, and now this humpback, were the first whales I'd seen for years that were unmolested by high-speed whale-watching boats. We wouldn't start seeing those again until farther south, in the more tourist-oriented Clayoquot Sound.

We approached the Bunsby Islands through a corridor of sentinel reefs, straining for a sight of something corporeal in this strange, limpid landscape. The fog lifted obligingly to show us the tricky entrance, and by the time we had anchored in Scow Cove, it was hot, and we could smell an intoxicating mixture of ocean and wet rocks and trees. Charley drew it in, quivering.

"Let's go," I said, wrestling the kayak off the foredeck and letting it fall overboard with a smack. "We're in heaven again."

How different this place was from Klaskish Basin, just the other side of the peninsula. Sheltered between islands rather than in a secretive notch, the place felt more open (a bit too open, as we found out later). The cedars still came to the water, but there were humped, mossy rocks too, and enough pocket beaches that Charley and I had our pick of landing spots. I even saw a few oysters, which meant the water got just warm enough for them to spawn. But there was fresh bear scat on this beach too, so we had to be careful.

I squatted over a tide line of rotting kelp on a gravel beach while Charley tossed sticks for himself in sheer exultation at being on solid ground. Higher up, the gravel was infiltrated by sea asparagus, then tufts of grass, then an abrupt curtain of salal and the wall of cedars beyond. A nurse log sprouted its own exuberant ecosystem; the place was teeming with life. Overhead, eagles wheeled and cried, a peculiar fingernails-on-blackboard sound I always found at odds with their heft and power. There were ravens here too.

"Don't go too far," I called out to Charley. Squeaky-voiced or not, eagles had been known to take a run at small dogs. Back in the safety of *Vera*'s cockpit, we spent the rest of the hot afternoon doing all the boat chores that had taken a back seat to navigation anxiety. I transcribed several days' worth of notes, forcing myself to listen to whatever I'd blathered into the digital recorder. Black flies arrived and were snapped at; a shoal of sardines erupted suddenly at the surface, chased by something bigger underneath; six kayakers glided silently past. I baked two loaves of bread, freed up sticking fittings, and nipped a garbage mutiny in the bud.

"It won't fit," complained Hatsumi, on her hands and knees pummelling a large white plastic bag into a too-small opening.

"How did we manage to produce that much garbage?" I asked. "Since Winter Harbour?"

It could have been worse. The first year we cruised, we brought everything ashore: kitchen scraps, tin cans, wine bottles. At least we had now learned to jettison what sank or degraded or could get eaten. We still had to pack our own effluvia around, though, gradually filling the dreaded "holding tank" that every vessel was now required to carry, counting the days and nights until bitter experience dictated we had deposited our fifteen gallons of bodily waste and it was time for one of us (me) to go forward, lift up the mattress on my side of the bed, insert the pump handle, and yank it back and forth until the polyethylene box beneath it was empty. In Canada, you were supposed to be three miles offshore when you did this, but, while I doubt many people let fly in a marina or at anchor anymore, I do wonder how many steam three miles out just to blow their tanks.

That night we contributed a rockfish carcass to the marine recycling service, one of several I'd jigged up absurdly easily from the dinghy. Hatsumi steamed it in sake and ginger and sweet rice vinegar, and for the first time in weeks, we crawled into bed with a feeling of accomplishment, and some relief. Cape Scott and Brooks were done; it was all downhill now. It was a noisy night, though, the anchor chain catching repeatedly on what felt like a miniature version of the Rockies fifty feet below us. We stayed put, because there was little wind, but it still sounded as though Neptune was down there trying to jump rope with our chain.

The real wind came the next day, a northwest gale blowing straight into Brooks Bay. By ten in the morning, our protected cove didn't feel so protected anymore, the wind finding its way in and whipping the water into whitecaps. The chain-grabbing and hobby-horsing became more than a mild annoyance; every now and then, there was a sound like an underwater gunshot, and *Vera*'s bow shook. I ran forward and put my foot on the chain, which was trembling like a live thing. I stared hard at a fixed point on land. My foot began to jump, and the tree I was concentrating on began to walk slowly forward. I raced back to start the engine.

"We're dragging!" I yelled and pushed the starter button. *Click*. Again and again. Finally, it responded. Hatsumi took the controls. We yelled at each other as couples will when their yacht and everything in it is drifting backward onto a remote beach. I got the anchor up, and *Vera* sprinted ahead to find shelter behind the hook of land where we should have anchored in the first place. When the anchor left the bottom, there had been no resistance. It had worked itself completely free.

Once the dust had settled and we had re-re-anchored ("Not there, *there!*"), I spent a frustrating hour tracing the starter system and pulling apart the instrument panel to try to figure out why it was balking. In a sailboat, when you need your engine, you usually need it *now*. Upside down in the engine room, I heard the automatic bilge pump suddenly turn on and found that the stuffing box, the wonderfully low-tech packing of wax-impregnated flax that keeps the ocean from coming in around your propeller shaft, was leaking badly. Entropy was coming at us from all sides. I retightened the packing gland using two enormous wrenches while squatting on the engine transmission, a platform about the size of a loaf of bread.

"Beer would be good," I said. "I'll deal with the starter later."

The wind whistled relentlessly around the cove all day. In Brooks Bay, totally open to the northwest, the conditions would be savage. That evening, the owners of the only other boat in Scow Cove, an aluminum trawler so big I'd taken it at first for a research vessel, putted over and introduced themselves. He was Conrad; she was Kate.

"I heard you on the Boaters' Net last night," Conrad said.

Conrad had made what must have been a fortune in real estate, because he'd designed and commissioned his boat himself. I admired him; his boat was as far as you could get from the usual millionaire's yacht with its marble countertops and flat screen TVs. Conrad's boat was both highly sophisticated and spartan, built to stay out for months, with redundant systems where anything could conceivably fail, and nothing that didn't serve a nautical purpose. I liked Conrad, who, like many powerboaters in their seventies, had put decades into long-distance voyaging under sail before going over to the dark side. I especially liked it when he said that circumnavigating Vancouver Island was a real separator of boaters.

"But, Conrad," I said, "people go to Alaska all the time!"

"Hell, you can go to Alaska in a *kayak*. Around the island — that's different." As for him, he'd already decided to go no farther north than where we were now.

"It just gets worse," he said. "As you already know. We'll probably see you in Kyuquot."

That was fine with me. We hadn't met anyone interesting since the lone sailor in Bull Harbour, and the idea of running into a familiar face as you progress from harbour to harbour is one of the attractions of voyaging.

Conrad and Kate left early the next morning, and we were alone again. The wind had blown itself out overnight, and the fog that replaced it drifted over us like a moth-eaten veil before vapourizing to reveal a brilliant sunny day. A school of sardines flowed around *Vera*'s bow, the occasional silvery back breaking the surface with an audible plop. The only other sound was an odd one for such a place: the thrumming of an airplane, throaty, low-down, and slowly getting closer. The twin-prop de Havilland Buffalo came toward us out of the sun, a few hundred feet up, and went into a tight turn, the light catching the red markings on the bright yellow fuselage. The six Buffalos based in Comox were the coast's search and rescue workhorses, and this one wasn't flying over the Bunsby Islands just to admire *Vera*. Somebody was missing.

I rowed back to *Vera* while the Buffalo completed another circle, then droned and dwindled away to the north. The people inside that plane would know every cove and reef and shipwreck along this grim coast. To them, *Vera* was just a shapely green yacht in an emerald pool; they would be looking for something harder to spot. The Buffalo disappeared in the direction of the Brooks Peninsula.

I switched on the VHF radio. We listened to the forecast together — not much wind, a good day to raise anchor and motor down to Kyuquot Sound — and then came the bad part.

"Pan-pan. Pan-pan." The international signal for an urgent situation, one level below "Mayday." A twenty-foot aluminum "sport-fishing vessel" had failed to return to Winter Harbour yesterday. There were four men aboard. The name of the boat was the *Qualicum Rivers Nine*.

"Qualicum Rivers? That was the fishing lodge right next to us," I said. "We probably saw those guys on the dock."

"They went fishing yesterday?" Hatsumi said. "In a gale?"

"Apparently." I shut off the radio and we looked at each other. Yesterday, the wind had been strong enough to blow us off our anchor, and we were on the *south* side of Brooks, in a more or less protected anchorage. On the north side of the peninsula, in a nineteen-foot boat . . . well, we had turned back once, and it hadn't even been a full-fledged gale.

"I guess we should keep an eye out for them," I said. But I didn't think anyone would find the *Qualicum Rivers Nine*, or its occupants. If the boat had capsized, its wet grey hull would be near-invisible. And even if the men had been wearing life jackets, how long could they last in this freezing water?

We were safe here, and now I felt even less like leaving. I had plenty of "work" to do — there was still about a third of my father's trial papers to get through — but it was getting harder and harder to step back into that morass, especially after we had rounded Cape Scott and seemed to be encountering a new navigational challenge every minute. Hatsumi was feeling the additional stress too and was spending several hours each afternoon plotting out the next day's transit. While I had been plugging through files on hydrocephalus, she had been sitting in front of her computer, surrounded by paper charts, planning our path through the upcoming rocks and inserting waypoints into her navigation software.

I realized that, if something happened to me, we'd lose an expert on medical-legal conundrums from the late 1970s. If something happened to my wife, we'd *be* lost.

"I'll finish it soon," I told her. "Really, I will."

Experts and Apgars

Now that the examinations for discovery and their flashes of high drama were out of the way, I turned to the "expert medical opinions" with dread and what I hoped was by now a thick skin. Here was where the "primary data" in the case got filtered through subsequent interpreters, in the same way a pile of "facts" will be confronted and interpreted by a journalist. In this case, the journalists were doctors. What they had to say was drier than the examinations, but deadlier.

First, I read through the doctors' reports, the summaries of Billy's progress that were prepared as part of a doctor's job, not as an expert opinion for a trial. As I went through them, I had the image of a house in a rainstorm. At first, the water stayed outside. But, as the rain built to a deluge, rivulets found their way over the pristine floor, wobbling and expanding and joining with more incursions from all sides, until the place had become a muddy mess.

The rivulets were errors, small ones, but they built up, so that by the time the lawyers were paying other doctors to write expert opinions, the muddy water was ankle-deep. Little things like: the kind of meningitis was incorrectly recorded; or its date of diagnosis was wrong; or a doctor said the shunt was out for weeks, when it was really days. Reduced vision became severe vision loss. One doctor read what another had written, accepted it, and added another layer of opinion. Very few, it seemed to me, went back to the original records — something I was sensitive about, having just ploughed through them myself.

By the time the paid experts came along, I could see they would fall into two camps: "damage at birth" and "damage by negligence." The first camp couldn't see why you would ascribe damage to later events when there were perfectly good explanations written all over Billy's chart from day one. On the other side were the experts who were more comfortable with a flesh-and-blood culprit. For them, what happened on Labour Day was the straw that broke the camel's back.

There were three opinions for the plaintiff, Billy's mother, and four for the defendants. I picked up the first of the defenders, a professor of pediatrics. His analysis was straightforward: Billy was born prematurely, was slow to breathe, had respiratory distress syndrome, jaundice, meningitis, and hydrocephalus. His brain was irreversibly damaged from birth. He had multiple handicaps long before the Labour Day crisis — just look at his Apgar score.

Apgar score? I went back to the hellish pile of hospital photocopies and found it on page three. I remembered the births of my own children, how their performance in Virginia Apgar's ridiculously low-tech screening (Apgar stands for appearance, pulse, grimace, activity, respiration) had seemed so important. My children's scores, like those of most newborns, were both tens. Less than 1 percent of babies score below seven. Billy was a six, a score that quadruples the likelihood of neurologic disability.

Expert number two for the defence was a pediatric neurosurgeon who had been practising for twenty years. Here were the Apgars again, and a summary of observations on twitching and jerking and abnormal vision even before the first shunt. He too noted all the predisposing factors for brain damage (young mother, prematurity, anoxia). There were poignant reminders of how things had progressed in twenty years: now, a CT scan can tell you far more than a ventriculogram; now, a shunt reservoir can be injected with antibiotics so that you may not even have to remove an infected shunt; now, a CT scan can eliminate the agony of deciding whether or not to do a lumbar puncture. In this neurosurgeon's opinion, difficult decisions were made with the tools of the day and nobody was negligent.

Next up was an M.D. specializing in rehabilitation of patients with brain injuries. His report was simply a picture of the child at the time of the trial. He described the eleven-year-old Billy: myopic and falling frequently, having seizures, with learning disabilities and wet underwear. I had an image of all those clinics and rehabilitation centres I'd never had any reason to visit. All those kids, all those parents, struggling with their own little hell of eternal catch-up that will never happen, while the rest of the world worried about their kids making the hockey team, getting good grades, shouldering a backpack for a trip to Europe.

The last of my father's champions was a pediatric neurologist. He described a child struggling to keep up in school, still having mild seizures. Billy was "insecure and pathetic," epileptic, visually impaired, and with an overall mental age, despite his verbal precocity, several years behind what it should be. Based on the Apgar scores, this expert suspected a brain hemorrhage at birth. Billy had been an already compromised baby — but it wasn't all black and white. There had probably been further damage from the events of "the fateful night." The rise in brain pressure must have had an effect, especially on vision. There was no way around that.

❧

The plaintiff's champions certainly thought so. For them, no way around it meant there was no need to look anywhere else. The reason for Billy's constellation of problems was staring the judge in the face.

The plaintiff's first expert was another pediatric neurosurgeon. This doctor had treated Billy for five years, so he should know him pretty well. He glossed over Billy's perinatal problems and got the kind of meningitis wrong, but what mattered to him were the Labour Day events. The LP, he felt, was just *wrong*; Dr. Beamish, the pediatrician who a different expert described as a life-saver, should instead have done a ventricular tap right off the bat. Maybe Dr. Harvey was called and maybe he wasn't, but the lumbar puncture caused most of Billy's problems.

Billy's family doctor submitted a confusing pair of reports, the second written after a request from the plaintiff's lawyers for something stronger. I'd already run across these. The most intriguing thing about the first version was the two missing pages, the ones that my father's lawyer had finally wrestled from the other side during the actual trial. Comparing the two, it really looked as though she'd switched from one camp to the other, and I doubt if the prosecuting lawyers would have used either of her letters; here was a witness parked firmly on the fence.

The last expert was a professor of pediatrics, another neurologist, and, as it turned out, the prosecutor's star witness in court. His opinion was based on his own treatment of Billy for vision problems. Vision was Billy's "major handicap," he said. The epilepsy and all visual problems were caused by pressure and so was the cerebral palsy. This was the simplest and blackest condemnation. The expert's prognosis, which ran to two pages, was grim: Billy would never have a "successful marriage" (I wondered what that could possibly mean — maybe he could at least have an unsuccessful one?), and he couldn't ride a bicycle (contrary to what his physiotherapist had said). And, like any good speechwriter, this expert knew how to end with a bang:

"Finally, one has to address the question of how Billy would be today if Dr. Harvey had replaced the shunt earlier. No one can tell exactly, nevertheless, he would not have epilepsy, he would not be visually impaired, his coordination and strength would be close to normal, and he would not have severe learning disabilities."

All I could do was write, "Wow. Sunk by a neurologist." My father had some reservations about neurologists. He felt he could read an EEG as well as anyone and that they had the luxury of sitting back and recommending a surgical treatment without actually having to wield the scalpel. Most of his generation of neurosurgeons felt the same way.

～

While reading all these opinions, the fact that I already knew the outcome seemed unimportant. It was like seeing a movie whose ending has already been hashed over in reviews; if the story's any good, you watch it anyway. This story was getting better all the time, and the meat of it was in these expert opinions. They were like a doorway to the side of medicine that I had always known my father detested: the politics.

These experts were all so . . . *sure*. My father had read them all, of course — what had he made of them? I found his own opinions in the form of six letters to his lawyer, ending with some handwritten notes on a phone call made during the trial. I have an old habit of reading magazines back to front, so I read the last note first: "I doubt if I would be happy with an out-of-court settlement. Important to dispute claims of negligence. Might win."

Then the letters, and I read them rapidly, like someone jumping feet-first into a chilly lake. I needed something to get me through this painful little pile, something that would transcend the medical detail and help me understand why, despite not even remembering Billy's case, my father still wanted to fight.

And I found it. It was the *tone*. On page after page, he wrote not like a man fighting to get out of a tight spot, but like a professor facing an avid class: intelligent, open-minded students eager not only for the facts but also for a model upon which to fashion their own lives. He was polite, fair to a fault, and painfully honest. I began to wonder whether he understood how much trouble he was in.

"Dr. S. might like to reconsider his statement regarding the child's visual impairment," he wrote. What planet was my father on, to write this way? Or to say, in commenting on Billy's "spastic quadriplegia," that "the term quadriplegia refers, of course, to involvement of all four limbs, whereas the primary involvement here seems to be in the legs. In any event, the 'plegia' portion indicates a complete paralysis, which is not present in this child."

And that was the edited version! It went on and on like this. Lay out the facts, let the intelligent reader draw his own conclusions. Truth and reason will prevail. I might as well have been reading a handbook for my own upbringing: here's the info, *you* decide. My favourite was his including "a scientific paper of mine" from his Ph.D. research in 1951, showing that ten minutes of squeezing the middle cerebral artery in monkeys wasn't nearly long enough to produce any impairment (Billy's episode of increased pressure lasted ten minutes). All I could think of was, So that's what those monkey skulls in the box in my basement were all about! That and, How naïve can you get? But he believed in the written record, so for him it made perfect sense to include a portion of the "voluminous literature" on lumbar puncture and respiratory arrest.

Nor, in his view, did you have to go any further than the equally voluminous literature on prematurity and a newborn's lack of oxygen to find a simple explanation for Billy's disabilities. It just wasn't *logical* to ignore all those predisposing factors! Hence, "one might reasonably bring up the possibility of the twitching which was noted by the nurses being an indication of cerebral damage or an inborn tendency later manifested as epileptic seizures."

One might, might one?

"Well, I wasn't about to tell the lawyer how to do his job, was I?" A bony hand plucked the sheaf of onion-skin copies from my fingers and shook it in front of my nose. It made a noise like rustling leaves.

"*There* you are," I said. "You missed all the excitement. We went around the Brooks Peninsula!"

"It looked cold," he said. "And dangerous. The whole thing was irresponsible."

"Now you're going to warn me I could get sued," I said.

"That's not funny."

"Sorry. But did you have to admit that" — I snatched the papers back — "that the infant suffered a very significant cerebral insult after the lumbar puncture?"

"Why not? Anyone can see that he did. The point is he *recovered* from it. Lots of people do. And anyway, I wasn't there."

"No kidding."

"What do you mean by that?" He snatched the papers back again and stabbed at a long paragraph. "I would never have signed this patient off to another neurosurgeon. Labour Day or not, it wouldn't have made any difference. You know that."

I thought about all those years of blood-spattered glasses, the car door in the middle of the night, the holidays cut short.

"Yes. I do."

"Look at this. One of the defendants was just a pediatrician on call! What does he know about this baby's history? I told the lawyer, my advice to my own family is don't get sick on the weekend."

"That would have gone over great in court," I said. "Would you have done an LP?"

"I would not," he said, jabbing at the pile. "I doubt I was consulted about it either."

"So the pediatrician made a mistake."

"Well, he wasn't a neurosurgeon, and it was a neurosurgical problem. But he was quite right to be worried about the infection. He had a dilemma. It took some courage to do that lumbar puncture. Whatever he did could have turned out wrong. Doing a ventricular tap wasn't such an easy option either, because you're going back through the burr hole, through an infected area."

My father sneezed violently.

"Look. It was medicine," he continued. "If I had a newborn grandchild with a horrible problem, I'd still say, get Dr. Beamish."

"Should I talk to him? Is he still alive?"

"I haven't noticed him around here," said my father, gesturing vaguely.

"Maybe he went somewhere different?"

"I doubt it."

I took a deep breath. "The nurses say they called you at ten thirty."

"I don't remember. I just don't. That's all there is to it. Maybe they did. Nurses were always leaving messages with the answering service. Sometimes the messages never got to the doctor. Anyway, they should have called again. And again. Until they got me. Instead, she called some interns. The *interns* should have called me. If I'd got a message, of course I would have gotten in the car. It was only ten thirty. I wouldn't even have been asleep."

He probably wouldn't have slept much anyway, with a hydrocephalic baby dangling between infection and the effects of rising intracranial pressure. It would be like trying to sleep in your boat, at anchor, in a gale.

"One of their experts was awfully young."

"You saw that, did you? I doubt if he ever had to make a major decision without a CT scan. No wonder he can't imagine what happened that night. It couldn't happen now."

"What about all those things the mother said? That you'd help her get a normal child?"

"Impossible."

"Told us it wasn't hydrocephalus?"

"It *was* hydrocephalus."

"The bit about the shunt being a safety precaution?"

"Nonsense."

"And the shotgun? That's my favourite."

He gave me a crooked smile. "I would have remembered *that*."

The Emperor and the
Butterfly Net

When I managed to extract the anchor from the bottom of Scow Cove the next morning, it was neatly hooked through an ancient loop of rusted cable. No chance of dragging here. We took advantage of a break in the fog to crawl through rock-peppered Gay Passage, which I couldn't resist looking up. Walbran had named it himself, in 1897, after a character in Charles Dickens's *Dombey and Son* — Bunsby was another one. Sometimes it felt as though we were getting an education in English history, not navigation.

Walters Cove, at the entrance to Kyuquot Sound, was only two hours away, but we played dodge ball with rocks all the way, Hatsumi calling out a new course every ten minutes or so. I kept my mouth shut and did as I was told, speaking up only when I spotted another humpback rolling lazily through the smooth water. There was little Pacific swell along this route, but the fog caught up to us just as we approached the cove that was home to most of the residents of Kyuquot Sound. The last half hour turned into a tiptoe down an obstacle course of navigation buoys and the ghostly forms of shaggy islets before we popped through the final narrows into Walters Cove.

A cheerful, bearded man in an orange life jacket and a red ball cap waved us toward a spot on the public dock. Horn-rimmed glasses gave him a professorial look. He was seated in the bow of a fourteen-foot aluminum skiff, paddling vigorously backward.

"Helluva party boat you got there!" the professor bellowed. A tiny dog perched on the seat in front of him caught a whiff of Charley and began to bark. It looked like the sort of lapdog you normally see attached to refined, middle-aged ladies.

"Rufus, for *Chrissake*!" He swung his paddle at the dog. It barked louder.

"That's us," I said. "Party central."

The man dug his paddle into the water and zigzagged off across the cove. We tied up at the public dock, across the water from the First Nations village of Houpsitas, where most of the houses were. There was no road access here; the closest one ended at Fair Harbour, a half hour up Kyuquot Sound and itself three miserable hours by logging road from Highway 19. I'd driven it myself a year earlier, to research a story on a "green" aquaculture facility in Kyuquot Sound. Now I felt absurdly satisfied with myself to have returned the hard way.

The village of Houpsitas was pretty much all that was left of the Ka:'yu:'k't'h'/Che:k:tles7et'h' people, whose traditional territory extends south from Solander Island almost to Nootka Sound. The Ka:'yu:'k't'h'/Che:k:tles7et'h' are the northern-most of the fourteen Nuu-chah-nulth First Nations. Decimated by disease and dispossessed by European colonists, they now number around five hundred. In the three days we spent in Walters Cove, it seemed like half of them walked past *Vera* on their way to and from the store and post office at the head of the dock. And the *Uchuck*, Dave's old boat, called in here every Thursday; it would tie up right behind us. We had clearly not picked ourselves a tranquil hideaway. That was fine with us. We needed people around.

Even if they were slightly crazed. The professor was back, "helping" some Indigenous men load a boat they were taking to Fair Harbour. They seemed to tolerate him; in a place like this, what was the alternative?

"Have a good one," he shouted as they motored off. "Bring me back a woman, okay? Dead or alive!" A couple of shirtless kids raced down the dock on skateboards, making a sound like thunder.

Walters Cove was tantalizing. You had to be persistent. The place seemed literally to come and go with the fog. Sometimes the fog fell vertically, as though poured down over the trees; other times, the grey vapour seemed to be finding its way in through the natural openings to the cove. There was a tide-revealed reef near the western entrance to the harbour, guarded by a single basalt pinnacle like a twisted, rotten tooth. You could be sitting there, in the sun, when a wall of mist flooded silently in from the sea, enveloped the rock, obliterated the opening. In the evening, what might have been a brilliant sunset became weirdly transmuted by fog, the sinking sun first a pale disc, then an enormous pink ball.

But the fog only obscured physical things. When it lifted, there wasn't any doubt about what you saw: trees, houses, a rock you were about to steam straight into. Socially, Walters Cove revealed itself more slowly, and it was obvious that, as visitors for a few days, our impressions would be superficial — even wrong. Was I right in seeing a more than physical separation between the Indigenous village and the people on the side where we were tied up? Probably, and we would see the same thing, even more pronounced, in the two communities in Ahousaht, farther south. But beyond that single crude assumption, all we could do was snatch at impressions, the way Charley snapped at flies.

The fishing lodge, for example, a hundred yards across the bay. This place wasn't very old (five years, it turned out), and it made the lodges in Winter Harbour look like Super 8 motels. Someone had poured money into a land-based cedar building, with extensive docks and a fleet not only of the same aluminum twenty-footers we'd seen in Winter Harbour (one of which was still out there, still lost), but also some bigger fibreglass cabin boats with radar and twin 225hp Mercury outboard engines. These ones were all called *Kyuqout Avenger*, although what they might be avenging escaped me. The people with something to avenge lived across the way, in Houpsitas.

We wandered over to the fancy lodge in the afternoon, past the collapsing shack where the professor appeared to live ("Keep Out!" said an unnecessary spray-painted sign). When we passed, he was standing at one end of a long rickety float, legs braced, rocking it violently from side to side. His little dog, way down at the other end, was barking and scrambling to keep its feet. It looked like a lot of fun. I never did get the chance to hear his story; maybe he was a retired neurosurgeon.

We tramped down the gangplank to the Walters Cove Lodge. "Can we go in?" said Hatsumi, ever mindful of propriety.

"Why not?" I said. "Everybody's pretty laid-back out here."

But they weren't, at least not when presented with two people off a sailboat and a dog with a beard, white eyebrows, and an attitude. A young First Nations guy was filleting a hefty halibut at a stainless steel cleaning table. He wore a West Coast Resorts ballcap and blue mirror shades.

"Do something for you?" He drew the long knife along the backbone, and the halibut fell open like a book.

"How far out do you go for a fish like that?" I was thinking of the missing boat in Brooks Bay. Maybe he was too.

"Three miles? Sometimes ten. Maybe more." He worked the

fillet free and turned his back on us, hosing the blood away. I realized we were trespassing. We beat a retreat back up the gangplank.

"Just a peek," I said, pulling open the lodge's massive cedar door.

"But can we . . . ?"

She was right. We couldn't. A fire burned in the grate, leather chairs glowed, pastries glistened, but it was "Can I help you?" all over again. This time it was the manager who was pursing his lips.

"You're going to have to take the dog outside."

"I just wondered," I said as Hatsumi winced, "what do you charge for a night? We thought we might, you know, try it out? Take a break from the boat?"

"We don't charge by the night," he said, handing me a brochure. "Packages only. Five thousand for five days."

We took the hint. The company, I read in the brochure as we continued along the path, ran several lodges. Walters Cove was the most economical. We walked a little farther, following a narrow path through a forest that seemed to arise from the sea itself. "Coffee," said a hand-lettered sign tacked to a tree.

"That looks more like it," I said. Charley was already out of sight. We followed a string of yips and growls, emerging at a clearing with a porch, some bemused looking men in deck chairs, and a boardwalk leading to three simple cottages.

"Geez," said one man. He was wearing an RCMP uniform. "Is this your dog? And haven't I seen you before? McNeill, right?"

He'd looked different wearing shorts and washing the deck of his boat. We'd chatted, in the normal way one does on docks (except, of course, at expensive fishing lodges, where chatting is only available as part of a package).

"So, how was Cape Scott?" he asked. "And Brooks?"

"Horrible," I said.

His name was Lee; he and his partner covered the top third of the island. Now I understood why he had seemed so happy just to squat on his deck and sluice soapy water over it; his workweek had him in and out of boats and helicopters dealing with everything from domestic violence to pot farming. You can read about these nasty everyday infractions in the local newspapers, which often publish a weekly account, a sort of criminal social page. There were a lot of what the RCMP termed "consensual fights"; a favourite weapon was the hurled beer can. I should have asked Lee about the axe murderer on Minstrel Island.

The screen door banged open, and a perspiring, goateed man in an untucked shirt, jeans, and slippers threw up his hands and sat down heavily on the steps.

"I ordered tomatoes, but we got cabbage instead. We're running out of things to do with cabbage."

This was Eric Gorbman, and his place was called the Kyuquot Inn. Eric's style was about as far from the fishing lodge's as you could get. For one thing, he was positively delighted to talk to us, including in Japanese. It turned out his father, a fish endocrinologist, had been stationed in Japan after the war, part of a program meant to rebuild bridges between the conquered and their conquerors.

Fish endocrinologist?

"Your father was Aubrey Gorbman!" I said. "Small world or what! When I was a grad student, I used his textbook."

"Yeah, well, one of his students at Tokyo University was the emperor's brother," said Eric. "When I was five or something, we visited the emperor's butterfly preserve. I took a swipe at the emperor with my butterfly net, put it over his head." He let out a guffaw. "My God, those guards, they were *fast*! Hey, you want a coffee or something?"

I looked at Charley, who was wrestling with Eric's Jack Russell, Charlotte. "Deal with it," I said. We went into the restaurant equivalent of a butterfly net on an emperor's head. The room had the same million-dollar view as the Walters Cove

Lodge, but there weren't any leather chairs or fishing prints. A few oilcloth-covered tables ran along the windows, and three more had been pulled together for several Indigenous women and assorted grandchildren, who were working their way through large plates of fish and chips. A toddler in diapers spun past our table, lost his balance, and was scooped up by a long-suffering older girl. The queen squinted down on it all through the smoke from a wood stove on the end wall.

"No cabbage, I promise." Eric brought us our espresso and homemade apple pie. We'd ordered from a teenage girl with a sad, faraway look; now she was gone.

"What happened to your waitress?" I asked between mouthfuls. The pie was faultless. Eric rolled his eyes.

"A personal problem." It looked as though he was taking this one in stride; he probably got near-constant practice. He disappeared into the kitchen, and Hatsumi handed me a local newspaper she'd been flipping through.

"Look at this."

"Do I have to?"

I had forgotten about the sordid fight over salmon farms that I was supposed to dive back into when we returned to "civilization." Other things — wind, weather, fear, my father — had seemed more important. But here it was again, in a long article lambasting the farms and sundry colluding governments. I put the paper down. The diapered toddler ricocheted off my chair, howled, was retrieved, and began spinning again.

"Life's too short," I said. I could hear Charley defending the door. I might as well have been talking to him, for all the sense I was making, but I had to get it out. "Nobody's going to win this battle, or if they do, it won't have anything to do with science. So why am I getting involved again?"

"Because they're going to pay you?" said Hatsumi.

"Well, however much it is, it won't be enough."

That felt good, just saying it, but even as we got up to rescue

Charley, the other thoughts came crowding in. Whatever I wrote on salmon farms, how many people would read it? How would my words be bent and re-formed to suit other peoples' agendas? Why was it worth writing about at all when there were so many other things that people would rather read about, would enjoy reading about, would even, God forbid, actually *pay* to read about? From where I was sitting now, Eric Gorbman's chaotic little restaurant was a lot more interesting than salmon farms, and probably not just to me.

We said goodbye to Eric, detached Charley from the cops trying to drink their coffee on the stoop, and wandered down to the dock where the RCMP patrol boat was tied up. It was mid-afternoon, and the sport-fishing fleet was straggling in. The dock at the lodge began to fill up again with aluminum twenty-footers.

"Shit boats," said a man standing next to me. We watched the fleet come in together.

"They don't look very safe to me," I said.

"Get a big wave, split one of those things wide open." The man spat into the bay.

"They seem to be on a schedule," I said. Another one was coming around the corner. Middle-aged men were clambering out of the earlier arrivals, whooping and high-fiving.

"You got it," said the man. "Eat, fish, get shitfaced; eat, fish, get shitfaced." He spat again. "That one last week, they'll never find the bodies."

The Coast Guard had upgraded the *Qualicum Rivers Nine* to "missing." The search was widening. The Buffalo circled Walters Cove twice, and I'd heard the sound of helicopters on and off all day, sometimes muffled by the fog, sometimes, it seemed, right on top of us like gigantic yellow dragonflies. The mayhem of Brooks Peninsula seemed far away, and when we walked back down the boardwalk to the tidal reef, everything looked calm, even immutable. A soccer ball I'd seen the day before had gone through three tide cycles and was still in exactly the same place. In here, a body would stay put.

Sometime during our exploration of Walters Cove, Conrad and Kate had arrived and tied up across from us. Later, we helped them eat a salmon they'd caught, and I found myself blurting out my quandary over doing the review of salmon farms. They were both successful, confident business people — what would *they* do? I laid it all out for them: the no-win subject, the inevitable wrangling and misquotes. Conrad wiped his trim grey beard and sat back.

"How much they gonna pay per word?"

I worked it out. Conrad whistled.

"What're you complaining about?" he said. "Do the minimum! Sub it out, even! Take the money and run!"

"That settles it," I told Hatsumi later, as we got ready for bed. "I quit."

The End of the Inlet

The next day, we left Kyuquot Sound behind, unexplored, and threaded our way out through rivers of fog. Once again, the engine had been reluctant to start. At least it ran fine once it got going. In fog like this, a reliable engine was non-negotiable. I couldn't ignore this problem much longer. We were heading south to Esperanza, the next big fjord. From there we could strike east, making a long detour up Esperanza Inlet, connect to Tahsis Inlet, and descend directly into Nootka Sound. That way, we would bypass some of the confused Pacific swell that made nearshore travel so uncomfortable along the coast, and we would get to visit the mill town of Tahsis. We left Walters Cove as we had entered, by stealth, so close to the fog-hidden rocks we could smell the bird shit.

On this first leg, the view came in glimpses permitted by a break in the fog or snatched through binoculars between the drunken rolls *Vera* was making. When the fog did relent, the views were often startling, like Jurassic Point, where a shaft of sunlight suddenly spotlit a gentle curve of pebble beach, backed by rolling hills of an intense, golf-course green. Another wave, another roll, and the fog-curtain fell again.

The Rolling Roadstead, a protected channel just before the entrance to Esperanza Inlet, was a gorgeous, shallow corridor of beaches where the swell finally abated. We could pick out brilliantly coloured kayakers' tents that studded a sandy spit like beads. The beaches on this side of Vancouver Island were bites taken from black rock; behind them were salal and the wall of cedars. We hung a left through spectacular Birthday Channel, beneath an eagle riding high with wingtip feathers spread, as though gripping the air. "Many rocks!" my log entry says, in a jiggly hand. Then down past the Catholic church in the village of Chenahkint and into Queen Cove for the night.

It was a clammy place in the fog, the only sounds the whine and crash of timber being torn from the surrounding hills. A school of young salmon flowed around *Vera*'s rudder, and I tried not to think about the job I had decided to walk away from. That night, we ate below with the propane heater purring, and I wondered how conditions were at the Brooks Peninsula. On the VHF, the search was now focusing on debris.

We had both had enough of playing pinball with rocks. Fog or no fog, the next few days would be in protected waters that were free of the sentinels that guarded the west coast. This was territory that Dave — had he fixed that water pump yet? — had known like the back of his hand as he took the *Uchuck III* in and out of the inlets between Kyuquot and Port Alberni. And when we left the next morning and I turned to look behind us, there she was, entering Birthday Channel not ten minutes after we'd gone through.

The *Uchuck III* caught up to us less than an hour later, as we passed the ancient, abandoned Indigenous settlement of Ehatisaht. We watched through the binoculars as she came on astern. She seemed to float above the water, her two long lifting booms angled out from the mast on her foredeck like the antennae of a shiny black moth. As she passed us, I saw red fuel barrels on the foredeck and passengers taking in the sun. Ehatisaht, even overgrown and obliterated, was a lovely site, the hills opening to a symmetrical valley through which the creek emptied into the sea. I peered hard, trying to imagine the village, and for a moment thought I caught something leaning in the trees. A totem? I took a picture, but when I blew it up there was nothing, just the stern of the *Uchuck III* slipping away.

There was plenty of evidence of more recent human activity, though. The scars left by clear-cut logging are notorious; viewed from a low-flying plane, the scale of tree-scalping on these mountainsides is profoundly depressing. But even here, chugging along at sea level, we saw many patches, maybe a few dozen acres each, where crews had moved in, taken everything, and dumped it down skids into the sea. Centre Island, where I could just make out the remains of the skids, looked hollowed out. The loggers weren't lacking in derring-do; one old swath snaked like a ribbon along the hillside above Hecate Channel at what seemed an impossible angle. Directly beneath, a salmon farm lay fallow, the smooth galvanized decking, yellow buoys, and bright blue flotation blocks making it look for all the world like something from IKEA.

Again I wondered, which was worse, the clear-cut or the farm? So often we saw them together, and every time, I found myself asking that question. At least you could tow an offending farm somewhere else or close it down. The clear-cuts, and the havoc they wreaked on streams and hillsides, weren't going anywhere. I decided that comparisons were a distraction. Both fish farming and logging needed to clean up their act.

Once past the farms (there were three of them in Hecate Channel, all apparently fallow), we went through the back door of Tahsis Narrows, the shortcut that would dump us practically at the landward end of Tahsis Inlet. We throttled down to find our way through, so slow that a silent squadron of kayaks actually overtook us. A lone sea otter watched us pass, toasting its toes in the sun. I took comfort in the reassuring Rorschach of the radar: old technology, stolid and simple, so unlike the gorgeous "you are exactly *here*!" images of the electronic charts, which I still couldn't bring myself to trust. Radar's shadowy pictures form and re-form with every sweep, in a way that says to me, "You can trust me. I'm *working*."

Once around the corner and into Tahsis Inlet, we did the last five miles under sail, the warm wind filling in strongly behind us. By now, I was so worried about the starter button that I left the engine running in neutral while we surfed past vast log dumps to Westview Marina in Tahsis. The marina was barely distinguishable from the strung-out remnants of the lumber mill and what remained of the town centre. We followed a big RCMP cruiser through a gap in the "breakwater" that was no more than a chained-together corridor of logs and tied up at yet another version of sport-fishing nirvana.

Tahsis used to be a mill town. It had two mills, in fact. The remains of the "old" mill, now little more than a bit of pier and parking lot, sat next to the marina; the "new" mill, at the end of the estuary, had closed down ten years ago. A large section of the bay was marked "booms" and "submerged anchors and cables" on the chart, but all of that seemed to be history. Tahsis the town was still emptying. There weren't many businesses left, although the family running the only food store was going flat out to get their new gas bar operation running. The young owner rang up our groceries while stage-directing his dubious-looking mother on which buttons to push. Their lone fuel customer, a geezer in ill-fitting jeans and a cowboy hat, waited patiently by the shiny new tanks. At the local building supply store, where we lugged our propane bottles, the owner filled me in on the town's pulse.

"What tips you off is the number of kids in the school. It's at the point where one family can make the difference, one way or the other. Every year you watch the numbers — who's moving in, who's leaving. There's thirty-five houses for sale right now."

"How do you know all this? I mean, about school numbers?"

The man laughed. He had a neat moustache, close-cut grey hair, good posture. The long socks beneath his neatly pressed cargo shorts gave him a military air.

"I was the school principal," he said.

Out back, his tired-looking wife filled our propane tanks in a near-empty lumber yard that had become a parking lot for old boats, the kind of mildewed fibreglass cruisers and fishing boats you knew would never float again. A few four-by-eight plywood sheets and some bags of concrete were all that was left of the building materials side of the business. Four enormous cellphone repeater dishes loomed over us, the only landmark left. Tahsis itself had no cell service.

Back at Westview Marina, a string of cottages had commanding views of the mudflats across the estuary of the Tahsis River. In front of one of them, roses struggled to find the light through the branches of a Douglas fir, trying, like Tahsis, to stay alive.

We made friends with the couple tied up across from us. Tahsis was the first place on the west side of the island where there'd been more than one or two cruising boats. Neil and his wife, Alice, had slogged north from Portland, Oregon, to Barkley Sound, as they did every year, a thirty-two-hour no-sleep nail-biter that, for them, got the worst stretch of the trip over with in a hurry. Neil and I exchanged books we'd already finished, and for the first time, I found myself forced to choose between titles. You didn't run into many people with books on Buddhism and Bach's cello suites. I don't usually ask people what they do for a living when I'm travelling, but I winkled it out of Neil: he and his wife operated a psychiatric and counselling clinic for trauma victims, mainly refugees. I would never have known.

It was "Steak Night" at the marina café, and we joined Neil

and Alice for dinner. The steaks, grilled outside on a barbecue, were serviceable, but what really endeared me to the place was the fact that our dog was welcomed in.

"Him?" said a durable-looking woman wreathed in smoke from the grill. "No problem."

Charley had a brief discussion with a German shepherd, agreed to the conditions, and flopped down under Hatsumi's chair. The bigger dog's owner was an affable paramedic who'd grown up in Tahsis. The German shepherd was a replacement for a dog who'd been killed by a cougar while the two were walking together at the edge of town. After dinner, we moved across the dock to an outdoor fire pit that fronted a gift shop, where an indifferent folksinger sang the same song over and over again, and sparks from the fire burned holes in my pants. Behind this cozy scene, sport fishermen laboured around a brightly lit cleaning table, like a team of large, casually dressed surgeons. As we walked back to *Vera* in the warm evening rain, three more of them huddled in the stern of a twenty-foot boat, fussing with one of the gleaming engines. The boat leaned crazily, and the men were getting rained on, but they had beer, an engine to fix, and the next day's fishing to look forward to. They were pretty happy.

⤳

After the steaks and the singing, I was ready to go to work, to finally get started on the trial itself. I had the feeling that, like the trip we were on, the home stretch was coming. The trial — such as it was before the deal to settle was made — seemed to consist of two days in court for the plaintiff's star witness, the neurologist-professor. Was my father in the courtroom? He must have been, and it must have been excruciating for him as the professor was led through his report, sentence by damning sentence. His eyes must have rolled when the witness misspelled septicemia for the judge:

"Let me just spell it for you. S-e-p-t-o-c-e-m-i-a." Later on, he got "parietal" wrong too ("Gee, I can't spell, my lord"), and the lawyer had to spell it for him.

Spelling was the least of this man's blunders. By page ten of the transcript, he was confidently describing a ventriculogram for the plaintiff's lawyer — except that the procedure he came up with involved injecting air into the spinal space, not the ventricles. He was hopelessly confused; that would have been the spinal tap from hell. None of this would get challenged, of course, until cross-examination, so the tag team pressed on, the witness strenuously repeating phrases like "critically ill," and "grave, grave significance," and "this unfortunate child." In one paragraph, he said "very significant neurological sign" four times.

His explanation, despite the gaffes, was pretty compelling. By the end of it, I was rooting for Billy. Who wouldn't? Unfortunately, the finger was being pointed at my father. It was a disheartening conclusion, and the page I was reading was marked with one of my father's inimitable bookmarks, a shaft of exposed photographic paper. This one was all black.

The plaintiff's lawyer lobbed a few soft questions; like a tennis player expecting a set-up, the witness slammed them away. Apgar scores? "Not that important." (*Wham!*) Neonatal hypoxia? "Never that severe." (*Thunk!*) One expert's opinion that there was brain damage from the hydrocephalus itself? "He's a good pediatrician, not a neurologist." Shot whistles down the line, catches the far corner, takes out a ballboy. Game over.

The cross-examination that followed was more interesting. At last the gloves were off. That game-winning shot, replayed in pitiless slow motion, now wobbled out of bounds. Mr. Thackray became suddenly unavuncular, more terrier-like. He started, of course, with the misdescription of a ventriculogram, a public poke at credibility that would undermine anyone's confidence. Soon he was reducing the expert's argument about hydrocephalus being benign to a string of *uhs* and dashes in the transcript. It got a little unpleasant ("I am not a neurosurgeon, I am a child neurologist"); at one point, the witness was stammering about "viral bacteria." And then complaining, after a particularly nasty broadside in which he was caught contradicting himself about the degree of complications from birth, "It's just the way questions are asked."

To which the Mr. Thackray replied, "I am not trying to make it easy for you."

It got nastier, until I really thought I was reading a movie script, not a transcript of a real trial.

"She simply *told* you the child was okay in that first month, didn't she?"

"What she said, what she didn't say, it's so hard for me to . . ."

Thackray piled it on. The witness's timing of the meningitis was all wrong, his timing of the shunt problem was wrong. The shunt didn't fail; it was infected. The expert's report was based on "what was given to me." He had no idea of the way Apgar scores are normally reported and interpreted ("Usually it comes with a form which tells us"). After a page of remorseless questioning, the witness agreed the Apgars "looked bad." Finally, an admission that there was significant neonatal stress. And then, thank God, adjournment.

When court reconvened two days later, the poor man felt compelled to re-apologize for getting the ventriculogram wrong. "I should have known and it's just one of these things. The test I described, it's called a neuro-encephalogram."

Wrong again. There is no such thing as a neuro-encephalogram. But there is a pneumoencephalogram, which is exactly the nasty procedure he had described. Replaced by CT scanning, a "pneumo" really hurt, and it took a long time to recover from. In the 1973 movie *The Exorcist*, the possessed girl gets a pneumo before she's shipped off to an exorcist. She screams a lot.

Mr. Thackray steps up again. Right off, he confirms that the damning report was based not on the hospital records but on the doctor's summaries (their consultation notes). In other words, I had read more aboard my boat than this man had in his office. And he'd *never seen* Billy's records from the first days of his life, when he had trouble breathing, when his incubator failed, when Billy was put on the respirator with a tube down his trachea.

One by one, the symptoms of brain damage *before* Labour Day were brought out and admitted to. Here, the lawyer read the witness his own words and forced him to take them back. It was like a movie again, the lawyer producing information the witness had never seen. And at one point, Thackray even tricked him, getting him to okay a "normal" ratio of red and white blood cells as being ten to one (it's more like seven hundred to one). Here I found my father's aggrieved highlighting in three colours, with a note: "He doesn't know!" Nor did he know Billy was on phenobarbital ("doesn't know phenobarb used in jaundice"). Or how shunt valves work (more outraged scribbles from Dr. Harvey). Again and again, the expert witness was forced to admit that he never looked at the nurses' records, the day-to-day history. "Well, I was given the consultations of the doctors." Exactly the thing I had been worried about.

It went on. I forced myself through it, knowing that these preliminary "victories" for my father would in the end get steam-rollered but still enjoying the discrediting of this guy. There was much discussion of where Billy's seizures came from (if from the frontal lobe, where the EEG — brain wave records — seem to point to, that was an area unlikely to be affected by the lumbar puncture). Again, the lawyer made the witness eat his own words about the EEGs; his own data showed the frontal lobe was exactly where they came from. My father's highlighter was heavy here, and I knew why: he prided himself on reading and interpreting his own EEGs. No neurologist necessary.

After two days of trial, the star witness seemed shaken, if not discredited. I later found a note my father wrote to his lawyer, saying, "Any good neurologist would have been con-vulsed with laughter." In my father's simple view, Thackray had just demolished one expert witness; surely he could have done the same to the plaintiff?

I found myself flummoxed too. Because those two days of trial were all I could find transcripts for. There was no defence. As far as I could tell, the scheduled fifteen-day trial was over after two. It was like watching someone from your team tackle a runner, cause a fumble, scoop the ball up, and break for the goal line — and then the game is, unaccountably, called. Why?

Maquinna's Ghost

We stayed a second day in Tahsis. I liked the place. There was a good walk up the steep hill to St. Joseph's Catholic Church, where Charley could relieve himself in an ecclesiastical setting. I also had to do something about the balky starter switch, which lurked in the back of my mind, clicking. Lying in bed that night and listening to the gentle hiss of rain on the water, it came to me: I would install a shunt! Simply bypass the starter button so that if it balked at a critical moment, all I had to do was open the hatch and flip a second switch.

The marina had a decently stocked repair shop. The next morning, I hot-wired the starter motor, tucked the new switch where it couldn't be activated accidentally, and *voilà*. Surgery my father would have been proud of. But he stayed away.

We left Tahsis in fog so thick we couldn't even see *Vera's* bow. I knew it was a straight shot out into the main inlet, but we still needed radar, GPS, and binoculars to get there. Ten minutes out, we were in the clear; behind us, Tahsis receded under a thick white cloud. Suddenly, six sport-fishing boats materialized out of it, fanning apart to blast by, like a squadron of fighter planes. No radar, no running lights. As though on cue, the VHF Coast Guard channel broadcast the news that the sport-fishing skiff from Winter Harbour had been found.

The *Qualicum Rivers Nine* had finally been spotted the day before, five days after disappearing, by another fishing guide from Winter Harbour. It was upside down in the middle of Brooks Bay. Only the tip of the bow was showing; not enough for the search planes' radar. Divers found one life jacket floating nearby; the other three were still in a locker on board. The ignition key was in the off position, so they had probably been jigging for halibut when the boat flipped.

I thought about that: three middle-aged guys braced against the wicked chop, perhaps joshing with the guide, cradling their rods and intent on any signal from a hundred feet down. Come on, baby, bite! But the monster — the rogue wave — came from above.

The search for the men was soon called off. High winds, freezing water, ten miles from shore with no life jackets — by any measure, their time had run out. An EPIRB — a radio beacon that could be triggered by the boat's rolling over — might have led searchers to them faster, but radio beacons aren't mandatory on such craft.

There wouldn't be much sailing today. Long and narrow, Tahsis Inlet runs almost straight north-south, and we had a dozen miles with the wind dead ahead in a channel only a half mile wide. Where the Tsowwin River entered the inlet, the sandbank off the estuary squeezed the channel enough to take three knots off our speed. The river cut deeply into the mountains at right angles to the inlet. Passing the Tsowwin was like gazing briefly into a lone, illuminated window — grass flats, silvered driftwood, the gentle V of the valley and the fog-shrouded mountain beyond.

We bulled slowly through while, in the other direction, a conga line of nine sea otters, head to tail, hitched a ride with the current heading back toward Tahsis.

We would spend the night somewhere in Nootka Sound. Of all the place names on this famous coast, Nootka may be the most familiar. Before I even knew exactly where it was, the name brought to mind explorers, swirling mists, angry rocks, Indigenous people in conical cedar hats. Friendly Cove, to give the main anchorage and settlement its English name rather than its real one, Yuquot, was where Captain Cook and his men became the first documented Europeans to land in British Columbia. The *Resolution* and the *Discovery* anchored there in 1778. British names, of course, abound; I didn't have to go to Walbran to recognize HMS *Bounty*'s master William Bligh, who has a large island named after him.

The sea otters that seemed to be monitoring *Vera*'s progress since Cape Scott should have been direct descendants of the ones that watched Cook's vessels arrive but, strictly speaking, they weren't. Once Cook's party demonstrated the profits to be had from otter pelts, later traders managed to extirpate the species in B.C. waters. Between 1799 and 1801, around 10,000 otters were being taken from B.C. and Alaskan waters every year. The ones we were enjoying now were transplants, the descendants of eighty-nine Alaskan otters released south of the Brooks Peninsula in 1969. There are around 3,000 otters along the coast now; not enough to restart a hunt, but a few were being shot and skinned, illegally, every year. I was glad we didn't find any of these grisly remains. For now, the biggest threat to the animals was oil spills.

We ended up in Friendly Cove, although it wasn't our first choice. Protection from wind and swell looked much better in Santa Gertrudis Cove, a notch just north. The Spanish name, like so many here, reflected the stalemate between British and Spanish traders in the area. Ten years after Cook landed, the

Spanish built a permanent settlement in Yuquot (they called it Santa Cruz de Nutka), but they lost interest and dismantled their fort as the otter pelts ran out. They were gone by 1795.

But the entrance to Santa Gertrudis defeated us. It was high tide, so the many rocks we needed to avoid were underwater. Even the vaunted GPS threw up its hands, offering seriously conflicting locations on two different electronic charting systems. Suddenly, *Vera* felt like a sumo wrestler in an airplane aisle. I lost my nerve, yelled at my wife, went into reverse, and backed out *exactly* the way we had come in.

In Friendly Cove, we were the only boat anchored, although the public dock was humming. The *Uchuck III* had just arrived, disgorging seventy families of the Mowachaht/Muchalaht First Nation for their annual summer residence on the grassy isthmus that separated Friendly Cove from Yuquot Point, on the outside coast. This place is the site of historic Yuquot, the summer home of Chief Maquinna and his Nootka people (their winter village was in Tahsis). It's now a National Historic Site (although, when I looked a little deeper into that one, it turned out that the original designation in 1923 was to recognize Cook's historic landing. It wasn't until 1997 that the Mowachaht/Muchalaht persuaded the Canadian government to "re-designate" the site to reflect First Nations history).

A cultural and interpretive centre was in the planning stages, and tourism was being developed, beginning with a half-dozen rental cabins. The whole effort was poked and prodded into being by a couple of Gold River entrepreneurs, both of whom we managed to meet. The first of these people we were obliged to find if we wanted to stay overnight; the second one found us when we tried to stay in the wrong place.

Margarita James was in charge of the band office and collected the twelve-dollar overnight fee. If we had tried to come at a more chaotic time for her, we couldn't have managed it, because seventy tents were being erected on the freshly mowed meadow.

A small fleet of off-road buggies was hauling supplies and equipment over the long roadway from the *Uchuck*'s drop-off, and already the area was strewn with ice boxes, lawn chairs, piles of firewood, backpacks, garbage bags, blankets, and wheelbarrows. Racing through it all were the kids, giddy in the brilliant afternoon sun. The sound of more firewood being chainsawed blew in from the long crescent of beach that looked south.

A few of the kids sidled up to check us out. One little girl wore white sneakers with flashing red lights. She sat on the edge of a picnic table, swinging her feet.

"Cool shoes," I said. She tucked them up. "Do you know who Margarita is?"

The girl pointed solemnly at a group of women beside a lime-green tent.

"It's my mom," she said.

Margarita was sturdy and energetic. She launched into a spirited argument for the cultural centre she was trying to raise money for, and how it would house the many artifacts they were doggedly working to repatriate from museums across North America. I knew the fisheries biologist for the band; did she know Roger too? Of course she did; he was out fishing with the rest of the men. Margarita pointed out the church on the shore, and the network of trails her people were tending and expanding, and sent us on our way. We forgot about Estevan Point looming somewhere out there waiting for us and set off, skirting the happy scene in the meadow and entering a green corridor of salal that ran along behind the beach that finally, after a month and a half of fear, frustration, and fog, felt exactly the way I wanted a west coast beach to feel.

"This is why we came," I said to Hatsumi as Charley raced ahead. "And about time."

Never mind that we could have found something similar by just driving to Tofino; we'd gotten here the hard way, and that made it sweeter. We cut through to the beach and stumbled, half-running, down the pebble shelf to the hard-packed sand where we could walk easily. Pinnacled black rocks were sprinkled throughout the bay. Squinting at them into the sun, I decided they looked like a fleet of ships. Hatsumi looked at the rocks and shook her head.

"Everything is *pointed* here," she marvelled. "It's just like Japan."

We walked. Charley harassed seagulls. To call them a flock seems inadequate; this was a sky-darkening mass, an airborne seagull division, yet a single schnauzer stage-managed them down the beach, running them aloft, waiting while they regrouped and settled a hundred metres farther down, then charging them again. If we'd been further south, someone would have taken us to task for allowing it. But there were no other people here. A sport-fishing boat buzzed the beach, cutting close to the toothy headland where the Spanish cannon had sat. Men in the back whooped and waved. They disappeared around the point in a cloud of exhaust.

"Assholes," I muttered. This time, when the seagulls rose, they didn't come back. But we were back at the church, an unremarkable wooden building built, in 1956, by the Mowachaht/Muchalaht community and decommissioned as a Catholic church in the 1990s. Unremarkable outside, that is. Inside, the Church of St. Pius X was unlike any "house of God" I had ever seen. House of Gods was more like it because St. Pius X was no longer a place for monotheists. The Virgin had left the building.

A carved killer whale on two stumps now blocked the path to the altar, whose alcove was taken over by two exuberant totems, too long to fit in the previous tenant's space. The dais was still there, with a small, engraved cross and facing angels, but they kept to themselves, as though fearing to look up at the bears and ravens and wolves towering above them. As though to emphasize the point, the pews were all turned sideways now. No longer did people face a single symbol of devotion;

now, they faced each other, along the axis of the building. The door we had tiptoed through, once we were inside and turned around to look, was itself flanked by more totems, in brilliant greens, reds, and blacks. A magnificent thunderbird spread its wings over them, and us.

Every Christian church I have ever visited has had the same point to make: this is God's house, here are his symbols and representatives, take your place and worship him. From the impossibly ornate Catholic cathedrals of South America to the stern stone of English High Anglican and the blandest of suburban Unitarian boxes, my reaction has always been the same: this is where you come for instruction, for guidance, for forgiveness, for solace. A kind of one-stop spiritual shopping, from one God.

It was difficult, standing in the warm gloom of this place while children raced around outside staking out their territories in the sun, to miss the point that was being made by St. Pius X in Friendly Cove. I felt no less welcome than in a Christian place of worship, but the enormous feat of accommodation that native people had made in this country, here so plainly symbolized by building their own meeting place inside the walls of what had for so long been a Catholic church, was more humbling than the thunderings of a robed minister. Maybe it was as simple as realigning the pews — what better way to "love thy neighbour" than to have to look at him in church? There was a sense of calm here, surrounded by an entire crowd of animistic representations, and you felt part of them all, not just answerable to one or two. In its serenity and inclusiveness, the church was a little like being in a Japanese temple.

It was all too much for Charley, who vomited in the vestibule beneath an incongruous stained glass titled "Reunion de los Capitanes Bodega-Quadra y Vancouver." Donated by the Government of Spain in 1957, the panel depicted the resplendent explorer-entrepreneurs inking their deal with their ships at anchor in the cove behind them. A few worried-looking natives watched from the sidelines.

"Jesus, Charley, not in a *church*!" But was this still a church? Maybe the spirits of killer whale and bear wouldn't be fussy about a little dog puke. I cleaned the mess up with handfuls of the grass that was trying to engulf St. Pius's steps.

~

I wish I could say that the church had a calming effect, but by this point in our trip, that was too much to expect. Friendly Cove, for all its revelations, was where you waited to go around Estevan Point, the last of the major obstacles on our circumnavigation. And as each of these obstacles had been fussed over and surmounted, something had been happening to us. The more spectacular the scenery got — and after a day in Friendly Cove, it was hard to imagine anything more beautiful — the more anxious and irritable we were becoming. As the wind rose and *Vera* began to twist uneasily on her chain, we realized that we needed to go. Get out, get around Estevan, hightail it south to Clayoquot Sound. We were familiar with Tofino and Ucluelet, the two main communities there; I'd been in Ahousaht before, and finally there was the "big reason" for boaters to visit.

"Hot Springs Cove," I reminded Hatsumi, who was glumly doctoring packaged ramen to look like a proper evening meal. "We'll be there tomorrow, row in and soak in the pools. You'll think you're in Japan."

She frowned, stirred, winced at the moaning in the rigging. Seven o'clock, and the perverse wind was rising again. Just across the bay, with the *Uchuck* gone, the dock was empty. Hatsumi looked longingly at it through the porthole above the stove. I sighed, started the engine, got the anchor up, and moved the boat.

But it wasn't a good idea. As darkness fell, the dock came softly alive again. Now it was a place for teenage trysting, and for younger boys to try out rod and reel. For the first time, I felt like an interloper, even when the murmuring stopped and the fishing lines came in for the last time. Finally, it was quiet again, but I knew it couldn't last. Margarita had mentioned that the men had all gone fishing. I hadn't seen any of them yet.

They started to straggle in around 10:30, one runabout after another. Men spilled out, happy, boastful, caustic, the usual result of hours on the water with a fishing rod and beer. I turned on the weather forecast, listening for conditions at Estevan Point.

"Do we have to move?" whispered Hatsumi. She was in pyjamas, and she didn't look as though she wanted to go anywhere. There was enough swell getting in around the corner to make *Vera* toss and turn against the metal dock.

"Winds thirty knots northwest of Estevan Point," said the voice on the radio. That was where we were — wasn't it?

Outside, the voices got closer. Then, knuckles on *Vera*'s hull.

"I'll deal with it." I crawled outside into the cool night air. A man in sweatpants and a Tilley hat squatted on the dock.

"Got a problem with your boat being here, buddy. I've got some guests showing up later for the cabins."

Guests showing up . . . when? Midnight?

"Oh," I said. There had to be a way out of this.

"You work with Margarita, right? Managing the place? We had a *great* talk. And you know what? She said she knew Roger, the fisheries biologist."

This was sinking pretty low. The guy scratched his head. He had fine, aquiline features. Replace the canvas hat with a conical cedar one and he could have been the legendary Chief Maquinna, who unfortunately presided over the conversion of Friendly Cove to a European trading post. Maquinna probably didn't sound like this, though.

"Sure, he was out fishing with us. I think he went up to the camp already. You want me to try and find him?"

This was better. I pressed on, disgusted with myself. "It's okay, I'll find him in the morning. Look, I'm really sorry about taking your space." I stuck out my hand and introduced myself. His name was Albert.

"Nah, we'll make it work."

"See," I said, getting off the boat so we could go eye to eye, "it's the wife. Long story, but she's, you know, a little freaked out. We've been having starter motor problems. I thought if I could get at it first thing in the morning . . ." We exchanged a conspiratorial, testosterone-fuelled look. If Hatsumi overheard any of this, I was dead.

"I got plenty of tools in my cabin," Albert said. We got to talking; that is, he did. Albert, once he was your friend, couldn't stop talking. I learned, variously, that he was a concrete contractor, born and raised in Gold River, that his business in Vancouver got skunked by the recession, and that he was now back home, running the Friendly Cove operation with Margarita. And doing it vigorously, I could see.

"I'm relentless," he said. "No patience at all! Today, out fishing? Got lost in the fucking fog, can you believe it?"

"You don't have GPS?"

"Fuck, no. But here we are!" Together, we shuttled *Vera* forward twenty feet, tiptoeing out onto the steel hoop that rode up and down the last piling so that we could tie her up as far along as possible. Albert talked the whole time. It was better than listening to the weather.

Early the next morning, the forecast was the same. I climbed with Charley up the winding steps and over the aluminum catwalk to the lighthouse buildings perched on the hill above us. A cedar helicopter pad shone wetly. Yesterday, the keeper's house and the light had been brilliant, red-roofed gems in the sun; now they were hidden in fog. I knocked on the back door while

Charley nosed around in the geraniums, looking for somewhere to pee. A flustered woman answered.

"Sorry," she said. "I was just filing our weather report."

"Then maybe you can explain the forecast."

"Forecast? Haven't listened to that part yet."

Hmm. "Well, they're calling for high winds 'northwest of Estevan.' What does that actually mean?"

"Northwest of Estevan? Well, I guess it could mean . . . hmm. Bajo Reefs? Up there?" She waved vaguely. "The thing is, we're in a tricky spot for forecasting. You know what the word Yuquot means, don't you?"

"Not yet," I said.

"It means, 'place where wind comes from all directions.'"

"We're thinking of going around Estevan Point today," I said.

The woman watched Charley rooting around in her potted plants. Behind us, a precipitous trolley-way led all the way down to the dock where the two Coast Guard Zodiacs waited for someone to have a maritime emergency. Except that they were hidden by fog.

"What a cute dog," she said. "Is he friendly?" Charley barked at her. "Estevan? Ah, you'll be fine."

A Little Piece of Japan

We escaped before Albert could wander down for more conversation and a spot of fixing the starter motor that I'd already fixed. Vague or not, the lighthouse lady had been right, the wind must all have happened somewhere "over there." We never saw a breath of it. But there was plenty of ugly swell, lumpy and short, that bedevilled us for the three hours it took to crawl around the rocky defences of the Hesquiat Peninsula. Off Estevan Point itself, the hitchhiking thumb of the peninsula, the sea coarsened like reptile skin as the waves caught on the bottom and began to break. It didn't last long. Once we'd completed our long turn, the swells lengthened and moved accommodatingly in behind us, and we rode them to the lights that mark the narrow entrance to Hot Springs Cove. We didn't really need the lights to find our way in; we could just have followed the water taxis from Tofino.

"We won't exactly be alone," I said. There were two water taxis tied up at the dock that services Maquinna Park, along with a fifty-foot power yacht registered in Montana. We hadn't seen one of those since leaving Port Hardy. We headed further into the inlet, looking for a spot to anchor, and a Tofino Air float plane materialized at the end of the cove, dropping fast and heading straight for us. It whacked the water three boat lengths away, throttled back, and chortled on to the dock.

"Let's get close to the edge," said Hatsumi.

Over the months we'd cruised together, my wife had carved out, not without some spirited back and forth, a number of niches where she indisputably excelled. Navigation was the big one; an offshoot was a knack for choosing a good anchoring spot. This isn't easy, because "anchoring spot" means not only the place where you begin to release your anchor but also the place where the anchor actually hits the bottom, the place where it finally digs in and holds, and all the other places where your boat is likely to roam at the end of whatever length of chain you pay out. The paying out of chain I was allowed to keep doing, and I still got to give Hatsumi polite arm signals from the bow that told her when to reverse (to set the anchor) and when to go forward (in case the damn thing hadn't grabbed). But calculating where our boat would actually end up, given wind, current, distance to land and other boats, was her responsibility. As to my hand signals, she ignored half of them.

"Over there," she said, pointing to a section of shore where the angle of the rocks suggested a drop-off. So did the chart.

"Are you . . . ?"

"*There.*"

She took us in to within two boat lengths, watching the sounder, then put *Vera* into reverse while I paid out the chain. When she shut the engine down, Hatsumi had a big grin on her face. To me, it looked as though I could reach out and pick a fir cone. At night, I knew, the shore would appear frighteningly close. But there would be no float planes in here.

"I guess I have to wear a bathing suit," she said. "In the

onsen." We could see the dock clearly; another taxi-load of tourists from Tofino stumbled ashore and set off along the boardwalk to the hot springs.

"Alas, yes. This isn't Japan. You'll probably be sitting next to a software developer from Seattle. But we can't go yet. The hot springs will be packed with tourists all afternoon. Once they leave, we'll be in there."

Waiting was fine with me. I'd left my father dangling after the confusing truncation of his trial, and I *knew* there had to be more. Above all, I needed to know why the trial was cut short. I wanted to get his story over with just as badly as we both wanted to stop worrying about rocks and fog. I sat myself down again.

Was that really all there had been? Two days, one mauled witness, then *poof*? I went back over the correspondence file, where there were still some odds and ends I hadn't yet looked at. It was time for some detective work.

First, I found a carbon copy of my father's expenses for three trips to Vancouver ($207.75). Frugal as always, he had taken the bus. Above the little invoice he'd reproduced a poem, "The Road Not Taken," by Robert Frost. The return date was five days later than the last trial transcript I had; something must have kept him in Vancouver.

Next, I found a copy of one of the newspaper stories, the one with Billy's mom defiantly staring down the camera beside the big, bold quote, "I got so upset, I told him if anything happened to my boy, I'd be at his back door with a shotgun." (Next to which he'd scribbled, "Then I would have called the police!") Sure enough, the story was written during the trial, so she'd had her day in court after all — I just didn't have the transcript. The date of the final disgraceful story ("Doctor Offered Mother

New Son to Replace Brain-Damaged Boy") tallied with his bus ride back to Victoria. Later in the story, the writer listed the expert witnesses heard; all were for the plaintiff.

So there *had* been more than two days of trial, and it had all been from the plaintiff's side. My father had sat through at least five days of accusations and lurid media reports and then his defenders had pulled the plug. Maybe, somewhere in the B.C. Supreme Court archives, those missing transcripts are interred as yellowing microfilm, but I haven't had the heart to exhume them. Maybe he'd had copies after all but had destroyed them. I wondered if, as he sat on the ferry back to Victoria, he had looked at Portland Island gliding past and thought back to the last weekend he'd spent there, relaxed enough to sleep away the day while my mother read and painted.

Missing transcripts or not, what mattered to me was his state of mind. I was trying to understand his reaction to the trial, short or long, documented or not. And he *had* left some clues. Here were his notes, made at the trial. Many were on Four Seasons notepaper, or in a cheap spiral notebook with a colour photo of two gaudy parrots side by side on a branch. One of them was confiding in the other's crested ear. He'd labelled that one "Laxton" (the plaintiff's lawyer) and drawn a balloon with the words, "Let's go for $4 million!"

A lot of these jottings were immediate reaction to testimony. I read them several times, and it began to sink in that here at last were the answers to the questions I should have been asking when he was still alive. These notes were as close as I was going to get to his feelings as the accusations emerged and he fought to refute them.

They ran from mundane to moral. Some were just technical: "He's wrong about the choice of shunt type." "He described a pneumo!" More important to me was his reaction to the charge of "failure to monitor": "Presumably Dr. Beamish was called at 0015. He wouldn't just wander in. Why him instead of me?"

This, I thought, was the kind of thing he was itching to say in court, if he'd had the chance.

This matter of the phone calls got murkier the more I thought about it. The nurses came across as heroic and frustrated and on the side of the plaintiff. "Something went wrong," they were said to have told her. "We called him five times." The media liked this — and used it. But how many times had I myself — has *anybody* — said, "Look, I tried to call you. A couple of times, really!" We know it's a lie, a little, ass-covering white lie, but it saves face, and who's to know? The hospital was being sued too, and that included the actions of the nurses. Maybe, with the nurses, that's all it was: damage control for them, and let the big-shot doctor fend for himself. I knew, from reading these anguished notes made at the trial, that he was incensed that a nurse's note of a single phone call "attempt" seemed to count for more than his statement that he would never ignore such a call, had he got it. It was her word against his. I guess he'd forgotten how Harvey Cushing's nurses felt about *him*.

From phone calls, his notes turned to the timing of the shunt replacement on Labour Day: "What's the big deal about a day or two of [raised intracranial pressure]? We see many head injuries recover from two days of pressure." And this one, which summed up the doctors' dilemma: "Would not have epilepsy if shunt replaced earlier? Might be dead too."

These were notes for his defence. There were so many, and in such detail (I haven't included them all here), it was clear he was itching to get back at the people who were questioning his judgment. Sometimes he complimented one of the hostile witnesses ("He described this okay"); often, he asked himself the unanswerable: "Did A.T. believe me? Does anyone?"

The saddest were the notes that described how he *felt* as the barrage wore on: "You find out who your friends are." There was even some Shakespeare, some lines from *Othello* he obviously knew by heart:

Who steals my purse steals trash; 'tis something, nothing.
'Twas mine, 'tis his, and has been slave to thousands.
But he that filches from me my good name
Robs me of that which not enriches him
And makes me poor indeed.

It wasn't hard to imagine him sitting in the courtroom, pulling out his pen and writing these words as his own good name was filched in front of him. And "poor indeed" is exactly how the experience left him.

During what I assume was Billy's mother's testimony, my father's notes became more urgent and longer. He could see which way the emotion was going. The nurses hugging the mother, saying, "Something had gone wrong" — and all the rest of what appeared the next morning in the newspapers. His writing became a scribble, with abbreviations and dashes as he raced to get it all down — even though it was exactly the same recitation as in the examination. But this time, for the audience that counted.

The next day, it was over. All he'd written was "Back to hotel. Vera there. Call from A.T., settled out of court. Problem: the lumbar puncture." And it was a lumbar puncture he hadn't even done.

The last note I found was dated just after the trial, after the newspaper stories had appeared. It said, "Fiona asked me if I had turned a little boy into a carrot." Fiona was one of his grandchildren. She was six.

These notes were excruciating reading. All I could think was, Why didn't you tell me any of this? Why did I have to go through a thousand pages of scribbles and photocopies, half-truths and hyperbole to find out what was going on?

"Nobody asked you to do any of that," my father said. He was still wearing the ridiculous hat I'd thrown into Haro Strait. I turned on him.

"On the contrary. *You* asked for it every time you got all defensive about the damn trial. Moaned and groaned."

"You wouldn't have understood."

"What, that some people screw up? That other people are perfectly okay with standing up in public and lying? That they wouldn't give a shit if you'd trained with Harvey Cushing himself? 'Truth and hard work is the best way' — look where *that* landed you!"

"Watch your language." He squinted, the way he did when he felt I wasn't taking him seriously enough.

"Honesty is the best policy? That got you on the front page of the newspaper. *Two* newspapers! At least, if you'd talked about it to your family, they would have understood."

"Understood what?"

"That your patients came first. That you wouldn't have left a patient hanging. That somebody screwed up, maybe a nurse, maybe one of the other doctors. I mean, we just had to accept that on faith. It took me *months* of slogging through all this shit to realize it was true! One of the other doctors blew it!" I tossed the hated transcripts across the cockpit, missed the seat, and watched them subside untidily into the scuppers.

"I'm trying to do yoga down here," said Hatsumi.

"Anyway," continued my father, "even if one of my colleagues made an error of judgment, and I'm not saying he did, that was his call. It could have gone either way."

"You mean the LP."

"Yes."

"So you just suffer in silence? The fraternity of medical brothers?"

"What would you know about it?"

"But you were constantly complaining about this or that

341

colleague, how they had terrible training, how they wrecked patient's backs, how they couldn't operate their way out of a paper bag!"

"Privately, in the family. But not publicly. It wasn't done."

"Wasn't *done*? What do you think that dickhead, who couldn't even describe a ventriculogram, didn't even know we have more red blood cells than white for God's sake, what the hell do you think *he* was doing? And for money!"

But my father was unflappable. He shook his head. "I wouldn't do that. And I wouldn't expect you to either."

"So you let yourself get taken down by a . . . a neurologist!"

Even that didn't get to him. "Neurologists are more knowledgeable these days, I'm told."

"By whom? Is there a whole bunch of you guys up there, wherever that is? Some kind of Wounded Ivy League Surgeon's Club that meets every Thursday afternoon to congratulate themselves on how they always put the patient first?" I was crying now.

"Leave him alone." My wife's face appeared in the companionway. Hatsumi looked serene, as she always does after touching her toes to her forehead on the cabin floor for an hour. "You've got it wrong."

"*What?*"

"Backward. It's not that he wouldn't talk to you. You wouldn't talk to him."

"How do you know? You weren't his son."

"I watched you. For ten years. And I helped take care of him."

"You're talking about me as though I weren't here," said my father. "That's rude."

"You're *not* here," I said.

"Of course he is," said Hatsumi. "You wanted to talk to Brian, didn't you? About all those things?" She waved at the transcripts soaking in the scuppers.

"So I didn't have to read all this?"

"I could have saved you the effort," he said. "But I am sort of flattered you didn't just throw it away."

"Which you told me to do."

"That was because you wouldn't talk to him," said Hatsumi.

"Because he was impossible to talk to! He always had to be right!"

My father extended two mottled fingers and tapped the pile of soggy paper, like a doctor sounding a patient's chest.

"Well," he said, "was I?"

Would a man wracked by guilt have written a book about it? Maybe. But would he have written one in which he never, not once, felt the need to say, "It's unfair. I'm innocent"? Not a chance. He never said that because, as I'd been taught so well, *one didn't have to.*

"Yeah," I said finally. "I guess you were. Somebody screwed up, made a call that went the wrong way, you closed ranks and took the heat."

"Something like that."

I played my trump. "Then why couldn't you get over it? You paid for the rest of your life. Why couldn't you just say, 'I know the truth, the rest of you are beneath contempt,' just, you know, fuck it? Oh, sorry."

I knew he didn't like swearing. But it didn't matter, because he was gone. I wasn't going to get the answer I wanted most. I gathered the remaining papers and stuffed them back in their bags. I never wanted to see them again.

"Can we go to the *onsen* now?" said Hatsumi. "He won't be coming back."

"Let me grab my bathing suit," I said.

⁓

As it turned out, we could have gone in naked, which is the only sensible way to take advantage of sweet, sulphurous spring

343

water that emerges from a crack in the earth, cascades over a rock shelf exactly at shower height, and meanders through a chain of rock pools to empty into the chilly Pacific. The reputation of the springs at Hot Springs Cove as a spectacular, intimate and unspoiled *rotenburo* (the Japanese word for an outdoor pool) was built on accounts from fifty years ago, when the only non-Indigenous users were the occasional intrepid boaters. You could still only get there by water or air, but the explosion of tourism in Tofino now meant a daylong stream of water taxis and float planes like the one that had dropped out of the sky on top of us. The three or so usable pools were hellishly crowded now; you had to stand in a towel, waiting your turn, until a rosy, steaming form emerged from one of the pools to make its way unsteadily to the changing rooms in the woods.

But the pools themselves were unspoiled, under protection of B.C. Parks, which acquired the land in 1957 from a long-time resident. All the cranky, stressed-out boater had to do was wait until six-thirty or so, when the last water taxi had returned to the restaurants and spas of Tofino, then row to the dock, walk the two kilometres of boardwalk, and slither into their own private pool.

Which we did, three times in the two days we stayed at Hot Springs Cove. We ignored the "no dogs" sign, as did the harassed-looking park ranger finishing up with his daily tidying after the pools had been used by — how many people? We must have passed thirty of them on their way back along the boardwalk, and it's probably unfair to say they were all loud, pasty, and smoking, but that's how it seemed to me after so many days in inaccessible places where the only tourists were there to fish. The boardwalk itself was something of a legend, a kind of yachtie roll call where the owners of visiting boats had carved, chiselled, or scraped the name of their boat into a plank. I found myself reading these planks compulsively, even upside down, which they were on the way back. On either side, ferns burst from the forest floor like green fountains, between waxy salal leaves and nurse logs and stupendous moss-wrapped cedars that had escaped the loggers.

We smelled the pools before we could see them. Hatsumi took the first shift, a look of wonder on her face as she disappeared around a dripping rock while I took Charley to the nearby beach and sat watching the hypnotic breathing of the ocean around the black rocks that guarded the cove. When Hatsumi finally reappeared, she looked beatific.

"Heaven," she said. "Go."

"Heaven" was a chain of pools carpeted with flocculent sulphur-slime and fed by a cascade. I stood under the waterfall, closed my eyes, and let the pungent steaming water pound out my noisome cargo of frustration, fog, fatigue. Too bad my father hadn't hung around for the hot springs; he could finally have gotten warm.

We walked back on rubbery legs, not talking, watched by the silent cedars. By the time we got back to the boat, the fog had found Hot Springs Cove, and *Vera* was a vague greenish form floating in liquid glass. We ate a simple dinner with the heater hissing and jazz on the stereo. There was wine.

"You look happy," I said.

"I don't have the dream now."

"The dead man?"

"Not since Cape Scott."

"So maybe that's all it was. Anxiety."

Hatsumi smiled.

When I rowed Charley ashore before bed, I rested momentarily on the oars and could hear only the distant tinkling of Oscar Peterson from our boat and, fainter still, small domestic sounds from the family in a sailboat that had arrived while we were in the hot springs. We fell asleep to the sound of the fog whistle on Sharp Point, a single note, attacking and fading slowly, a crystal wineglass out there in the dark.

Us and Them

Ahousaht is a strange place, a few hours around the top of Flores Island from Hot Springs Cove and down the long neck of Matilda Inlet. Actually, Ahousaht is two places. I'd briefly experienced the First Nations village, properly called Marktosis, which sits on a thread of land so narrow it looks both ways: inward, toward the inlet, and outward, to the Catface Range on Vancouver Island. I'd spent a strange night there, a few years ago, wearing my biologist hat, and had written about the experience. This time, I wanted to see the other side. I wondered, was Ahousaht-Marktosis the same arrangement as Walters Cove and Houpsitas? Whites on one side, Indigenous people on the other?

We passed a native longliner on the way, probably going after dogfish. Just before the entrance to Matilda Inlet, several salmon farms were tethered in the shallow channel. There was another concentration of farms here, extending from Estevan Point to Barkley Sound. Not as many as in the heavily peppered stretch around Johnstone Strait and the Broughton Archipelago, but enough for visitors like us to notice.

Ahousaht — the white version — was a string of sagging concrete docks beneath a blue general store with a carved sign featuring an extravagantly endowed mermaid. Next to the store were a restaurant and a shed that served the fuel dock. I knew we were on the fuel dock because a long snake of diesel hose extended in lazy waves down a gangplank and along the dock, as though waiting for someone to come along and squeeze the trigger. This, I learned, was more or less how you got fuel in Ahousaht; I watched a string of locals, in everything from run-abouts to trollers, pick up the hose, gaze expectantly landward, and be rewarded with the appearance of a stern woman who shaded her eyes and yelled, "Diesel or gas?"

This person was the sister of the store owner, a toadlike man in his seventies out of whom, for a while, I made it my business to try and coax a smile. I wasn't successful, unless you counted his mirth at my expense, which he shared with a crony whose troller was hauled up on the ramshackle marine ways behind the store for bottom-painting.

"What's that up on your mast?" said the fisherman.

"Yeh, looks like a fender. We been thinking, why's that sail-boat got a fender up its mast?" Har, har.

"Radar reflector," I said. Charley was making friends with the man's dog, leading it on a chase up and down the gangplank. "The kind that works."

A cheap radar reflector, which is supposed to make you visible to everybody else's radar, looks like two metal Frisbees welded at right angles inside a shoebox. A better one, like the one *Vera* had, has all the metal elements encapsulated inside a smooth white plastic lozenge. It does look a lot like a fender, or a really big suppository.

"Yeh, well," said the store owner. I noticed the "For Sale" sign in the window behind him. No wonder. Inside, the place was dim and untended. He had some eggs, some plastic-wrapped bread, candy bars. The store served as the local post office, and I'll give it this, there was a fine selection — although it was beginning to look more like a collection — of the practical stuff needed to keep a working boat working: chain, pipe elbows, electrical wire, many boxes of screws. No sissy stuff like jiffy salmon smokers or solar showers. I didn't buy anything.

I led Charley on a stroll around the grounds and took my own inventory of a place in collapse. Or maybe it was just transition, like so many outposts along this coast, because, on closer inspection, there *were* things happening here, they just weren't what the present owners had signed on for. In behind the docks where the salmon boats used to come to off-load their catch, where the fat cocked elbow of the fish chute still swung in the wind like an amputated limb, there was evidence of life.

A bunkhouse housed miners contracted for the exploration of the Catface Range — unpopular in Tofino, but business. And next to the old torpedoes and dried-out flower boxes in front of the restaurant was a shiny blue undersea rover the size of a toddler's wading pool, fitted with tiny propellers and bearing the logos of suppliers and sponsors. A nice young man with an English accent told me it was for his research; he was from the University of Bath. Most of the funding was from the U.K., but the rover also bore an Earthwatch sticker, which explained the fleet of kayaks at the hostel.

Earthwatch provides a "field science experience" by inserting paying "volunteers" into research projects around the world. The project in Ahousaht, I found out, was about tracking grey whales, although the dockside briefing I watched a young man give a group of middle-aged kayakers seemed more to do with his research on sea otters. It was all very confusing: English and American researchers, using funding from their own countries and from a global grant-maker with offices in London, Boston, Melbourne, and Tokyo, teaming up with the science tourists who flew in to "help" them.

The fuel-selling sister was renting out her "rustic but comfortable" hostel to the visitors. She had them figured out.

"It's all bullshit," she told me.

The restaurant, also glowingly described on the Earthwatch website, wore a sign in magic marker on a scrap of cardboard: "The Restaurant Is Not Open." When I looked more closely at the shot I had snapped, a native troller was reflected in the window with the testy sign, and I remembered the man who had tied up, come into the store to collect his mail, and left. I also remembered asking the store owner about the marine ways in the First Nations village, which had been an impressive facility for boat repair when I'd first visited.

"Huh," he said. "*They* only used it once. *They* left it in the water. It's ruined."

I wondered who had ruined all the equipment littering his own property — the abandoned cement mixer and forklift rusting in the bushes, the boat trailer overgrown by blackberries, the collapsing large-vessel dock nearby, its walkway furred with lichen like an old man's patchy beard. The loading area was littered with batteries and propellers and a couple of huge Mercury outboard motors, on their sides like dead hippos.

One night in white Ahousaht was enough. We rowed across to the village of Marktosis in the evening, and my visit a few years before came slowly back: the desperate look of the houses, the graveyard of wooden fishing boats lining the shallows. On a rock at the entrance, a carved cedar representation of a man in a traditional conical hat raised one arm to the outside world; the low sun made the weathered cedar gleam. The salute seemed ambiguous to me because the arm was lifted only to waist level, like a person measuring off a child's height. Surely it was a gesture of welcome, but, given the indignities being suffered in that unfortunate place, it might as easily have been farewell.

The next morning, as we were preparing to untie and head for Tofino, an Indigenous family in a small runabout dropped by for fuel. An older man, who I guess was the patriarch, ambled along to where I was untying lines. He looked *Vera* up and down.

"Nice boat," he finally said. Was there a twinkle in those brown eyes? I've worked with enough Indigenous people to recognize their sense of irony, which, given their history, is highly developed.

"Should put some trolling lines on it. Might catch some fish."

He *was* giving me a gentle dig. I didn't mind.

"It's a good year?" I asked.

"This year? Unbelievable. I don't know what it is, I know we overfished in the past, but this year . . ."

"What are you catching?"

"Sockeye. Tons of 'em."

"But there aren't that many strong stocks out here." I'd worked with a neighbouring First Nation on the sockeye stocks near Tofino; they'd been depressed for years.

"These ones aren't local," the man said.

"Where are they from?"

"Fraser River."

I thought back to the prediction of the woman in Sointula two weeks ago. "The sockeye are coming," she'd said. "I can feel it." I didn't ask the man, "So why are we mounting a royal commission on the disappearance of Fraser sockeye if you're getting a bumper crop?" But it certainly looked like the decision to bail out of my part in it was turning out to be the right one.

"Have a good one," he said. "I'm going fishing."

Sporties

"Don't dock in Tofino."

Many people told us this. We didn't listen. We should have. We did dock in Tofino, multiple times. It was more like crash-landing.

Tofino is a natural halfway stop between Ahousaht and Ucluelet; from Ucluelet, the run to Bamfield, in Barkley Sound, is manageable. So it makes sense to take a break there, but there are two problems. First, the approach from the north, which we would follow, becomes congested, confusing, and very shallow. Basically, you find your way around sandbars. There's a lot of sand here, the pebble beaches of farther north having given way to smooth grey tourist-friendly curves.

Second, currents run very strongly past Tofino, which sits on the end of the Esowista Peninsula exactly where water racing in and out of several major channels collides in the rush to enter the open Pacific. This means you have to time your arrival for near-slack if you don't want to be suddenly playing catch-up with a dock. A friend who lives in Tofino says, "Nobody should come in here without a pilot!"

And there's a third reason, which probably just flows from the first two: Tofino isn't set up for recreational boaters. It's not boater-friendly. There aren't enough spaces, so people end up cruising the fingers for a glimpse of someone doing the equivalent of opening a car door in a crowded parking lot. The land-based visitor to Tofino, of which there are zillions in the summer, never suspects any of this. Lots of little boats coming and going beneath a backdrop of sparkling sea and the Catface Range high above: "Hey, honey, that looks like fun!" Well, it isn't.

By the time we entered the pinball-alley of navigation buoys that takes you through the sandbars into Tofino, neither Hatsumi nor I were in perfect mental shape. Ahousaht had gotten us down, and the prospect of playing bumper cars in a crowded approach weighed on us. Suddenly, with Tofino in sight, it was the rapids all over again, this time with the current behind us. *Vera* slipped sideways so fast that, even steering a course that was 45 degrees off our destination, we skidded around buoys so close I could have reached out to touch up their paint. And it was shallow — thirteen feet, eleven feet, ten — at one point, there was only four feet of water under *Vera*'s keel, a situation you don't want to be in when you're having trouble keeping your boat pointed in the right direction. Assuming there is a right direction.

The current fired us at the fuel dock like a projectile, and I had to go hard in reverse to get the lines onto the wharf. After refuelling, we cruised along the docks available to visitors, finally settling on an open-looking spot at the Weigh West fishing lodge. Here, docking meant the equivalent of doing a U-turn in a river. When we were finally secured, our tempers were shot, and both of us were grabbing our shoulders and hoping we hadn't done irreparable damage. I took a picture later: the ocean-river was cresting around *Vera*'s elegant stern as though she were forging along backward at six knots. All around us, the water boiled in angry whorls. We might have tied up in the middle of the Yuculta Rapids.

And, of course, we were surrounded by sport fishermen, although the commercial fishery was still in evidence here. At the Lions Gate Fisheries' dock next door, an aluminum vessel unloading its cargo of sardines was so low in the water that you could have sat on the rail and paddled your feet. But our dock was all sporties. Right behind us, an exuberant party just returned from the fishing grounds was celebrating in the cockpit of their shiny Trophy cruiser. Country music washed over *Vera*'s cockpit, "Got muh ass in the sand, a cold beer in muh hand." We collared Charley and set out for the grocery store, breasting a tide of tourists.

The sporties woke us up the next morning, gunning into the channel at top speed. We waited another hour until the current subsided, then worked our way through another sand-maze into deeper water for the five-hour run down to Ucluelet. The greasy swells came on the beam now, and *Vera* rolled in her own faint cloud of diesel stink as familiar landmarks came and went. Long Beach, the six-mile stretch of sand that lines Wickaninnish Bay, emerged obligingly from a grey bolster of late-lying fog as we crept past. As teenagers, my friends and I had viewed Long Beach as a rite of passage, struggling up the unpaved, muffler-eating road from Port Alberni to emerge, finally, at the gap in the trees where you left the road and high-tailed it down the hard-packed sand in your car. The beach was part of Pacific Rim National Park now, with proper parking lots, machines that took your money, interpretive signs, and no trace of the dozens of vehicles that had got stuck in the sand and sank slowly out of sight, back in the day.

Ucluelet Inlet is the indentation that follows Amphitrite Point. Scientifically, *Amphitrite* is a genus of worm that burrows into mud or sand and waves its tentacles about to feed. We must have passed over billions of them, crooking their fingers at *Vera*'s keel. Amphitrite Point can wave its tentacles at the boater too if you're not careful. The rocks glisten in the surge from breaking waves. If you can't see the point, you listen for the dolorous groan of the fog signal (not too close, or you're on the rocks) and the clanging bell that marks the inner boundary of the safe channel. If there's any wind, this strange duet is joined by the keening of the whistle buoy a half mile further out. The whole effect is eerie, like being serenaded by a trio of idiots.

With the tone-deaf chorus behind us, I looked forward to Ucluelet, halfway down the inlet. Ucluelet has always been the "poor cousin" of Tofino. It's the working harbour, blue-collar where Tofino, if not exactly white-collar, was popularly seen more as a no-collar-at-all kind of place. Of course, the stereotypes don't hold, but I've always preferred Ucluelet anyway; if I really *must* have an espresso macchiato, I can drive the thirty miles. Certainly my preference held up when it came to visiting in a boat because the Ucluelet Boat Basin was everything such places should be: decent docks, shelter from the wind, bins to dump your garbage in, and a bellied, bearded Dane selling fresh shrimp off his boat.

"I know you," I said, digging for my wallet. "Cowichan Bay, right?"

"Yeh, could be. Or Nanaimo. I get around."

This was the guy who, spotting Hatsumi a few years ago, had deftly beheaded and peeled a couple of shrimp, popped one in his mouth raw, rolled his eyes, and passed the rest to us. His fingers looked like they'd recently been inside an engine. Hatsumi's parents had been with us that time, from Tokyo, and they sampled too. Please, God, I thought, don't let them get sick from raw Canadian fish. Of course we didn't, and the shrimp were delicious. This time, the man didn't peel me any shrimp, maybe because I was alone. But I bought a big bag anyway.

People who live in Ucluelet don't usually say "Ucluelet."

354

It's either "U-kew-let" or, more commonly, "Ukee." Steve, the hyperkinetic manager of the Ukee Boat Basin, was too busy to take my payment; I saw him briefly as he sped along the dock on a bicycle, balancing a courier package on the handlebars.

"Gotta get this to one of the fishing boats before he leaves," he shouted over his shoulder. Steve wore baggy shorts and a sleeveless T-shirt. His shoulders were seared.

"We'll figure out the money later."

"You look busy," I said. "But I mean, it seems pretty quiet. The place is only half full." It was true, we could have had our choice of spaces.

"Wait," said Steve.

I never saw him again and ended up calculating what we owed and slipping it under the door of his tiny office, where he never came to rest long enough for me to trap him. The thing he had told me to wait for was the annual fishing derby; we had arrived on the Friday afternoon before the big event. By seven o'clock, when Hatsumi was getting down to doing something with all those shrimp, the Boat Basin was jammed with sporties, most of them in twenty-footers they'd trailered from as far away as Washington State and were now loudly shoe-horning into Steve's little kingdom. Some of the boats were rafted three deep. One dock was reserved for charter boats, and I walked past three skippers cleaning up after the day's clients had wandered into town to get started on the evening's partying. One fellow was washing dishes on the dock, humming.

In behind the marina, the cluster of modest motels was solidly sold out, and a tent city had sprouted in a cleared area nearby. It was Winter Harbour all over again: pickups, trailers, sizzling meat, and a beery haze above clusters of deck chairs. In the basin, the commercial fishermen were having a gathering of their own, the sounds of merriment and clanking beer cans rising into air that was blue with diesel exhaust. Behind it all, Mount Izzard glowed purple in the rosy twilight.

After my little meltdown in Hot Springs Cove, I felt able to finish up the final document, which was in another notebook my father had titled Epilogue. I'm glad I left it till last because in it was the draft of a long letter to his lawyer that, if he ever sent it, didn't seem to have survived. I started to read and found myself back inside his head. Maybe this document held the answer to his long decline.

It turned out not to be the simple answer one hopes for, the "all is revealed" that snaps everything into focus. But if there was a bright spot in the whole affair, this notebook seemed to be it, beginning with the fact that he was addressing his thoughts to the person who represented the process he felt had failed him — his lawyer. Respect for an individual trumped anger at a system.

Why, he wrote, had they settled? That settlement rankled: was justice served merely by "appeasing the accuser with large amounts of money"? His reputation had been dragged through the mud, and he'd wanted to fight. Even though "you might have been the only person in that courtroom who believed me," he still wanted to clear his name. If it really was the lumbar puncture that was the sticking point, well, he wasn't the one who did the lumbar puncture.

Maybe his total lack of recall had been the problem? Were they afraid he would cave in? "If so, your fears were groundless. I was sure of my position, and I believed in the power of truth." *That* was what I had been looking for. He knew who he was, and that person wouldn't have refused to get out of bed and attend to a sick child. In his world, that should have been enough, and if some people were suggesting he'd gotten the call, rolled over, and gone back to sleep, well, who were they? Who was *he*?

He finished the letter with a few words about the book he was trying to write about the whole experience.

"Sorry about the bits about the Mercedes and the black robes," he said, and I remembered the clumsy pokes at the legal profession in an early draft of *The Game*. "I have been combating a tendency toward this sort of nonsense all my life, but sometimes I slip." And there was a bright side: the trial had at least given him the opportunity to see a fine lawyer in action. "I wouldn't have minded a little more of that."

There were peculiar details that made me shake my head. In his first draft of *The Game*, he wrote to Thackray, he'd worried about using real names; once the newspapers had published everybody's name, he'd dropped that scruple. But he'd chosen a pseudonym for his little patient, and what had he come up with? The same one I had dreamed up: Billy.

He knew he was on shaky ground writing about the experience. He admitted that "my computer has taken the place of a psychoanalyst's couch," and that whatever he wrote was in danger of becoming "an exercise in self-pity." I had *The Game* with me on *Vera*; before we returned to Victoria, I decided, I needed to complete the voyage with my father by reading it properly. Somewhere in Barkley Sound, where we were headed next, I would finally sit down and work my way through the story he could never bring himself to finish.

But I already knew something important. His frustration, and probably his inability to get over it, really seemed to stem from being unable to defend himself publicly. His accusers stole his good name and, just like in *Othello*, that was infinitely worse than taking his money. I didn't know how to feel about that because I'd never elected to spend my life on a highwire, doing something like neurosurgery. Growing up with a man who had, I'd probably heard enough dinner-table stories to make sure my own career would keep me well out of that danger zone.

Immersing myself in his life and his troubles had at least got me to understand that the reason I had chosen not to live by the sword was because I was raised by someone who would die by it. At some level, I must always have known that.

Barkley Sound

The sporties turned the air blue the next morning, climbing stiffly into idling boats and peeling away from the dock by 5:30. By mid-morning, Ucluelet was hot and still. We'd done our provisioning at the Co-op up the hill. We were two days away from Victoria, even if one of those days would be a marathon seventy-two-miler, the first half completely exposed to the Pacific and the second a run down the Strait of Juan de Fuca, a long wind funnel that small boats were always relieved to be out of. But we were finally in Barkley Sound, where the Broken Group of islands offered weeks of cruising opportunities.

"It's up to you," I said to Hatsumi as we lugged our shopping bags back down to the boat. "Go now, hang around here, whatever you like." There was no point in pushing her, especially when I was ambivalent myself. Getting here had been hard work, and the near-daily business with my father had taken the stuffing out of me.

We settled on motoring over to the Broken Islands, finding somewhere interesting to stay, and then nipping into Bamfield

Inlet the following day to wait for a favourable forecast. Dave and Nancy would be in Bamfield for a few hours, on a jaunt from Port Alberni aboard the *Frances Barkley*, the "other" coastal supply ship and ferry. We'd hook up, get reacquainted, and head home when the weather looked good.

The Broken Islands *were* beautiful; if we'd hit them early in our trip, we might have stayed for weeks. But neither of us could settle down. We crept over a shallow bar into a deserted cove called Joe's Bay and dropped the anchor for lunch. In the Gulf Islands, a place like this would be stuffed with boats; generators would be muttering, inflatable dinghies whining past like motorized bagels. All we had to do was — nothing. Relax. Read a book. Nap.

Instead, we pulled up the anchor and moved to Effingham Bay, a few islands distant where, for the first time since the Gulf Islands, the anchorage was actually full. I was irritated with all those other boats, irritated with myself for making so little of such a remarkable place. We anchored within spitting distance of the shore, and by mid-afternoon the place wasn't only popular with boaters, it had filled up with sardines. The water was brown with algae, and it simmered with fish. As they flowed around *Vera*, I caught the occasional flash of silver in the tarnished water and could see, just for an instant, a mass so dense I could have raked them from the sea. From the shore, where I rowed Charley and sat staring out into Effingham Bay and the lowering sun, the surface of the water became pointillistic. Each little puncture of the surface tension was a crystalline explosion.

I picked a fistful of goosetongue to dress up our salad and rowed back toward the fiery ball of the sun. It set like a red-hot poker; I almost expected to hear the sizzle. By nine o'clock, when we went to bed, so many fish were breaking the surface, it sounded like a room full of people chewing. They kept it up all night.

In the morning, we motored around the corner into Bamfield Inlet, a place I'd last visited as a graduate student. Bamfield is the end of the road from Port Alberni. It's always been a fishing village, but since the 1970s, it's also been the location of the Bamfield Marine Station, a research facility shared by five western Canadian universities. The place, originally built around the old trans-Pacific telegraph cable station, seemed huge to me now. We didn't drop in, although the dock in front was almost empty. Nobody was likely to remember me, especially as I seemed to be retiring myself from the biological field. That empty dock was enticing, though, because the so-called public dock was mostly reserved. We got the last spot.

Bamfield is funky and appealing, although I think the owner of the general store had seen one too many tourists on the day we visited. We got there on a long and tortuous boardwalk planted at intervals with boxes of flowers. Many of the cedar cottages we passed had their own docks; some of these still had commercial fishing boats alongside. You could practically read the history of fishing technology in their backyards; in one, derelict boats, chunks of Styrofoam, wire, crab pots, and the odd wheelbarrow were slowly being engulfed by blackberries. A whimsical, many-signed post worked its way up through "Dog Shit Alley" past the "Bamfield Cat House" (both, I'm sorry to say, were pet places), and ended, at the top, with "Neckache." Well, somebody had gone to a lot of trouble. And Charley loved the boardwalk; every inch had a canine signature on it.

The *Frances Barkley* disgorged Dave and Nancy, along with the rest of their Courtenay Camera Club, and we all straggled across a neck of land to Brady's Beach, a spectacular crescent of tan-coloured sand guarded by basaltic pinnacles and turrets. If I hadn't been so preoccupied with the next day's journey, I might have enjoyed it more; after Yuquot, it was probably the prettiest beach we saw on the whole trip (and perfectly reachable by land). As it was, I pestered Dave about the weather. But he was at his most noncommittal, and I didn't get much out of him beyond, "Get up early and check the forecast." Which was all anybody could sensibly say.

After the *Frances Barkley* pulled away, we wandered into the Coast Guard Station on the promontory next to the dock. Why not check the forecast at the source? A fellow in blue overalls and paint spatters said, "Something I can help you with?"

"I thought you might have the long-range forecast. We were thinking of going down to Victoria tomorrow. Is there anyone here who can . . . ?"

"Well, I'm the officer in charge, so I guess I could." He put down his can of paint. "Come on in and let's look." He sat us down in front of a computer and brought up the Environment Canada marine page. "If you want to print it out, give me a shout." He started to leave.

"Yes, but . . ." We already had these forecasts. "I mean, would you have any concerns about going tomorrow?"

He looked up at the sky. "Tomorrow? Nah. You'll be fine."

It was at moments like this that I disgusted myself the most. Wasn't there any way I could fast-track this learning process, eliminate this craven search for reassurance? Probably not. Probably, I was going as fast as I could.

That evening, Bamfield Inlet was a slow-motion thoroughfare, an aquatic horse-and-buggy town where small boats puttered up and down the main street. We were serenaded by a questionable band at the Pirate's Cantina, who murdered reggae, blues, rock, and the Beatles, finishing up with a country and western tune of their own making. It featured endless fish jokes and bad puns. It was called "Wet Dream." I went down below, where at least I couldn't make out the words, made a cup of coffee, and pulled out *The Game*. In two days, we would be home, and I wanted to be through with my father's archive before we got there. *The Game* was the last document on the list.

The Man Who Could Turn
a Little Boy into a Carrot

At the end of all my digging into the medical mess that resulted in *The Game*, I was left with the most unexalted of conclusions: of *course* things went wrong. They always do, always will. Most catastrophes are crudely engendered and obvious. A bus driver fails to do a shoulder check and wipes out a cyclist. A weekend sailor mis-times a squall, takes a flogging jib sheet across the face, and finds himself spitting teeth onto the cockpit floor. Simple systems, misjudged for an instant, the squibs popping away in the background of our lives. On the face of it, my father's experience was meaningless: a lawsuit was launched, he got caught in the headlights for a medical procedure he didn't even do himself, and he couldn't answer the complaint about "failure to attend" because he didn't remember. The plaintiffs and their lawyers walked off well satisfied. Without the chance to defend himself, he just limped home to brood.

As to why he could never get over it, the best answer I'd

come up with in two months of digging was the public damage to his good name. "Get over it," was easy to say, and maybe he should have. But when I asked myself how I might react if I were publicly shamed, I realized I had no idea. We're exhorted to empathize with others, and that's what I'd been trying to do for my father, but how good could I be at empathizing when I was unable even to predict my own reactions to something as calamitous as what he went through?

After spending a year on just one medical condition, and how its "going wrong" caused so much pain and suffering to such a large cast of characters, I decided that the amazing thing about modern medicine, even in my father's time thirty years ago, was that things went *so well*. Especially with the brain — no, not just the brain, the *developing infant* brain, bathed in its cushion of fluid, consolidating its spectacular inner architecture for monitoring, processing, controlling, executing all the conscious and unconscious commands the organism needs to move, to see, to eat, to communicate, to live independently of the mother ship. That such complexity even exists, and works as well as it does, is a potent reminder of why Charles Darwin kept his theory of evolution so close to the vest for so many years. Something so complex as the human nervous system flew in the face of reason. It was just too much to expect. Divine direction was so much simpler.

But the developing infant brain does exist, and we understand it pretty well, and most of the time, it does what it seems built to do. Babies get born, they cry, they suckle and grow. When something goes a little off the rails — a touch of jaundice, an ear infection, croup — medicine steps smoothly in and puts it right. But what happened when many things went wrong? Like an insidious, undetected ventricular bleed long before birth, followed by an untimely early appearance and a struggle to get the oxygen so desperately needed before all those developing systems begin to falter and reorganize themselves into worrisome variants of the normal? That, I decided, was when our expectations of medical knowledge and the ability of its practitioners might be a little over-optimistic. Maybe the doctors could fix a "bad baby." *But maybe they couldn't.*

And if they couldn't, society felt compelled to award a consolation prize: the malpractice settlement. The better medicine got, the more people expected from it, and the more severe their displeasure when things went wrong. Try as I might to be fair to Billy's parents and lawyers, I couldn't shake the conviction that he'd been born into a perfect storm of neurological disasters that, doctors or no doctors, shunt or no shunt, would inevitably have compromised his life and the lives of the people who would care for him. My father sailed into that perfect storm, and when he had done his best to keep the ship afloat and come out the other side, the legal system was waiting for him.

That's how I felt when I finally reread *The Game*. It was never published, although he had a publisher interested. The problem was he couldn't finish it. The pain was still there, but the fire to get it on paper had finally flickered out. I'd been through it years before, when many of its chapters had been parts of a larger memoir that I'd nagged him for years to complete. The entire manuscript was on now-unreadable floppy disks, and I'd had it all laboriously retyped so that he could refine and rearrange without the frustration of computers. And he did it, spreading the chapters out on the kitchen table and annotating in an increasingly wavering hand. But whenever he came to the material on the trial, the whole process ground to a halt.

"I can't face it," he would say.

"Okay, let's put it together some other way. Defer the trial stuff until later." The result was a slim and entertaining memoir and the manuscript for *The Game*. The memoir got printed and distributed to friends and family, but *The Game* died with him. Now that I'd finished with every scrap of evidence, the trial itself and its aftermath, I was finally ready for it. In Bamfield, to the accompaniment of a bad pub band, I read it.

It was so much better than the memoir. He'd taken chapters about his youth, his training, his experience as a doctor, and alternated them with the story of Billy, from the summons at the door to the stories in the newspaper. Told this way, the malpractice case ran as a malevolent countercurrent to his career, and the back and forth pacing worked just as it should in the telling of any good story. It was good writing, and not just in the architecture but the details too. In a chapter called "Water on the Brain," his description of the cerebrospinal circulation made my own efforts seem ponderously journalistic. He compared the ventricles to "a chain of lakes," and the choroid plexus, where cerebrospinal fluid is produced, to "frilly curtains" projecting into the ventricles. His primer on shunting managed to be breezy and authoritative at the same time. "Infants outgrow their shunts," he wrote, "just as they outgrow their shoes."

But most of *The Game* wasn't breezy. It was sad, angry, defiant. When he wrote about waiting for the trial so he could rid himself of his "secret monster," it wasn't funny. His feelings about lawyers and the operation of the legal system were there, and strong, but he didn't entirely lose his sense of humour. When his own lawyer remarked it had been a tiring day, he said, "It has. But you can send in your bill for it, and I can't."

Everything he'd concluded about medicine and the law was contained in a fine chapter called "Two Solitudes." In medicine, he said, truth has "few absolutes and many exceptions." Yet, "the doctor in court encounters an inquisitor who insists on yes or no answers, who urges him to turn biological grey into legal black and white while at the same time telling the truth, the whole truth, and nothing but the truth." But despite the pain, there was an undisguised love for medicine, even if it didn't turn out the way he'd hoped. He loved teaching and, at least at the beginning, even the surgery. His whole professional life was in *The Game*, good and bad, including the drop-out periods when he tried to escape the grind. He called his brief sojourn at the University of British Columbia, "The Easiest Full Professorship in History," and reprinted all of Robert Frost's famous "The Road Not Taken."

There was a high point, when he had a Chicago-trained partner and got the respites he desperately needed, allowing him to join the violin section of the Victoria Symphony after "seven years of being the neurosurgical Lone Ranger." But his partner didn't stay long in Victoria, and my father went back to his escape attempts. Eventually, he got another partner, but by then he was winding down. Finally, in his mid-sixties, he packed it in. The telephone stopped being an enemy. "I would look at it when I climbed into bed and say you're not going to ring tonight. It was a good feeling." He was just getting used to that, eight years later, when the summons came.

The rest of *The Game* is a diary of the case. It takes over his life, infiltrates sleep: "It is always the same dream. I am in the operating room, in the middle of a craniotomy, when I suddenly ask myself, why am I doing this? I'm retired. I have no malpractice insurance. The operation is never finished; it goes on and on. And then I wake up in a sweat." To get ready for his appearance in court, he quotes Polonius:

> This above all, to thine own self be true
> And it must follow, as the night the day
> Thou canst not then be false to any man.

It's easy to belittle the use of a famous literary quotation to justify one's own actions, but he really believed in truth. Reality, though, was his lawyer entering court dragging "a little two-wheeled cart like the ones you see in airports, and on it was his own giant briefcase beneath a stack of loose-leaf folders three feet high." Reality was the freezing cold inside the glass-walled atrium of the Vancouver Courtroom, where lawyers gathered in whispering clusters during recess.

"Always remember," his lawyer told him, "you're in enemy territory here."

Above all, reality was the abortive trial itself, which turned out to be a *game*, a contest between lawyers with the judge as referee.

Finally, near the end of *The Game*, I found the thing that was as close as I would get to a bombshell. It was this: for him, the real story of the trial wasn't the defeat and the shame. It was "how a gifted individual managed to make such a mess of things." Everything in his life — from the tiny prairie town to violin trophies and top of the line professional training at the University of Chicago, then the sputtering practice in Victoria, the isolation, the conflicts and defections, the escapes and the restarts — everything was connected. It was a process, and it led to the final straw that broke his back. The trial confirmed what he already believed: he'd made a mess of his life.

Of all the surprises I'd encountered in nearly two years of invading his past, that admission was the biggest. Thinking back over the man I had known, it wouldn't surprise me if his disappointment in himself had driven him through his entire career. The conclusion I'd come to the day before — that public humiliation had been the thing that broke him — wasn't wrong, but it wasn't everything. Now I knew: the trial was the last nail in a coffin he'd been building all his life. I'd thought I was finally getting to know him and now this.

It explained what he said to me between the stroke that eventually killed him and his final day, when the nursing staff tucked him into bed with his bloodstream full of tranquilizers, stage one in the death routine such places can practically set their watches to. And not just what he said, but how he said it. He was still in his ratty velour recliner, cardigan cross-buttoned and slipping off one chicken-shoulder, white hair flying as though we were braced against a gale rather than sweltering in the hothouse of a care home. Two days before, we'd arrived for a visit and found him on his face on the hallway carpet, his legs still in the bathroom where he'd fallen. He couldn't move, and he'd given up calling for help. Now he was only a few days from the end. He leaned forward, or tried to, and looked me in the eye.

"I was a very good doctor," he said.

Seventy-Two Miles without a Pee

The alarm went off at 4:30 a.m. It was pitch black *and* foggy. Hatsumi made a thermos of coffee while I walked Charley, whose bladder would be tested today. Then we followed the shape-shifting black blotches of the radar for the next four hours. The first leg, which took us around the invisible Cape Beale, where we finally turned south, was unsettling. The wind came from the wrong place, there was much more of it than we'd expected, and the fog made everything clammy and opaque. *Vera*'s windscreen wept steadily, and I had to mop my glasses with a disintegrating Kleenex every few minutes. Once, as we neared the cape, a bobbing cluster of red and green lights materialized astern and winked past us at high speed, like a squadron of fireflies. The sport-fishing boats were heading out. I checked to make sure our own running lights were working.

But the fog stayed with us for hours, even as the wind dropped. The sun was there, a pale disc climbing steadily as we ground our way south, but visibility was only a few boat lengths. I began to mutter about assholes in small boats.

"Remember that old horn?" I asked Hatsumi. She was huddled in the cockpit, staring into nothingness. "The one my dad left, that you were blowing on the Nahwitti Bar? I think we're going to need it."

The sporties found us as we entered the Strait of Juan de Fuca. Four sudden radar blips astern, closing, passing, gone. I made out, for an instant, a ghostly white shape. Off Port Renfrew, a lousy anchorage but a popular marina for fishing boats, the radar screen was suddenly infested. I stopped counting at seven blips and concentrated on peering into the murk. Without warning, two white speedboats came right at us, one practically on the tail of the other. I yanked *Vera* into a hard right, grabbed the ancient horn, and emptied my lungs through it. They had no running lights, no radar. I screamed uselessly at their sterns, letting out two months of fear and frustration that nobody but my shocked wife and cowering dog could hear.

"Fucking assholes!"

We'd made it through tidal bores and river bars, past lurking rocks and through dense, soul-sapping fog. This was not how I wanted it to end, with some cretin's Bayliner wedged in my rigging.

"Mother*fuckers*!" I was shaking.

After Port Renfrew, we were left alone. The fog finally burned off, giving way to a hot sun and a fresh breeze behind us. We sailed now, rolling down Juan de Fuca with the suddenly brilliant Olympic Mountains seeming to herd us home. It didn't *feel* like the Graveyard of the Pacific.

But there were more hazards. From here south to Becher Bay, where we planned to spend the night, military area WH (Whiskey Hotel) ran across the international boundary to within a mile of the Canadian shore, and the entire thing was bordered by designated shipping lanes. We were in big-ship territory, and some of them had guns.

"The hell with it," I said. "If we're in the way, they can come over here and tell us." We were already close to the Canadian shore but still inside the test area. Unlike Whiskey Golf, where all the testing is underwater, Whiskey Hotel is a surface range. I heard a distant noise: *parp, parp* and grabbed the binoculars. Silhouetted against the fog bank that clung to the base of the American Olympics was a gunship. Nearby, a smaller vessel encrusted with antennae watched and waited. Two miles ahead, I could see their target, an anchored hulk. We sailed slowly out of hearing, past the confused chop at the mouth of Jordan River. Nobody came after us.

"Must be the end of the ebb," said Hatsumi, and I was suddenly absurdly happy for her. A statement like that was a long way from the pedal boats in Inokashira Park. It was three o'clock in the afternoon. The wind fell to the point where we wouldn't even make Becher Bay under sail by nightfall, so we motored the rest of the way, rounding the corner by dinner time. We anchored between the docks of two waterfront mansions, over a rocky bottom that ground relentlessly against the chain. Perversely, there seemed to be more wind inside Becher Bay than outside in Juan de Fuca. But a night here wouldn't kill us. We were only a couple of hours from Victoria.

"We did it," I said. "Almost."

Hatsumi looked haunted. I poured her some wine and went on deck to wrestle the kayak into the water. It was cold and blowing hard. I wished we were tied up to a dock, not anchored; emotionally, the trip was over for both of us. Hatsumi handed Charley down to me and we set out to look for a landing place on the rocky shore.

"Won't be long," I said.

I really wanted to get out, away from this cold, crappy anchorage where there were no other boats and where the wind and the current grabbed *Vera* like a tag team, twisting her this way and that. And the worst of it was, we still had to get past Race Rocks.

I had forgotten about Race Rocks, a collection of lumps that was home to one of B.C.'s oldest lighthouses (it was first switched on in 1860) and, since 1998, one of the first official Marine Protected Areas in Canada. Race Rocks was notorious for weather so bad the place became invisible; one of its first keepers had died after nine days of flying the Union Jack at half-mast to try to attract the attention of passing ships. In good visibility, the shortcut through Race Passage was supposed to be fine, but you had to time it with the current, which shot through like a river. Going around the outside meant going *way* around. We worried about it for a while, read some guidebooks, and went to bed.

The wind moaned all night and was still whistling into Becher Bay the next morning. I knew it was foggy before I even got out of bed; I could hear the fog signal. I double-checked the tide tables: we needed to go *now*, fog or no fog. It took fifteen minutes to chase down the anchor because *Vera* had swung and circled all night, as though replaying the twists and turns of our circumnavigation. We left at full flood, trusting to chart plotter and radar, and even with the tide on our side, it was slow going in the lumpy seas. To work our way safely around Race Rocks would take another hour.

"Screw it," I said. "Let's go through the passage. It's not the Nahwitti Bar." We turned, the current caught us, and in ten confused minutes we were through, running an invisible gauntlet between the rocky shore and the demented whistle of the fog signal. And like that, the picture changed dramatically, as though one backdrop had hastily been substituted for another. The water flattened, *Vera* slowed down, and suddenly we could see. When I looked astern, there was a fog bank, with the red beanie of the Race Rocks light poking through it. It was as though we had left an entire world behind.

"By the way, good morning," I said. "Let's stay the night in the Inner Harbour. A treat. What do you say?"

"Yes," said Hatsumi. "*Yes!*"

"Then tell me how to get there."

I watched the prison at William Head slide by on our left while Hatsumi pulled out the chart of Victoria Harbour. The prison looked like a pleasant place, unless you were locked inside and watching a green sailboat chug past. Every now and then, someone would make a break from William Head, astride a log or a jerry-built raft, but they never got far. Now I knew why.

What would my father have made of all this? For two months, he'd been popping up, unbidden. Whatever schedule his visits had been following, it hadn't been mine. Now, though, with Race Rocks receding behind us and our sailing adventure all but over, I realized that my parallel adventure with my father's past wasn't quite done yet. Now, on my own terms, I wanted a word. Try an overture, see what happened.

"Remember that time you took us into the O.R. to watch you do a ventriculogram?" I said.

"Sure." He wasn't up on the bow this time or perched on the stern rail. He was right beside me, next to the wheel. He grabbed the smooth stainless steel and gave it a weak, experimental tug. "I'm not sure I'd like one of these things," he said. "They take up too much room."

"I've gotta agree with you on that one," I said. "We never had a wheel, did we?"

"Never needed one."

"But you did need to show your sons how to do a ventriculogram."

"I thought you might be interested in what your old man did for a living."

"Did the guy live?"

"You think I can remember that? But yeah, probably."

"Were you disappointed none of us went into medicine?"

It took him a while to answer. We were closing in on Victoria now. Finally, he said, "At first, yeah. Then later . . ."

"You mean, after all the stuff that happened?"

"Even before that. Trust me, you made the right decision."

He didn't sound unhappy, or even cranky. For the first time since he'd popped up that chilly morning in Princess Bay, he didn't seem cold either. He watched the land stream past and his knobby fingers worked slowly at the buttons of his red wool jacket. I knew I should say something — reassure him, even thank him. At least help him get that damn jacket off. But the things that came to me all sounded trite, or maudlin, and when I finally opened my mouth, a seaplane emerged from the harbour, engines screaming and climbing fast. I craned my neck to watch it pass over us, so close I could see the rivets on its white fuselage. By the time I could be heard again, my father was gone.

~

Entering Victoria Harbour was surprisingly easy; all we had to do was stay on the right side of the well-marked seaplane lane. It was high summer again, the end of August, and we tied up right off the tourist-clogged causeway that ran beneath the Empress Hotel. Buskers played banjos and violins, street artists scribbled awkward renditions of tourists, and Hatsumi, responding to some deep instinct, fell to flaking the mainsail. A lugubrious older man stood over me as I retied a line. He looked like an elderly beagle waiting for its owner to return.

"Where have you come from?" He had a thick German accent. I figured he was a tourist.

"Bamfield," I said. "Well, not directly, we stayed somewhere else last night." Who cared about the details? This guy wouldn't know what I was talking about.

"I am going there," he said. "In the next days. Then we continue around the island."

I stared up at him. Probably I looked surprised.

"Just we are waiting for the wind a little bit to settle down."

"You have a boat," I said.

"Oh yes. Every year, I do this." He nodded morosely. "The wife, she is just now doing shopping."

You're going around the island *in reverse*? At the end of the season? I hope you have radar, I thought. And a good engine. And a strong stomach. Because you're nuts.

"Better you than me," I said.

Hatsumi and I passed the rest of the day in a kind of daze. I led Charley through a forest of tourist-calves to find flower beds to pee in. We took a harbour ferry across to the liveaboard marina on the other side of the harbour, where we fantasized about buying a bigger boat and moving in. After dinner, I listened half-heartedly to the weather forecast (another gale in Juan de Fuca) and decided to deal with it tomorrow. That evening, Chris and his wife, Karen, stopped by on their way back from chemotherapy in Vancouver. Two ferry trips and a day spent sitting with tubes in his arm, yet here he was, clambering aboard to welcome us back. I was profoundly happy to see him.

"You just came to see the engine," I said.

"I don't need to. I know it's fixed."

The next day was windy as promised, thirty knots finding us the moment we rounded the massive breakwater that protects Victoria Harbour. Even under reduced sail, *Vera* galloped past beaches and mansions like a dog straining at the leash. It was the best sail of the entire trip, and it only lasted an hour. When we shot through Enterprise Channel and came in sight of the breakwater that marks the Oak Bay Marina, I found myself wondering, What would happen if we just kept on going? If we turned right instead of left, back up Haro Strait again? Would my father reappear at Portland Island, as though nothing had happened?

But a lot *had* happened in the last two months. Hatsumi and I had finished what we'd started, and my own obsession with my father's collapse had led me to a place where I was unlikely ever to run into his ghost again. I swung the wheel. *Vera* came through the eye of the wind, we did the usual things with winches and jib sheets, the sails filled again, and we headed home.

Notes

Sea Trial is a work of non-fiction that spans many decades, fields, and locations. There is ample opportunity for errors of fact or usage; where these are found to occur, they are my own.

Some people's names have been changed, the criterion being whether I felt there was any risk, no matter how small, that someone might not be completely happy with being identified. Spelling of First Nations place names follows usage on official band council websites current at time of writing. Other place names are spelled as they appear on the Canadian Hydrographic Service marine charts for the area.

Water depths are expressed in feet rather than metres or the seldom-used fathoms. Speed through the water follows the universally accepted convention of knots (nautical miles per hour); the same goes for wind speed. One nautical mile is 1.85 kilometres.

Acknowledgements

Writing of this book was made possible by generous support from the British Columbia Arts Council and the Government of British Columbia and from the Canada Council for the Arts.

Many people were involved in the events related in this book or helped in its creation. I would like to extend special thanks to Allan Thackray and William Bullock for encouragement and critical reading of the manuscript for legal and medical aspects, to Charley Brown for sharing his memories of practising medicine with my father, and to my brother and sister, Rod and Sarah, for filling in crucial memory gaps. My wife and navigator, Hatsumi Nakagawa, was always there to remind me what really happened on the boat, and thanks are also owed to our parents and children, for putting up with our being out of touch for months when we should have been closer to a phone. Finally, the Victoria Medical Society Library helped me out with technical references and provided a home for many of my father's framed photographs.

Friends with boats who in one way or another helped us through many tricky passages include Chris Denny and

Karen Platt, Stuart and Anthea Piets, Dave and Nancy Young, Gordon and Bruce Jones, Yoshio and Fumie Asanuma, and Ivan Boyadjov.

For the actual work of writing and production, I want especially to thank David Greer for his unfailing encouragement and endless capacity to read and advise on whatever I write. Amanda Lewis and Shaun Bradley provided critical analysis of earlier drafts and suggestions for revisions, while Emily Schultz and Jen Albert continue to be the best editors a writer could hope for. Jack David of ECW Press did me the honour of believing in this book, while other members of ECW's amiable, creative, and efficient team, including Rachel Ironstone, Jessica Albert, Laura Pastore, and Amy Smith, made production a real pleasure.

BRIAN HARVEY grew up on the west coast of Canada and trained as a marine biologist. He began writing newspaper columns and science-travel articles for magazines in 1997. His first full-length book for a general audience (*The End of the River*) was published in 2008 and was followed by two works of fiction (*Beethoven's Tenth* and *Tokyo Girl*). He lives in Nanaimo, B.C.